ISSUE 31 n+1 SPRING 2018

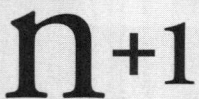

OUT THERE

THE INTELLECTUAL SITUATION

1   **Bringing the War Home**
    Gun violence and American foreign policy

POLITICS

7   **Bad TV** ANDREA LONG CHU
    Would #metoo jump the shark?

14 **Code Red** ALEX PRESS
    Organizing the tech sector

22 **Fire in Jakarta** ADAM BOBBETTE
    City politics and the rise of conservative Islam

FICTION

57 **Superking Son Scores Again** ANTHONY VEASNA SO
    The Magic Johnson of badminton

95 **Two Stories** HELEN DEWITT
    Fashion is out of structuralism

TRANSLATION

137 **You Can't Read** ROSE RÉJOUIS
    They need to feel you've been properly flayed

143 **Letter to Freud** ROSE RÉJOUIS
    Any cracked mirror will do

ISSUE 31
SPRING 2018

ESSAYS

CHRISTINA NICHOL **An Account of My Hut** 33
I don't want to live in a spaceship

MARISSA BROSTOFF **Missing Time** 75
As usual, Mulder was right

NATASHA STAGG **Two Stops** 119
You identify as hairless?

BELA SHAYEVICH **Day of Memory** 147
People, don't kill each other

REVIEWS

A. S. HAMRAH **On Oscar movies** 165
NICHOLAS DAMES **On spy fiction** 175
NAMARA SMITH **On Zadie Smith** 185

LETTERS 195

Clickbait Minotaur; on liking "On Liking Women"

n+1

n+1 is published three times a year by n+1 Foundation, 68 Jay St. #405, Brooklyn, NY 11201. Single issues are available for $14.95; subscriptions for $36; in Canada and other international, $55. Send correspondence to editors@nplusonemag.com. *n+1* is distributed by Ingram, Disticor in Canada, and Antenne in the UK and Europe. To place an ad write to ads@nplusonemag.com. *n+1*, Number Thirty-One © 2018 n+1 Foundation, Inc. ISBN 978-0-9970318-9-8.

WWW.NPLUSONEMAG.COM

EDITORIAL

Editors
NIKIL SAVAL
DAYNA TORTORICI

Senior Editors
CHAD HARBACH
CHARLES PETERSEN
NAUSICAA RENNER
NAMARA SMITH

Associate Editors
RICHARD BECK
LAURA CREMER
ELIZABETH GUMPORT
EMMA JANASKIE

Contributing Editors
KEITH GESSEN
MARK GREIF
MARCO ROTH

Founding Editors
KEITH GESSEN
MARK GREIF
CHAD HARBACH
BENJAMIN KUNKEL
ALLISON LORENTZEN
MARCO ROTH

Special Projects
STEPHEN SQUIBB

Senior Writers
KRISTIN DOMBEK
A. S. HAMRAH

ART AND DESIGN

Design
DAN O. WILLIAMS

Art Editors
IAN EPSTEIN
EMILY LYVER
RACHEL OSSIP
SU WU

FOUNDATION

Publisher
MARK KROTOV

Business Manager
COSME DEL ROSARIO-BELL

Subscriptions Manager
EMILY LYVER

Managing Editor
DAYNA TORTORICI

Production Manager
RACHEL OSSIP

Board
RONALD BARUSCH
CARLA BLUMENKRANZ
KEITH GESSEN
JEREMY GLICK
MARK GREIF
CHAD HARBACH
JYNNE MARTIN
CHRIS PARRIS-LAMB
NIKIL SAVAL
DAYNA TORTORICI
ROGER WHITE

THE INTELLECTUAL SITUATION

A Diary

Bringing the War Home

IT'S DIFFICULT TO THINK ABOUT THE MASS shootings that have become a regular feature of American life because the conversations that follow them repel thought. When Nikolas Cruz got out of his Uber ride on February 14, 2018, and entered Marjory Stoneman Douglas High School with an AR-15, he reanimated a gun-control debate that had been dormant for only four months, when Harvey Weinstein's firing in October knocked the Las Vegas shooting off the top of the *New York Times*' website. The gun-control debate is a Frankenstein's monster, undead and therefore unkillable, shedding bits of flesh with each passing year but senselessly marching along, no different from what it was after Orlando, San Bernardino, Sandy Hook, Virginia Tech, Columbine. There is no other public debate so thoroughly permeated by bad faith. Democrats do not "love" and "respect" the Second Amendment (they are just too frightened to say so). Republicans do not think an AR-15 is for hunting (they are just too frightened, for now, to state their belief that an unlimited capacity for violence is the birthright of all white men). Neither party is at all troubled by the quantity of violence the United States exports to people all over the world.

This time around, magical forces—that is, young people—were supposed to save us from the gun-control debate. There was something unsettling or self-serving about the excess of praise adults heaped on the Stoneman Douglas students who boarded charter buses bound for the Tallahassee statehouse just a few days after watching their classmates die. "This shooting is different from the other ones," a 16-year-old boy told a *Times* reporter. "I just have a gut feeling—something is going to change." It's understandable that the student should feel this way; no previous school shooting had happened in *his* school, to *his* friends and teachers, and no previous group of school-shooting survivors had organized so quickly, on such a scale, in response. But his representatives quickly demonstrated that it was not different enough. Florida's legislature voted down a motion to debate an assault-weapons ban. Later, at a nationally televised town-hall meeting, a Stoneman Douglas junior brought the crowd to its feet by asking Senator Marco Rubio whether he would refuse further donations from the NRA. Rubio said he would not refuse them, and he was not hesitant or ashamed to explain why. "I will always accept the help of anyone who agrees with my agenda," he said. "People buy into my agenda." These government officials may sincerely care about the safety of the children they represent, but they do not care about what the children themselves have to say about what would make them feel safe.

In March, the students had another go at making their representatives listen, with #MarchForOurLives protests organized all over the country on the first Saturday of spring. Just as the Women's Marches had turned tens of thousands of previously depoliticized middle-class women into community activists, candidates for local office, and Democratic campaign volunteers, these marches, too, looked like a moment of genuine political awakening. In many of the speeches you could hear a demand for drastic change learning to voice itself. A striking thing about this demand, however, was that when voiced in its most powerful form, it quickly moved beyond school shootings to broader concerns: the economic despair of working-class communities, the racism at the heart of American policing, the steady and intentional impoverishment of the country's public schools. A number of speakers said the name of Stephon Clark, the young, unarmed black man who was shot twenty times in the back by police in his grandmother's backyard less than a week before the marches. You could sense these young activists realizing what kind of country they're being raised in, the kinds of lives they're being prepared to live, and mustering all their energy, all at once, to try to change something. To see that desperate energy was inspiring and awful in equal measure.

In Washington, however, and in much of the media coverage of the marches, children were portrayed as calling for little more than the most toothless of what Obama always called "common-sense" gun-safety measures: restrictions on assault weapons, intensified background checks, closer communication between police and mental health professionals, bans on bump stocks. Some of the teen activists really were just calling for these things. In the *Guardian*, the staff of the Stoneman Douglas student newspaper published what they called a "manifesto" for new gun laws, demanding the reforms listed above and funding for armed police to patrol all of the country's public schools. The caution of these brand-new activists was visible here, as were the guiding hands of the adult liberal wonks and politicos who have uselessly pursued these half measures for years—adults who clearly believe that with traumatized children to speak for them, they'll finally get what they want.

What they'll get, it looks like, are the bump-stock bans, plus a raise in some states of the minimum age to buy a gun from 18 to 21, plus federal funding for metal detectors and more police officers in schools. By now we know that these legislative measures will increase, not decrease, the number of guns in schools and public places. They will intensify the surveillance and criminalization of mental illness, and when specially trained and certified teachers begin to keep guns in their desks in case the worst happens, the worst eventually will happen, and then we'll have teachers gunning down their own students while trying to save them. An armed police officer was stationed at Columbine on the day of Eric Harris and Dylan Klebold's massacre, and more than a dozen police were assigned to Virginia Tech's campus when Seung-Hui Cho killed thirty-two people over the course of two hours. Cops don't stop shooters. What they do is target children. Police have conducted around one million arrests in public schools since Columbine. But because "evil walks among us," in the words of NRA head Wayne LaPierre, we will "harden our schools."

THIS DYSTOPIAN VISION of American life is one the country has been actively pursuing for nearly two decades. Soon after September 11, 2001, Americans made a collective decision that in response to a once-in-a-lifetime catastrophe, an event whose scale and devastation were unrepeatable, large swaths of American life, as well as the country's relationship to most of the world, would be militarized on a permanent basis. Since then, the ways in which politicians and journalists have responded to terrorist attacks and school shootings have been so consistently similar that it seems foolish not to think of the shootings as extensions of the war we are waging around the world, epiphenomena of the war on terror. Public discussions of terrorism and mass shootings both lean heavily, for example, on an exaggerated sense of danger that bears little resemblance to the risks that actually menace us. On American soil, more people have been killed by falling furniture and appliances than by jihadist terrorists since September 11. In schools, roughly two hundred children have been killed by gunfire since 2000. That's almost twelve children a year—or, to put it another way, about three-hundredths of 1 percent of the thirty-three thousand Americans who have been killed by gunfire every year, on average, over that time period. To allow school shootings to drive the policy debate on gun violence, as they currently do, is like allowing traffic safety policy to be dominated by discussions of the drivers who die when a piano being moved by a crane slips out of its harness and drops onto the roof of a sedan.

Numbers are not everything. The murder of an ordinary person will do little to register in the public imagination beyond a day or two of news coverage, while the murder of a head of state will provoke an international crisis. The symbolic resonance of a violent act matters, and a society that guns down children in school is one in which something has gone very wrong. But as with terrorist attacks, the symbolism of school shootings mutates into spectacle, and if symbolism resonates like a plucked guitar string, the spectacle is the sound of that string fed into an amplifier and then trapped in a feedback loop, increasing in volume and intensity until the only possible response is panic and anger. Al Qaeda achieved what it wanted on September 11 insofar as the attacks were successfully spectacular, a series of Hollywood-style explosions in real life, filmed and photographed from every possible angle, in the biggest news-media town in the world. The broadcast images of September 11 *were* as much the attack as the destruction of the buildings and the people inside them. The power of school shootings similarly derives in part from their spectacular qualities, the photographs of children sobbing in each other's arms, the aerial footage of students streaming out of school in a line, hunched forward with their hands aloft as SWAT officers scream at them to get clear of the building. Stoneman Douglas added an element not seen before: cell phone videos shot by the students as they huddled in a classroom corner and waited for help to arrive. One video, shot from the back of the group, showed that a number of students were all filming at the same time. Police officers with assault weapons entered the room and told everyone to put their hands up. One set of hands, at the very edge of the frame, was shaking uncontrollably. The officer told everyone to put down their phones, and a few students began to sob as the video ended. These images are like the sound of a sick infant wailing, so viscerally upsetting as to make one feel that anything to make them stop would be justifiable.

Debates about how to stop the attacks, however, have been at pains to confine themselves to the tools used to carry them out and to methods of physical prevention: how to keep potential shooters from buying weapons, how to improve police-response times, how to ensure that FBI screenings don't miss any red flags. These debates have stayed away from questions of motivation that bear equally on preventing attacks. Why school shootings? Why not supermarket shootings? Why mass shootings? Why assault weapons and crowds of innocent people and suicidal attacks? The school shooter's reasons for carrying out his attacks, like the terrorist's, are treated in public debate as either totally unknowable or pathological, outside the realm of rational thought. In the time since the Stoneman Douglas shooting, President Trump has described Nikolas Cruz and mass shooters in general as "mentally disturbed," "a big problem," "a savage sicko," "cowards," and "bad people." The less vulgar among us use different words that mean the same thing, assuming that shooters must be mentally ill. We talk about terrorists in the same way, as "cowards," "fanatics," members of a "death cult." In the first major speech he gave after September 11, Bush said that the terrorists "hate our freedoms." In America, "hate our freedoms" is how you use the vocabulary of a civics class to call someone mentally ill.

But the motivations of terrorists and mass shooters are neither unknowable nor pathological. Al Qaeda carried out the attacks on September 11 because of the sanctions levied against Iraq by the United Nations in 1990, the presence of American troops in Saudi Arabia after the Gulf War, and America's support of Israel, Egypt, and other repressive Middle Eastern regimes. Since then, America's military adventures throughout much of the Middle East have continued to serve as a potent recruiting tool for jihadists. The profile and motivations of mass shooters are also more or less understood by psychologists and sociologists. Mass shooters are socially isolated young men who are angry because they feel they are not getting the social standing, attention, and recognition they deserve. Their attacks are efforts to force the people around them to recognize them at last.

As for the cultural environment that makes mass shootings seem like an attractive outlet for these feelings of isolation and rage, some investigators have plausibly cited video games as a contributing factor, not so much for their explicit violence as for their obsession with narratives in which almost exclusively white male heroes remake the world around them, all on their own, by killing people. The intensely competitive atmosphere of American education may also play a role. As Malcolm Harris wrote in an editorial for Al Jazeera, "In a society that pits each kid against the whole world for a shrinking number of success slots, shooting up your school seems like a misunderstanding. You're only supposed to figuratively kill all your classmates."

Terrorism is another of these factors. Today's mass shooters have all grown up in a country that lives in constantly reinforced fear of a kind of violent spectacle in which an individual who is willing to die selects a public place and kills as many people as he can. No other violent act is more feared, more discussed, more capable of causing society to change itself—nothing gets more attention and recognition. The mass shooting is our domestic variant of the jihadist terrorist attack. Were the US to abandon the specter of terrorism as the organizing principle of the country's foreign policy, travel laws, and security procedures, the mass shooting would lose much of its dark appeal. But during this century so far, America has responded to terrorist attacks by deepening its fears and further entrenching itself in militarism and surveillance. It is responding to mass shootings in much the same way. So long as that pattern holds, angry and unstable young men will continue to act in accordance with the world they've inherited. +

WHAT IS OUTSIDE IS INSIDE.

Ace Hotel New York @acehotelnewyork
Stay over with code **KEEPREADING** for a smart deal

CELESTE RAPONE, *KAREN*. 2017, OIL ON CANVAS. COURTESY OF THE ARTIST.

POLITICS
Memoranda

ANDREA LONG CHU
Bad TV

THE DAY THE KEVIN SPACEY ALLEGATIONS broke, I was sitting with my girlfriend on our couch in Brooklyn. By accident, we found ourselves playing a dark game. One of us would name a male star, as if removing an article of clothing, and the other would respond on instinct—first, with the chances of his being outed as a sexual predator, then with how disappointed she would be in the event of his fall from grace. The goal was to pick men who scored high in both columns. The whole thing smacked of truth or dare, or spin the bottle: games of needless, voluntary exposure, games about the risk of being caught wanting things you shouldn't.

The secret, of course, was that the red-skied reckoning that had followed a blitz of sexual misconduct allegations against film producer Harvey Weinstein in October 2017 could be, whatever else it was, fun. Out there, in the fields of something like history, women were talking, telling stories of rape and abuse and harassment and weird texts and constant gaslighting. Most of these stories weren't new. Those that were cleaved so tightly to the genre that they bore the seal of instant recognition. Maybe nothing would change; maybe this was one of those *Matrix* things, where the system would just adjust and reboot. But there isn't anything especially feminist about being jaded. A world was ending, maybe. At any rate, the stars kept falling.

And then here we were, bae and I, kids playing hide-and-seek in a fallout shelter. We were enjoying it. Ours wasn't just the righteous satisfaction of justice finally served, or even the hot joy of revenge. For sure, there was real pleasure in the prospect of seeing bad men suffer. But there was also another, less flattering kind of enjoyment, floating right beneath the waterline of consciousness. For all the great to-do, all the scandal and vindication, there were certain stars of film and television—just a select few, we told ourselves, a special club—whom, in a week or month or two, once the fires were out, we would find it in our hearts to forgive. That's a lie, actually. We wouldn't forgive them. But we also wouldn't stop watching their shows.

Jeffrey Tambor hit particularly hard. I'd been avoiding starting the fourth season of *Transparent* on account of its multi-episode Israel arc, which filled me with the dread of Having to Have an Opinion. *Transparent*, for me, had never been about telegraphing a politics—for that, I had *Orange Is the New Black*, *Atlanta*, and *Insecure*. I had taken in the first two seasons with dumb luxuriance, as if ordering macaroni and cheese at a restaurant with three dollar signs on Yelp. The third I binged on a few months into transition, popping estrogen and waiting for the sadness to kick in. "I don't *wanna* be trans!" cried Tambor's character, in a bitter argument with her estranged sister. "I *am* trans!" Me neither; me too.

Then, shortly after the fourth season of *Transparent* went live on Amazon Prime, a former personal assistant of Tambor's alleged that the actor had engaged in what *Deadline Hollywood* was calling "inappropriate behavior." Tambor denied it. There was here, I knew, a brief window of plausible deniability: if I was going to binge with a clean conscience, it was now or never. But by the time *Transparent* actress Trace Lysette came forward with her own allegations—on set, she said, Tambor had told her he wanted to "attack [her] sexually" and mimed sex acts while pressed up against her—I still hadn't watched.

The irony was thick and frothy: a transgender actress sexually harassed by a cisgender actor playing a transgender woman, and doing so to tremendous critical acclaim, with a winsome humility it was easy to slip your belief into, like a pair of comfortable shoes. Tambor was a good woman. Accepting his second consecutive Emmy for the role in 2016, Tambor thanked a team of trans media consultants and said the show had changed his life. When a piano tried to play him off, he shushed it, his face sad and urgent. "I'm not going to say this beautifully," he warned, "but to you people out there, you producers and you network owners and you agents and you creative sparks, please give trans"—his voice failed mid-word, his mouth still moving, then he rallied—"transgender talent a chance." The audience, warm and charmed, let the slip slide. "One more thing," Tambor continued over the cheers. "I would not be unhappy were I the last cisgender male to play a female transgender on television," he finished, awkwardly flipping the words *transgender* and *female*. More cheers, louder and looser. Sure, he hadn't quite stuck the landing—but that could be forgiven, couldn't it?

TELEVISION WAS NEVER good for you. In 1950, there were, by some estimates, six million television sets in the United States; a decade later, something like sixty million—nine out of ten households. By the mid-Sixties, Herbert Marcuse was suggesting that the masses would rather chance nuclear annihilation than be deprived of television. What postwar critics were talking about when they called it a technology of mass consumption was how television broadcast, on a historically massive scale, the helplessness of desire in the face of its object. TV didn't have to be good to be good: all viewers asked for was the possibility of returning, over and over, to the scene of enjoyment's crime—hence the episode, the serial, the sitcom. Trash just had to be reliable. Even contempt could breed familiarity. If the barrage of televisual garbage that Americans were willing to consume proved anything, it was that once hooked, desire is very hard to spoil. This was perhaps the ultimate spoiler.

Hence early critics' second objection to television: its inherent quashing of the instinct for political resistance, or even just public life. "Television atrophies consciousness," wrote Theodor Adorno. For him, television's danger was its capacity for producing in viewers a feeling of social belonging that was in fact ideological cover for their increasing alienation under capitalism. The warm togetherness of the average American family gathered around a little box in their living room was a lie fabricated to keep people off the streets where politics might happen. Even Marshall McLuhan, no one's idea of a Marxist, thought that television was too "cool," too sensorially engrossing to drive political change. The political effect of television on the average American was therefore the formal inverse of the fascism of the Forties. Hitler's radio had uprooted one country; now, television was potatoing another. "The dreamless dream," Adorno called it, crowning it king of the culture industry. "The Timid Giant," McLuhan called it, quoting from *TV Guide*.

But at some point, someone poked it. One will be forgiven for thinking that the current tenant of the White House represents a full-on invasion of the political by television. Even the popular fan theory that the President is secretly a Russian patsy, credible or not, feels ripped from the plotlines of some drama on USA. Equally, more than ever, television is political. "The Great Awokening," the journalist Molly Fischer called this in the Cut, describing how wokeness—as in "stay woke," an exhortation to political awareness popularized by Black Lives Matter—has consolidated as a televisual aesthetic. Witness *Black-ish*, *Girls*, *Insecure*, *Louie*, *The Handmaid's Tale*, *I Love Dick*, *Transparent*, *Master of None*, even the rebooted *Will & Grace*. At worst, woke TV has all the moral subtlety of an afterschool special. In one episode of *Master of None*, Aziz Ansari's character has sexism explained to him by his female friends. The tone is self-congratulating and neogallant, as if pointedly sparing a lady the chivalry of an opened door. Writes Fischer, "This is not a blow to the patriarchy; this is *Sesame Street*."

The promise of woke TV is that the naysayers of the Sixties were wrong: watching television can be a kind of political act, if only minor and tenuous. If this sounds like wishful thinking, that's not simply because wokeniks like Tambor and Ansari left themselves vulnerable to getting called on their shit. It's also because in the very act of delivering on its promise to make people feel political, woke TV accidentally proved that political was something you could be made to feel. That *Transparent* can make you feel political—the way, say, *This Is Us* can make you feel sad—implies that the political is essentially a special effect, a trick of the light, TV magic. The full discomfiture of this claim can be shrugged off as long as you maintain the fantasy that somewhere out there, in the bleeding wilds of the world, there exists a secret glade called Politics where the gods of history dance. This will let you cleanly cleave the world in two: true and pretend, genuine leftism and performative wokeness, real life and the stuff of television. The scarier thought is that feeling political is all that politics is. In truth, you can't book a direct flight to the political. There are always layovers in aesthetic form: in tone, mood, shape, and everything else a work of art might employ to try to get you to feel part of something bigger than yourself.

The other way to say this is that politics is just a very special episode of belonging. Belonging is television's forte. Television was never just a box; it has always been primarily a social event. When Adorno complained that television was a "substitute for a social immediacy," he had forgotten that every public is a fantasy, projected by rituals and shibboleths that if held up to the light just so will, like the medallion in *Raiders of the Lost Ark*, point the way to God. This applies as much to the halo of national pride that in 1969 descended, like Apollo 11, onto the rapt faces of viewers at home as to the numberless moons of fandom now wandering the internet's night sky. Mediation, televisual or otherwise, has always been necessary to make the leap from me to you, individual to group. All communities are imagined, as Benedict Anderson taught, simply because they could not be otherwise.

But the fear of missing out is real. This is truer than ever today, when twenty-four-hour streaming services have succeeded in making live television live forever. Hence the recap: a new genre of internet writing that mixes summary with commentary while being neither, anchored by the gravity of a show's sacred lore but prone to flashes of passion and diaristic longing. More than reviewing plot or assessing style, the recap's first job is to record the achievement of holding a shared object. Here in the Golden Age of Television, the point is not just to watch but to have watched—to have been there, in a sense not wholly imaginary, for that twist, that fire, that wedding. Death emcees most of these ceremonies. (Jimmy Kimmel, the rest.) Take *Game of Thrones*, a high-fantasy program whose appeal rested in its defiance of the economy of celebrity. Central characters whom other shows would have clad in plot armor could be cut down with the ignominy of an extra. It could be anyone, at any time. They even had a saying in Braavos, the financial capital of the *Thrones* world: *Valar morghulis*, all men must die. And so the nation got hooked on a show about famous men falling when you'd least expect it.

AS *GAME OF THRONES* sailed off toward its final season, a new show rose to fill its slot. #MeToo was another kind of fantasy drama, one that resuscitated the dream of Seventies feminism: arrows dipped in anger, fletched with optimism. Time's up. Ban men. Burn it down. Only this time, the revolution would be televised. Allegations rolled out like your regularly scheduled programming. A political movement could be a form of entertainment; America had just learned this the hard way. Now justice was on prime time, and everyone was watching. In coffee shops, on public transit, all across social media, the whisper network was suddenly, shockingly loud, as if someone had forgotten to cut its mic. Soon, it was congressmen, journalists, professors, radio hosts, talking heads, celebrity chefs. The news reports popped up on our phones like recaps of a phantom show no one had ever seen. Even the hashtag was an impossibility, an improvised attempt to build a universal out of nothing but particulars. Me, too. The singular, multiplied.

Those who called it a witch hunt had clearly never watched the short-lived series *Salem*, whose premise was that the witches hunted you. But the backlash came all the same. Before long, the devil had enough advocates to hang a shingle. Could all women really be believed? That was a lot of women. Someone with money started calling in op-eds. The standing orders were clear: for every twisted panty, a wrung hand. There was bad sex, and then there was bad sex. The thing had degrees. It was complicated. Some, calling themselves allies, cautioned that sex panics are never good for queer people, people of color, sex workers. If it wasn't careful, they said, the movement would jump the shark.

For others, it was already too late. Aziz Ansari, who for years had played a failed pickup artist on NBC's *Parks and Recreation*, had finally badgered a nerve into letting him touch it. A woman with the pseudonym Grace told the lifestyle site Babe that Ansari had pressured her into a blow job and kept wheeling her awkwardly around his apartment looking for a space to park his dick. Everything was consensual-ish. "You guys are all the same," she had told him, "you guys are all the fucking same." The internet went up in flames. Harassment in the workplace was one thing, but a national referendum on heterosexuality? What were we supposed to do, *not have sex*? Bari Weiss, with the *New York Times* feeding quarters into the back of her head, figured that if Grace had been assaulted, so had every woman, including Bari Weiss, which obviously wasn't the case. Someone in the *Atlantic* compared Grace to the weak female protagonists of the moralizing chick lit of the Seventies, at once slutty and hapless. Suck it up, honey. Spit it out. Call a cab.

What they were really saying was that Grace's story played like bad TV. It was all too tropey: wine, tears, countertops. This wasn't real life; this was Shondaland. They shouldn't have described her outfit; they shouldn't have included that sex thing with the fingers. Grace needed a better editor. But it was quickly becoming clear that #MeToo could turn broadsheets to tabloids with a single, unwanted touch. The truth was, many of the allegations read like outlandish episode pitches. Even Frank Underwood of *House of Cards*, who once had a bisexual threesome involving a Secret Service agent and also, like, *murdered people*, didn't have a button under his desk that locked the door behind female colleagues he wanted to bone. At some point, the most unimpressed feminist could allow herself the trashy pleasure of disbelief briefly unsuspended. What do you mean, he masturbated into a potted plant? That was something out of *Quantico*, or *Billions*, or *Scandal*. It's a twist we could have seen from miles away. It turns out that the men on TV act like the men on TV.

GOOD TV, OF THE long-form, narrative sort, is believable. Believability is never about reproducing reality. Time travel may be believable; a kitchen sink may not be. Believability is, essentially, an aesthetic of proportionality. It consists in the invention of an imaginary but plausible relationship between character and plot: that is, in negotiating some kind of correspondence between the squishy sentimentality of interiority and a few discrete, relatively high-impact events that interrupt, like meteors, the atmosphere of everyday life. In the land of television, critical acclaim is handed out to whichever shows manage to bridge these twin peaks most attractively. Usually, this means keeping the writing within a few standard deviations of the premise at hand: no secret clones, unless it's *Orphan Black*; no acts of God, except on *The Leftovers*.

Sexual violence is, however, notoriously difficult to portray realistically on television—hence its relegation to the fringes of good taste, from the family melodrama to the police procedural. Even HBO's female-driven *Big Little Lies*, which follows a clique of affluent women in airy California beach houses as each gets caught in a riptide of abuse, couldn't help draping rape in the lush folds of Emmy-nominated cinematography. The show's failure—and, equally, its success—was to have made abuse believable. In this way, *Big Little Lies* predicted, a little too well, how Harvey Weinstein would fall. The *New York Times*'s Weinstein report was a believability project years in the making: it systematized abuse, turned it into a pattern your eye could follow. There were interviews, emails, audio recordings, legal documents; facts were double- and triple-checked. But its paradoxical consequence was to set the bar far too high for every subsequent story whose breaking it had made possible. What's a little masturbation between friends when the king of Hollywood kingmakers had employed former agents of the Israel Defense Forces to silence his accusers? In one final act of gaslighting, Weinstein made all other abuse look not so bad and all other evidence look not so good.

But trauma rarely announces itself the way it does in the *New York Times* or on HBO, in the dramas that win big men statues of little women. In real life, trauma is soapy. The soap opera is distinguished not by the tremendous suffering borne by its characters but by the requirement that the *degree* of this suffering feel unwarranted. An unexpected death may be mourned in minutes; a personal slight can be grounds for arson. It's always too much, or not enough. This is why, despite all *Big Little Lies*'s high production values and A-list stars, there were still male critics who classified it as an "upscale soap." When *Vogue* asked Reese Witherspoon (who both acted and produced) for her response, she laughed at the question. "This is how women really speak to each other," she said. "There are a lot of dynamics where women are not telling each other the truth, and I think it's deeply relatable." *Big Little Lies* wanted to tell the truth about the truth about abuse, which is that the truth will always sound like a lie.

This is why the case against #MeToo rested, ironically, on charges of disproportionate response. Calm your tits, its critics said. Most men aren't monsters. Most things aren't rape. Of course, the thing about moral panics is that it takes one to know one. Women are panicking, they said, panicking. But it's genuinely worth considering whether panic is the only form of publicness available to the airing of sexual grief. Sexual harm is constituted by the impossibility of its being proven. Outside of statutory provisions around age, consent is basically immaterial. Rape and its cousins are ultimately determined not by the presence of physical violence but by the victim's mental state. Of the latter there can never be direct proof, only secondary indicators. Sexual assault is therefore, by definition, all in your head. Hence the slogan "Yes means yes," a spell for conjuring a world where people always say what they mean and mean what they say. But usually, they don't—and usually, they can't, since people are rarely any more transparent to themselves than they are to others. Events are not self-narrating. Violence is rarely realistic. You're expecting a break, but instead you get weird, curved continuity. Someone missed their cue. That can't be the line. What did he just say? Where are we going? Did I ask for this? No one calls cut. No one checks the gate. Not knowing what happened becomes part of what happened.

It is impossible to have a proportionate response to something that never, strictly speaking, occurred. That's why the beautiful risk run by all the public blacklists, unchecked facts, and internet yelling that coalesced alongside the due-diligence journalism like #MeToo's evil Twitter twin was its wholesale refusal to play ball with believability's evidentiary regime. No smoking guns, no blue dresses. Saying so would be proof enough. This was breathtaking, the way the open maw of deep space is breathtaking: nothing, catching fire. Nuance exists, obviously. We're big girls. Women hoard subtlety in a world where belief is something you have to save up to buy. This is a secret of femininity: paying careful attention to the world's complexity can mean letting it walk all over you. But to admit this was to concede too much. We deserved some recklessness. It can look like violence when women afford themselves the luxury of generalization.

That's certainly how it went in *Big Little Lies*. Nicole Kidman's abusive husband cannot be defeated until he is revealed, in the season finale, to be Shailene Woodley's rapist. For a split second, two different women's experiences of abuse are perfectly aligned, like lenses in a camera, each bringing into focus the objective reality of the other. The monster must be shared to be slain. And he is—falling down a long staircase in what the show's women tell the police was an unfortunate accident. They're lying, obviously. Abuse's solution ends up as unspeakable as abuse itself. The season's final shots depict the women spending a day at the beach, touching each other affectionately and looking out onto the breaking waves. Among a group of women accustomed to wielding niceness like a telescopic baton for knocking out each other's kneecaps, it's a scene of genuine female solidarity.

The price of this was murder, of course. Maybe it always is. #MeToo never actually killed anyone, though that might have just been an accident of opportunity. The desire to kill was real enough. While sensible people, garden-party appalled, wondered aloud if important men should really lose their careers in the small of some woman's back, we sat at home knowing that getting fired was mercy, not vengeance. But the desire to punish, for better or worse, isn't the same thing as punishment. Unlike the women of *Big Little Lies*, most of us will never get the chance to watch our abusers die. That mass murder would be morally untenable, or at least practically tricky, only whets the poignancy of the thing. That is the dark comedy of the desire we call feminism: we are ethically compelled not only never to get what we want, but never to stop wanting it, either. The only real justice would be unforgivable injustice. Separatism, the only answer, is also the wrong one. That fucking sucks. It means that justice is the biggest little lie of all.

THE THING IS, it's all of them. It's every single last one of them. Not just the famous ones. Not just the ones you don't personally know. Never let anyone persuade you otherwise, even if they write for a fancy magazine. But let us say, too, that it is a specious compassion that would make us reluctant to admit these things. Whether or not men deserve forgiveness—and if so, which ones—is not the question, much less the answer. In fact, there is no question. The reality is harder. What hurts isn't when the people we love do unlovable things. What hurts is when, afterward, we still love them. This goes as much for the neon of celebrity identification as it does for the quieter affections: friends, mentors, exes. What this means is that all of us will be caught wriggling on the flypaper of apologism before this thing is over. Lines in the sand blow away eventually.

No wonder, then, that the ninetieth Academy Awards, the first held after Harvey Weinstein's expulsion from the academy, passed largely without incident. The Oscars are prom for famous people. There is a white-people jazz band. The writing is cut from cardboard. The whole thing is equal parts ham and cheese—hardly the place to hold a protest. Viewers who had tuned in expecting *#MeToo Live!* were met with gentle ribbing. Host Jimmy Kimmel jokingly praised the male Oscar figurine for having "no penis at all." Emma Stone announced the Best Director nominees as "four men and Greta Gerwig." People said the word *women* a lot. The closest anyone got to the wrath of yesteryear was Best Actress Frances McDormand, butcher than usual and dependably electric, who ended her speech with the enigmatic phrase "inclusion rider," pronouncing it like code for something dangerous. Perplexed viewers scrambled to Google, whose guess was as good as theirs. The next day, the media clarified that an inclusion rider was a way for A-listers to stipulate diversity in casting and staffing as a condition of their fancy contracts. Oh, we said. That sounded like probably a good idea.

Like most finales, the Oscars were a disappointment, masquerading as a shock. If anything, they were a reminder that #MeToo never stood a chance. The celebrities were just doing what we've always wanted them to do: acting out our fantasies, not because we can't, but so we don't have to. Television is Westworld for people who can't afford to leave their living rooms. That its stars were all just trying to get paid made them no worse than those of us who were just trying to pay them. And just like them, at some point, we will cut to a commercial; at some point, we will change the channel. This could be an indictment, but it doesn't have to be. Politics, too, can be a guilty pleasure. A political movement is no more tarnished by its finitude than a romance, or a childhood, or a good TV show. Maybe it will be a relief to remember that #MeToo accomplished what every guilty pleasure accomplishes: itself. Weigh us; find us wanting. Wanting could be enough. Desire isn't revolution. But it might play one on TV. +

ALEX PRESS
Code Red

CASES OF MODELO SIT ON A RICKETY wooden table near the elevator, two laptops open to a Google sign-in sheet beside them. A few people mill around the table, welcoming newcomers. I enter my contact information on one of the laptops, take a half-sheet printout of the meeting's agenda, and find a seat.

We're in a start-up office in an unexceptional high rise in Manhattan. There is little furniture to speak of: dozens of black rolling chairs assembled in a haphazard circle, whose occupants scoot to make space for the people trickling in.

There are fifty-two people here, more than the organizers expected. Latecomers stand outside the circle, leaning against the bare columns scattered throughout the room. It is mid-July of 2017, and this is the first official meeting of Tech Action, a working group of the New York City local of the Democratic Socialists of America (DSA).*

"Raise your hand if this is your first DSA meeting," says Fred,† a mild-mannered, thirtysomething software engineer in financial technologies, or "fintech," and one of the men (it's mostly men) leading the meeting. Five hands go up.

"Raise your hand if you work in the tech industry," Fred continues. Almost every hand in the room goes up.

A few years ago, a room full of techies—shorthand for white-collar tech employees, usually software engineers or computer programmers—gathered to organize their industry was unthinkable. Press coverage of the industry was boosterish and sedulously uninvestigative, as journalists tended to embrace Google's old "Don't be evil" motto as a factual description of its aims. After all, tech was our path to utopia—it would "connect" us, reduce our environmental footprint by eliminating all paper and books, and free us from the tyranny of work by replacing us with robots.

But the gap between tech theory and tech practice has grown increasingly difficult to ignore. Even the tech press—*Wired* and its ilk—has lost faith. Many now know the tech elite as a hive of misogynists and sociopaths, and their companies to be indiscriminate vacuums of sensitive personal data that they package and sell to the nation's intelligence agencies (and the Trump campaign). According to polls, the majority of the public still maintains a positive view of the industry's biggest companies. But the scales have fallen from the eyes of many of its workers.

After Fred introduces himself to the meeting's attendees, members of Tech Solidarity and the Tech Workers Coalition (TWC), two leading grassroots tech organizations, give reports on their recent

---

* I am a dues-paying member of the DSA.
† When only first names are used, individuals' names have been changed.

activity. Tech Solidarity was created by Maciej Cegłowski, the founder of Pinboard, a social-bookmarking website. Following Donald Trump's election, Cegłowski and Heather Gold, a Bay Area comedian, put out a call for techies to meet up in San Francisco. They wanted to talk with other people about how to act on their discontent. More than a hundred people attended the first meeting. Soon Cegłowski was flying to other US cities to host Tech Solidarity gatherings.

Compared with Tech Solidarity, TWC may be, as Moira Weigel calls them in a recent piece for the *Guardian*, "the most radical Tech Left group." Created by Matt Schaefer, an engineer, and Rachel Melendes, a cafeteria worker and organizer, the group began meeting in 2014 and saw an explosion of interest after Trump's election. Focused on building a coalition of blue-collar and white-collar tech workers, TWC devotes the bulk of its efforts to supporting union campaigns among the low-wage workers who are increasingly employed through third-party contractors, a practice that allows tech companies to avoid directly employing the legions of custodians, cafeteria workers, and security guards that sustain their sprawling campuses. TWC's coalition work has the potential to reshape the tech industry from the inside out: not just how people work in it, but what it creates and does.

HOSTILITY TO UNIONS has been foundational to the tech industry. In its idealized self-image, tech is a meritocracy governed by speed, efficiency, and competition, in which companies can acquire and shed workers as needed. Insecurity is a value. There is freedom in hopping from job to job, and the idea that someone might want to remain anywhere for long is unthinkable. By making it difficult to fire employees and limiting other arbitrary company decisions, unions (supposedly) make labor markets less fluid. They are dinosaurs, and the tech industry is an asteroid.

In the 1960s, an increasing number of low-slung boxy offices replaced the oaks and orange groves of the southern San Francisco Bay Area, making what would become Silicon Valley. Around this time, Robert Noyce, the cofounder of Intel, asserted that "remaining non-union is essential for survival for most of our companies. If we had the work rules that unionized companies have, we'd all go out of business." Emphasizing the industry's need to retain "flexibility," Noyce's ethos held even as Intel and the industry at large expanded beyond the production of microchips.

Escaping East Coast unions had been a major reason behind tech companies' settling in California to begin with. As AnnaLee Saxenian writes in her book *Regional Advantage*, Silicon Valley overtook Route 128, the tech corridor just outside of Boston, as the industry's main hub in part because it could take advantage of looser labor markets. In a 1983 profile of Noyce, Tom Wolfe wrote, "Noyce disliked many things 'back east'":

> Labor-management battles were part of the ancient terrain of the East. If Intel were divided into workers and bosses, with the implication that each side had to squeeze its money out of the hides of the other, the enterprise would be finished. Motivation would no longer be internal; it would be objectified in the deadly form of work rules and grievance procedures.

Nonetheless, tech employees have tried to unionize since the industry's earliest years. Wolfe mentions several attempts to organize Intel in the late '60s and early '70s—campaigns Noyce viewed as a "death threat" to the company. The lead author of a 1976 article in *Science for the People* titled

"Rumblings of Organizing in Silicon Valley" writes of his experience in a "unionization drive among the chemists, physicists, engineers, and technicians" of the Smith-Corona Marchant (S.C.M.) Corporation, once famous for its typewriters. As the author recounts, intense workplace pressure jump-started the campaign:

> The company maintained an artificial crisis atmosphere by claiming severe urgency for almost every project. By implying a loss of job or status, the management was able to get large amounts of free overtime ("remember, you are a *professional*"), and justify almost constant harassment. Two fatal heart attacks of workers in their early forties occurred within one year in this small facility alone, and there were several other nonfatal attacks as well.

Though the company defeated the campaign, similar organizing drives popped up less than a decade later, as employees at Atari fought wage cuts and layoffs in the early 1980s. After all, despite tech executives' insistence that their industry is incompatible with unions, labor organizing among scientists is common enough. Take the Society of Professional Engineering Employees in Aerospace, a union that represents more than 22,650 professionals, or the faculty and graduate-student unions that represent many white-collar professionals, many of whom go on to work in tech. Add the Alliance@IBM, a union of dues-paying IBM employees that existed from 1999 to 2016; WashTech, formed by contract workers at Microsoft; the union-like Institute of Electrical and Electronics Engineers, which boasts a worldwide membership of more than 423,000, mostly made up of electrical engineers; and the Programmer's Guild, which "advances the interests of technical and professional workers" in IT. Taken together, these organizations make the anti-union fortress of tech begin to look less impregnable.

UNION CAMPAIGNS in tech companies have scored some notable victories in recent months. In January 2017, three thousand security guards on Silicon Valley campuses like Cisco, Facebook, and Genentech won union recognition. Last summer, cafeteria workers on Facebook's campus—assisted in small part by TWC, which includes Facebook engineers—voted to unionize with UNITE HERE, following Facebook's shuttle drivers who voted to join the Teamsters in 2015. The cafeteria workers are employed by Flagship Facility Services, a contractor, but they used their proximity to the image-conscious Facebook to pressure Flagship not to fight the union. Eric Murphy, a security guard employed by Allied Universal on Facebook's campus, told me that while some techies expressed support for the campaign, the physical segregation of techies and contractors hindered solidarity. The UNITE HERE local that Flagship's workers joined now represents cafeteria workers at Agilent, Cisco, Intel, and Nvidia, all Bay Area–tech companies. There are now approximately five thousand unionized workers on Silicon Valley campuses.

Tech Solidarity and TWC fall somewhere between workers' centers and community organizations. Tech Solidarity asks techies to bring in their contracts, so labor lawyers can analyze industry standards and assist in workplace organizing campaigns. Cegłowski himself has come to focus on electoral politics, particularly the 2018 midterms and fundraising for progressive candidates.

TWC is less interested in electoral politics, focusing instead on the working environment of blue-collar workers on tech campuses. When security guards at

Facebook began to unionize, the group was well positioned to help. As Kristen Sheets, a Bay Area–based technical analyst and TWC steering committee member told me, Facebook employees who were members of TWC distributed information to security guards about the campaign when union organizers were not allowed on campus. TWC also helped organize protests outside Palantir after Trump's election to pressure the data-mining company not to build the administration's planned Muslim registry.

Neither TWC nor Tech Solidarity is a union. The potential power of a true tech union would be enormous. Techies may not sweat it out in a warehouse, haul cargo at a port, or fix cars on an assembly line, but they occupy a critical point in their company's operations. Cary, a web developer at a marketing firm, explained to me how techies can create strategic interruptions in the system. Because "management often doesn't have specific programming knowledge," he said, "it's possible to monkey-wrench and slow things down in more complicated pieces of code."

Jason, a software engineer in a Boston-based company, told me that "because tech products have been cobbled together over the course of years, the learning curve to run a specific one is incredibly steep, unless someone can teach you about the quirks." And while a digital picket line wouldn't be centralized in any physical sense, the symbolic barrier could be made visible to the product's users. "If the developers from Slack decided to strike," Jason offered, "they could without too much difficulty push out a change that made it so that any message that got sent would push a message about the purpose of the strike [to the user]."

Techies operate in a tight labor market, one with more job openings than it can fill. Many tech jobs require highly skilled workers and months of on-the-job training. The extent to which tech CEOs worry about the power workers hold in this arrangement was revealed in 2013. A class-action lawsuit was filed on behalf of more than one hundred thousand tech employees against Adobe, Apple, Google, and Intel for conspiring to suppress wages by creating "no-poach" lists, an agreement among the companies not to recruit each other's engineers. The lawsuit, based on a Department of Justice antitrust investigation launched in 2010, resulted in a $415 million settlement. "It's not hard to find a coder," Fred told me. "There's a shitload of coders. But when you're at an elite tech firm, they have an understanding of what an elite, skilled worker is—some of which is not legitimate, some of which is—[and] the engineers are understood to be very highly skilled and not easy to replace. Which gives [workers] a lot of power, and a lot of cover if we're doing anything political."

WHY WOULD TECH workers organize? They're not poor. They have a relative amount of power in their industry. But even the most well-paid tech job can have grueling hours, which is why tech workers are lauded for spending nights at their desks and punished for having children. Tech is also not known as especially welcoming to people of color. Michelle Miller, cofounder of Coworker.org, a platform that helps workers organize, explained that it's no longer so unusual to find a room full of techies who want to organize at work. "We've had people from every major tech company you can think of contact us in the past year saying, 'I want to organize a union.'"

Miller and her cofounder, Jess Kutch, were working for Service Employees International Union when they decided to create a digital platform to help tech workers organize in

2013. "There wasn't a bridge between what was happening in so many people's non-unionized workplaces and what was happening in the labor movement," said Miller. She and Kutch wanted to share their organizing knowledge, but unions, hobbled by waves of anti-union legislation and strapped for funds as their dues-paying bases diminished, couldn't provide the means.

Coworker.org has since been used to create in-app tips for Uber drivers, increase staffing at Starbucks, and fight sexual harassment at Comcast. But Miller says that until last year, the idea of organizing tech workers was not on their radar. Tech is filled with well-meaning people, but it took Trump's election for many of them to realize that even if they identify as liberal or left (tech companies were four of the top five employers of Sanders campaign donors), their companies do not.

Tech companies often tout their internal feedback systems as more effective and flexible than union grievance procedures. Once she began to work with techies, Miller said, employees who'd previously told her they didn't need tools like Coworker.org returned with stories of frustration. "They've discovered that when you push your company on things that impact their bottom line or the power they have in the economy, or impact their monopoly over data, they stop listening to you," said Miller. "Their gentle, friendly systems for employees' voices stop working."

But trust really began to erode over more ideological issues. For many of the tech giants, internal feedback systems center on weekly all-hands meetings in which employees use Reddit-like platforms to up-vote or down-vote topics submitted before the meetings, which are then addressed by high-ranking executives. These systems are limited, especially when it comes to matters of politics. Miller explained that the James Damore memo revealed to some techies that "the alt-right contingents inside these companies have been organizing to game those systems, to 'thumbs down' important issues that people wanted to talk about." To them, Damore's memo revealed an organized effort by right-wing employees to suppress open discussions of misogyny in tech.

Google's response to the Damore memo infuriated more than a few employees. Googlers — as the company's white-collar employees are called — say the company "was on fire for a week before the memo broke publicly," with conversation about the "women-are-dumber-than-men memo" (as one female engineer put it) pervading the company's otherwise apolitical offices. Google scheduled a company-wide town hall devoted to the topic within days of the memo's publication, but canceled it for reasons having to do with "the safety of employees." Their stated cause for concern came from Googlers leaking the names and writings of colleagues upset by the memo "directly to the alt-right." Far-right blogs still display these leaks. Aside from a statement from the company's VP of diversity, "there hasn't been an official communication about the memo since that town hall was canceled," said Jake, a software engineer at Google, which suggests that the company remains ill-equipped to handle difficult workplace issues.

Faced with the Damores of the business and their alt-right allies, the left-leaning techies recognized their relative weakness. As they saw "how their internal platforms were being used against them, and were neither perfect nor optimized for good," said Miller, they began to suspect that if their executives couldn't address problems of racism or misogyny within the workplace, they were unlikely to do so in public, "where there are profits at risk."

Similarly, Miller described a group of workers at a social platform who "had been raising issues about the use of the platform to disseminate hate and [to] attack people for months and months and months, but all the processes that had been set up [to address them] . . . deliberately led to dead ends" or made the problem "impossible to solve." The workers were frustrated, Miller said, and "it eroded their trust in the company, making them feel that they were part of the problem and couldn't do anything about it."

Alex, another techie, knows the feeling. Before he became a systems operator at an ad-tech firm, he worked for Securus, which describes itself as a provider of "leading edge civil and criminal justice technology solutions"; Alex described it as "Skype for prisoners." He has worked in the tech sector for twelve years and only lasted a few months at Securus. He recounted his time there:

> There were discussions about how US policy on prison reform was going to affect our bottom line. Meetings were held as company-wide conference calls: the CFO would say, "Excellent news, we can raise the rates on our product without Justice Department interference." They would have projections on the recidivism rate and that if it'll remain high, we'll expect a great year. The thinking within the company about prisoners was, "You fucked up. If you didn't want to be exploited by our company, you shouldn't have gone to jail; we have no moral qualms about mining you for whatever you're worth." I couldn't sleep, so I had to leave.

Alex isn't the only techie struggling with the glaring contradictions of an industry that claims to make the world a better place. "At my last company, we did email marketing," Markus, a systems administrator at a social media management company, told me. While performing routine maintenance, he discovered that some of the company's customers were "not just conservatives, but Breitbartesque, right-wing propagandists." After talking to colleagues about his discovery, he asked the CEO to cancel the contract. "The CEO said we can't discriminate based on ideological beliefs." But Markus and his colleagues organized an after-work meeting to discuss next steps to pressure the company. "We met at a bar, fifteen to thirty of us in a company of one hundred employees, and decided to raise this through our company's internal feedback channel. We didn't expect the CEO to agree since it would hurt his bottom line, so we planned to form an organization to push this issue." But much to Markus's and his colleagues' surprise, the CEO caved when they raised the issue as a group.

His current company, however, isn't giving in to pressure so easily. "The Trump campaign was one of our customers," he explained. While his current CEO likewise insists that the company can't discriminate based on a customer's political beliefs, Markus isn't easily discouraged. "We're waiting until the next election cycle to raise the issue. It'll be a perfect time for us to say, 'We won't allow you to support Trump's campaign with the tools we created.'"

ROOTED IN THE traditional organizations of the labor movement (in the Bay Area, the group meets in a UNITE HERE building), TWC is leading the way in broadening the definition of "tech worker" to include blue- and white-collar workers alike. Divisions between classes of workers are often more visible in tech than in other industries, as low-wage workers are employed by third-party contractors and white-collar workers are themselves stratified, with badge colors signifying where they can go, what facilities they can use, and in some cases, who they can talk to.

At Intel, "they fired every cafeteria worker the day before Thanksgiving and told the new [non-union] company not to rehire them," said Murphy, the security guard on Facebook's main campus. Before he worked at Facebook, he worked at Intel, and before Intel, Apple. As Murphy pointed out, the subcontracting model allows tech giants to access the services their operations require without having to bear the responsibilities or costs of direct employment. "The point of subcontracting is to make the labor force unstable," added Murphy. "It's why we pushed for the worker retention ordinance in the city of Santa Clara, where Intel is based—to mandate that when a company switches any of its subcontractors, the workers have the right to keep their jobs at the same rate of pay."

Recounting his conversations with techies during the Intel union campaign, Murphy said, "The techie mind-set is that they want to help and feel good about what they're doing. That's the cliché of Silicon Valley, 'making the world a better place.' So they want to feel like they're doing that. At Intel, if I had a personal relationship with someone, they'd say 'I want to support you.'"

Murphy believes the best thing techies can do to support service workers is to advocate for an end to subcontracting. "My coworkers and I dream about going direct with Facebook: that's where the money is, that's where the power is, and this artifice of subcontracting is just a scheme to hold down our wages and prevent us from getting a whack at the Facebook piñata." Fred, the techie who led the DSA Tech Action meeting I attended, shares this goal, saying that while he sees the same female janitor in his office every evening, he avoids asking her how she is, whether she gets maternity leave, or anything else about her working conditions because he doesn't want to put her job in jeopardy: "I don't know what policies she's governed under and whether I'd endanger her position by asking her about it." If tech did away with subcontractors, he explained, "I'd know that anyone I see in the workplace is a coworker, and that we have the same hierarchy above us."

While none of the TWC organizers I interviewed named the end of subcontracting as a goal, their actions suggest they'd be amenable to the approach. In addition to organizing Facebook subcontractors, TWC members joined delegations of blue-collar workers in delivering petitions to tech CEOs demanding that striking immigrant workers not be fired for their participation in 2017 May Day events. Says Sheets, "We were successful in getting Facebook and Google to agree to non-retaliation agreements for workers who decided to strike on that day." Similarly, Tech Solidarity in Seattle used Coworker.org to organize a petition for techies to sign in support of security officers unionizing at Amazon. It attracted 1,300 signatures. As Jeffrey Atkinson, a TWC-affiliated product manager in Seattle, told me, "We'd go out on lunch breaks and during evenings and talk to people on the street about what they thought about workers' rights. Between the street canvassing and online petition, we got those signatures, and delivered them with a sit-in action at an Amazon office on August 18, 2017."

The end of subcontracting may seem distant, but things are beginning to change. A few months ago, a union organizer showed up to a Tech Action meeting seeking contacts with Googlers. Fred connected him with Jake, the Google software engineer. Before long, collaboration between blue- and white-collar employees at the New York Google offices was under way.

THE TECH WORKERS I spoke with disagreed about what shape tech unions would take, if successful. When asked whether the old union mold would fit, Miller said, "We need something that acknowledges that it's not just managers and factory workers on a contained shop floor." Tech's dispersed workforce presents a challenge for the traditional union structure. As an industry strewn with independent contractors and subcontractors (far-flung "little fiefdoms" as Markus put it), tech may well call for a reconfiguring of union structures originally created to represent geographically centralized workplaces.

The dispersed workforce also presents a challenge for the traditional union process. While Markus says union organizers were "verbally supportive" of his efforts to organize tech workplaces in Chicago, he believes they're not interested in extending resources for a fight they don't think they can win, which would involve remote, contract, and other loosely connected workers: "They aren't ready to deploy organizers." Others spoke of reaching out to unions and never hearing back, or having union organizers lose touch with them over time. Concerned with retaining their membership amid an anti-union climate the likes of which we haven't seen in generations, many unions aren't interested in going on the offensive. With no union support on the horizon, the most militant among the burgeoning tech workers' movement are on their own. "The onus is on us," said Markus. "We'll build a movement, and the unions will come."

But as the tech sector reaches further into every aspect of our lives, organizing tech companies needn't be an isolated, insular project. At a company like Amazon, organizing could bring currently outsourced service workers under the company's umbrella, as well as the warehouse workers of Amazon's infamous just-in-time fulfillment centers. Because of their position in the US economy, these workers, if organized, could revolutionize the labor movement. An Amazon union could likewise incorporate the workers toiling on Amazon's Mechanical Turk platform, which allows companies to outsource repetitive, often demeaning tasks—labeling photos, transcribing a minute or two of an audio file—to what is often called "artificial intelligence" but is, in reality, a population of invisible workers from marginalized countries who are paid pennies. If the most advantaged of Amazon workers led the way, insisting on collective bargaining agreements that applied to everyone within the company, these denizens of the global Amazon fiefdom could be unified under one big contract.

From the baseline of a unionized tech sector, a picture emerges for the possibility of worker-owned companies, which could receive startup capital from the state (much as the military has underwritten tech's greatest successes). As Fred put it, "changing the way venture capital works, so it isn't four or so major firms deciding all the tech that will be funded," will be necessary to gaining popular, democratic control over the direction of the industry. Eventually, the goal is a model of investors unencumbered from the profit motive, who fund what is socially useful, instead of more apps to extract yet more ads.

Ceglowski suggests a public advocacy model along the lines of those in place at the Centers for Disease Control, or among librarians. An organization of tech workers could be a conduit between the public and the industry, with public concern and democratic pressure flowing into the organization's considerations, and expertise, advocacy, and cautionary information flowing from the workers to the general public. Rather than viewing tech as distinct in all ways from other industries, a self-enclosed innovation loop, Cegłowski's vision emphasizes the industry's entrenchment in society — its reliance on the same shared, social world.

Following this train of thought leads to other, utopian ideas: nationalizing the internet, which is already the beneficiary of hundreds of millions of dollars in public funding; making all software open-sourced and transparent, to allow for public scrutiny into the application of what could be racially coded or otherwise biased algorithms; the list goes on.

IN JANUARY OF 2018, workers at Lanetix, a logistics technology company based in San Francisco and Washington DC, filed with the National Labor Relations Board for a union election. Theirs would have been the first union in the US made up entirely of software engineers. About ten days after they filed the petition with the NLRB, Lanetix fired them, announcing plans to outsource its operations to Eastern Europe. Björn Westergard, one of the fired engineers, told me the organizing drive's proximate cause was "the retaliatory firing of a coworker who had consistently been a spokesperson for us on a number of issues, most notably paid time off." Regarding the grievances that drove the organizing effort, Westergard says, "We were tired of managerial caprice in compensation, working conditions, and assignments; this caprice often seemed to favor the more experienced men (myself included). Second, we wanted management to replace two highly qualified staff engineers who had left the company so that we could keep up with the skill demands of the industry."

While the union has filed an unfair labor practices complaint with the NLRB, in the immediate aftermath of the mass layoff, TWC and Tech Action were among the first to respond, releasing a statement in solidarity with the fired engineers. These organizers might still be in the early stages of building power, but the rest of us can only hope they succeed, and quickly. Markus summed up the possibilities: "We're inching toward a dystopia, and it's being created by people who see themselves as liberal. And we need to organize, or else venture capitalists and CEOs are going to destroy our society." +

ADAM BOBBETTE
Fire in Jakarta

A POOR-QUALITY, THIRTY-SECOND YOUTUBE video shows Basuki "Ahok" Tjahaja Purnama, the former governor of Jakarta, delivering a speech on one of the small tropical islands off the north coast of the city in September 2016. He stands inside a community center in a short-sleeve beige uniform, with a name card on a retractable cord fixed to his breast pocket. Members of his cabinet, all men in similar uniforms, sit behind him in kids' chairs incongruous with their station but fitting for the informal event: the governor dropping by for a chat with his constituents. In his usual frank style, Purnama explains that working people in the area are being ripped off by local elites, and fishermen are barely scraping by. His plan is to make this right, he says, and the people present need only look to his two years governing the city to find proof of his success.

Then he makes the comment that will lead to his downfall. "So if you choose not to vote for me because of the lies of 5:51 and things like that," he says casually, "you're afraid of going to hell or whatever, that's your right." The sarcastic remark is a reference to Sura 51 of the Koran, often interpreted to forbid Muslims from taking Christians or Jews as allies. Indonesia is 87 percent Muslim, and Purnama is Christian. He is also ethnically Chinese, a minority in Indonesia with a long history of facing oppression and violence.

It was an error of a magnitude he could not have foreseen. The video quickly spread: it was copied, edited, distributed, and widely posted. Many of the posts received more than a half million views in a few days. Duplicate videos distilled Purnama's hour-long speech to the single line, "the lies of 5:51 and things like that," repeating it over and over, sometimes with caption text running across the bottom. A few days after the speech, Amirsyah Tambunan, the Deputy Secretary General of the Indonesian Ulema Council, which purports to guide the moral behavior of Indonesia's 200 million Muslims, said on television that to blaspheme the Koran ought to be punished by "death, crucifixion, or at least hand amputation and expulsion." In Purnama's case, he'd settle for the state court's existing blasphemy laws, which can lead to years of imprisonment.

In the following weeks, the broad, leafy avenues that circle Jakarta's national monument — a giant travertine obelisk with a golden flame at the top, which commemorates Indonesia's independence struggle — were crammed with hundreds of thousands of men in brilliant white outfits and turbans. Muhammad Rizieq Shihab, leader of the ultra-right-wing political organization Islamic Defenders Front, stood on a truck in the middle of the crowd. "Jail Ahok!" he shouted through a microphone. Fists and banners shot up as the call echoed through the crowd. The courts summoned Purnama to stand trial on charges of blasphemy. When his testimony was live-cast, he wept and asked forgiveness; he meant no offense, he said. A gubernatorial election was called during the trial and Purnama was permitted to run against Anies Baswedan, a Muslim who drew the support of Islamist groups across the country. Purnama was found guilty and sentenced to three years in jail. He lost the election to Baswedan by a huge margin, even though he was, until that point, one of the country's most popular politicians.

ISLAM HAS BEGUN to redefine the highest ranks of Jakarta, one of the world's largest cities in a country with more Muslims than any other. But Islamist conservatism is also springing up from the grassroots. A video showed up on YouTube in May 2017 of kids shooting automatic weapons and burning their passports, encouraging their brothers and sisters in Malaysia, the Philippines, and Indonesia to join them in the struggle for the caliphate. Later that month, three people were killed by a bomb explosion in East Jakarta, which the police suspect was planned by a conservative Muslim. In West Java, statues commemorating national heroes were razed for idolatry. The Indonesian military deployed troops in June to guard the border between Indonesia and the Philippine province of Malawar, where president Rodrigo Duterte had recently imposed martial law and deployed military forces against the Islamic militants trying to take over the city. In July, an ISIS flag was hung outside a police station in Jakarta with a handwritten note: THE WAR HAS BEGUN.

In winter 2016, banners outside mosques claimed that lesbians and gays weren't welcome because they disturbed the Javanese spirit. A recent survey by the Kuala Lumpur–based Institute for the Study of Islam and Society found that almost 80 percent of religious teachers in schools support conservative Islam and are sympathetic to groups like Hizbut Tahrir Indonesia (roughly, Party of Liberation Indonesia), the Indonesian chapter of the conservative international Islamic political organization. More than half of all high school students in West Java were sympathetic with the establishment of a caliphate-based state. In the last presidential election, in 2014, the Islamist opposition concocted a Trump-style birther controversy, claiming president-elect Joko Widodo was actually a Christian. Had he not demonstrated his documents, his wildly popular candidacy would have been crushed. Rumors that Widodo was actually Chinese began to swirl. In response, Widodo went on pilgrimage to Mecca. He won the election.

At the G20 meeting in July 2017, Widodo gave a speech about taking seriously the spread of conservative Islam to potentially volatile regions like Southeast Asia. Back home, he reiterated through the media and his entourage of talking heads that Indonesian-style Islam is pluralist, liberal, and tolerant. Religious leaders from the major Islamic groups concurred and held press conferences about mutual respect with representatives from Hindu, Buddhist, Jewish, and Christian communities. Meanwhile, Purnama was carted off to prison for blasphemy. The governorship of Jakarta—the country's capital and largest city—was passed on to Baswedan. Prabowo Subianto, the oligarch politician whose PR team dreamed up the story about Widodo being a Christian, staged a media event where he publicly thanked the leader of the Islamic Defenders Front, Muhammad Rizieq Shihab, for supporting Baswedan's candidacy and "saving Indonesian democracy."

The Indonesian government's tension with conservative Islam escalated soon afterward, when Widodo decreed a ban on any organization that did not conform to the constitution, or what Indonesians sometimes refer to as the "state ideology."* This put militant organizations such as the Islamic Defenders Front and Hizbut Tahrir Indonesia in a league with previously banned organizations like the Indonesian Communist Party, whose members were all but exterminated in the 1960s because they threatened the "unity" of the state. According to the president's deliberations, these organizations could be made illegal, their rallies broken up by the police, and their organizers jailed. People charged with blasphemy could now also face up to ten years in prison. Journalists argued that Widodo was retaliating against the conservative groups for sending Purnama to jail. A week after the law was announced, Hizbut Tahrir Indonesia was listed as an illegal organization.

All this came as a surprise to the West. The rise of Widodo in 2013 had seemed like a turning point for Indonesian democracy. A furniture salesman from Surakarta, he came from outside the oligarchy and quickly rose through the political ranks, first as mayor of his small, provincial hometown, then as the governor of Jakarta. He was so astronomically popular that he was ushered in as the Indonesian Democratic Party of Struggle's presidential candidate before he had even

---

* The constitution of Indonesia is called Pancasila and is fashioned to uphold five core principles, the first of which is "Belief in the One and Only God." In the 1940s, early drafters of the constitution omitted which god, hoping to stem Islamic political parties' hold on power, ensure representational democracy, and protect non-Muslim communities. This did, however, delegitimize the many polytheistic traditions present in Indonesia at the time. Another principle is the "Unity of Indonesia," which, through flexible interpretations of its meaning, has long been used as a tool to suppress organizations.

finished his term as governor. Promising to end corrupt politics and the influence of big money, he would also invigorate and modernize Indonesia with a kind of humble technocracy. Good managerial practices mixed with roll-up-your-sleeves hard work would, his campaign suggested, finally bring the country sorely needed technological and infrastructural development. Widodo loved Metallica, looked and dressed like he was from the countryside, was liberal on social issues, and was keen to plug Indonesia into the Obama-era configuration of globalization. Both in the West and in Indonesia, he was projected as Obama's mirror image. The fact that Obama spent a few years as a kid in Jakarta only confirmed that Obama, and by extension Obama-era America, was at least in part Indonesian. But one of Widodo's closest allies, Purnama, was in prison for blasphemy, and the capital city voted its new governor into power on religious principles.

INDONESIA CAME into modern existence in 1945. Before that, it was controlled by the Dutch. Like the French and British, who also controlled parts of Southeast Asia, the Dutch were expelled when the Japanese took control of the region during World War II. After the war ended, some Japanese forces gave their weapons to the burgeoning nationalist groups vying to fill the power vacuum before the Dutch could return to reclaim the colony. From the veranda of a white modernist colonial building in Central Jakarta, Sukarno, the leader of the resistance and a powerful nationalist movement, read the "Proclamation" declaring the existence of the Republic of Indonesia. Soon afterward he became its first president.

Then he became its first dictator, claiming absolute political authority in the name of the anticolonial struggle. Sukarno was a leader of the Non-Aligned Movement and the third worldism that built political and economic alliances among new postcolonial states. He died in 1970, after he was replaced in a coup by Suharto, the dictator who defined Indonesia for decades as a country ruled by oligarchical power.

Though Indonesia has had several relatively free elections since 1999, Joko Widodo was the first candidate to emerge from outside the power structures inherited from Sukarno and Suharto: the corrupt judiciary, police, military, and civil service sector, and the small network of political families who hold an overwhelming concentration of capital. Even so, Megawati, the woman who financed Widodo's political career and brought him into the Democratic Party of Struggle, is Sukarno's daughter. His nemesis, Subianto, the oligarch behind the Widodo-is-a-Christian controversy, was a special-forces general under Suharto. Subianto married Suharto's daughter Titiek Suharto and is now head of the Great Indonesia Movement Party, one of the country's most powerful political parties. Widodo's vice president, Jusuf Kalla, is from one of the richest families in Sulawesi, an outer island east of Borneo, and was the chairman of Suharto's Golkar party until he shifted his alliances to Megawati. Aburizal Bakrie, whose conglomerates include Indonesian media, education, property, agriculture, mining, and manufacturing companies, took his place. Bakrie was then replaced by Setya Novanto, who was brought up on corruption charges in 2017 for orchestrating the redirection of $184 million in state funds to private coffers.

Where does political Islam fit into this picture? It is, by most accounts, a conservative populist movement eroding the country's already fragile liberal democracy. Some accounts suggest conspiracy, that the emergence of conservative Islam is not a true grassroots movement but a power play by the country's oligarchy to undermine Indonesia's liberal traditions. According to this view, radical groups are funded by entrenched wealth through opaque channels and encouraged to unleash vigilante violence; mobilize latent religious intolerance, social divisions, and scapegoating; and unsettle the stability of the popular president. Some writers have gone so far as to warn of coups planned by these shadowy forces.

JAKARTA SETS the political and economic agenda for the rest of the country. It is the largest stage from which the grand narratives of Indonesia are broadcast, and a magnet for Indonesian migrants with dreams of increasing their prospects and fortunes. The scale and complexity of the city are so vast as to be unfathomable: 30 million people living in a sinking estuary connected from the volcanoes in the south to the Java Sea in the north by the river systems that snake through it—river systems that carry 30 million people's worth of garbage and shit, which pile up during the rainy season and spill out over the edges for weeks on end.

About 5 million of these people live in slums, in pockets between roads and rivers and train tracks and overpasses. The concrete columns of the unfinished MRT light rail stand like ruins, their bases wrapped in faded banners bearing architectural renderings of the new, efficient city to come. Built on light deltaic sands, Jakarta is sinking unevenly, creating bowls for floodwaters to pool. The bay in the north slowly rises as global sea levels inch upward.

My low-lying neighborhood was a thicket of streets and cheek-by-jowl concrete housing. There were about twenty mosques in less than half a square mile. Five times a day, from four in the morning to six at night, muezzins raised their voices through speakers poised in minarets. They, too, are creating Jakarta, a city that speaks directly to God from the prayer mats laid out on tile floors.

I was living in Jakarta during Purnama's trial, trying to understand the confluence of city politics and conservative Islam that led to his downfall. Purnama had been an effective governor, promoting infrastructure projects that were meant to save Jakarta from floods and ecological devastation. But he made enemies in the city's slums when he attempted to evict the slum dwellers and move them into modernized public housing. The houses simply didn't take, and many former slum dwellers returned to their old neighborhoods or created new informal settlements elsewhere. These slum dwellers became part of the force behind Baswedan's successful contest for governor, and part of the overall transformation of Indonesia into a surprising home for Islamism.

Over and over, I found myself traversing the grounds of a cemetery in my neighborhood. I was first drawn to the goats that perched on top of cenotaphs for better views of the grounds, and came to understand that their herders lived in the small shanties woven around gravestones. The adjacent land was owned by Bakrie, the developer-politician, and from the graveyard you could see the two giant black-glass towers he'd designed for his company headquarters in 2009, known as Bakrieland. He also built a mosque only a few hundred meters from the cemetery and named it after himself. The song of the muezzin from Bakrie's mosque was the loudest in the neighborhood. After coming back from prayers, the people who lived in the cemetery worked under the shadow of those towers, sorting, burning, and selling the garbage from the nearby canals and neighborhood streets. They were right in the middle, stuck between the oligarchs, Islam, and the unstable ground of the city.

In August 2017, I spent weeks interviewing the cemetery's scavengers. They told me the story of a mysterious fire that consumed their village that July.

HARIS HAD WOKEN UP before sunrise to prepare his new coffee stall in order to catch the traffic from morning prayers. On the dirt shoulder of a three-way intersection, he had shimmed a wooden board between a lamppost and cement wall. On the board, he'd placed a couple of thermoses of hot water, a bucket to wash dishes, some cups, some saucers, and sachets of powdered instant coffee and tea bags. One red plastic stool for him, and two others—blue—for customers. Suddenly, his attention was drawn across the road. From deep inside the cemetery, rushes of sparks flickered into the night sky. At first Haris thought it might be fireworks set off by kids running around inside. But then the giant tree caught on fire, the tree that stood in the middle of the cemetery and gave shade to the workers and garbage piles and coffee houses that sprawled around the old cenotaphs and tombstones. Its leaves shriveled, and then the whole thing became a torch, illuminating the graveyard in a pulsing glow. Haris watched as the flimsy houses began to light up, catching fire like a bundle of matches.

Nazar, in his mid-seventies, was born and raised in the graveyard. That night, he was sleeping in his house in the eastern section, which runs along the concrete wall that separates the slum from the working-class neighborhood on the other side. The eastern section was almost like a different neighborhood, even though it shared the same graveyard as the others. The houses weren't connected: they used different makeshift showers and gathered their water in different cisterns. The families from the different sections knew each other but rarely spent time together. Nazar slept through the fire in his red sarong on a thin, faded mattress, which was raised on a plywood base to keep out the floods, rats, mice, and cockroaches. The roof above was a patchwork of wood, metal, and corrugated plastic abutting the concrete partition. Through his room's curtain door was the shop where his niece sold coffee and neighbors spent evenings watching television, and where his teenage nephew had played his ukulele the night before, singing pop songs with some girls.

But Sandi was awake for the fire, sitting on the couch outside the Betawi Forum clubhouse at the cemetery entrance. He was on the night shift, drinking coffee while his two friends slept inside. When the tree lit up, he roused and walked to the edge of the clubhouse porch. "Bastard," he said. "This one's big."

Karno was down the road sitting in his Bajaj, one of the blue, three-wheeled, beetle-shaped taxis that wind through Jakarta's small streets. He was smoking his first cigarette of the day, a fat Djarum Super, to get his stomach moving. Then he'd visit the public toilet at the market just down the road. He liked it there because it was usually empty that early in the morning. No one to ask for change at the door. The days when the market was full of promise were long gone. The stalls upstairs were half empty, the metal grates rusted shut from the humidity. In the corners of the food hall, high up toward the edge of the vaulted metal ceiling, black cobwebs had grown wild. When the market was first built, city officials said the neighborhood would be full of newcomers, but they never came. Everyone suspected it had been a way for someone in the neighborhood government to take a payout from a developer or construction company.

Like Sandi, all Karno could do was stand up and watch as the tree lit up and the houses erupted in flames. He didn't know anyone who lived inside the cemetery and had no one to call. He would just wait and see what happened.

Father Nudi was called father as a sign of respect. He was already awake when the tree caught fire because he kept irregular hours, sleeping through parts of the day in the graveyard if there was shade. Sometimes he slept as little as an hour a day, sometimes not at all. Perhaps this gave him the quality of delirium he was known for around the cemetery. A loner, he'd staked out a space among a few graves along the black iron fence and formed modest-size mounds of the plastic he collected throughout the day. Some of it had been there for a long time and begun to fuse with the ground. His red T-shirt slumped over a concrete tombstone that read, HERE LIES TJIE FEN SIONG, 18 NOVEMBER 1969. It was hard to know what Father Nudi thought about the fire. It was hard to know what he thought about anything, because he talked like he was continually surprised by his own existence. "Fire, there was fire, fire, there was fire, my name is Nudi." He said that over and over again.

Fire trucks with BAKRIE in big letters across the front finally raced past Haris's coffee stall. Nazar continued to sleep in his red sarong. Sandi sat back down on the couch, but he'd woken his friends, who joined him to drink more black coffee and watch the houses burn. Karno settled back into the front seat of his Bajaj to watch. Nudi hadn't moved much at all. By that point, the fire had engulfed forty tightly spaced one-room houses. People ran around with buckets of water, screaming at kids to get out of the way.

As the sun began to rise over the burned-out swath, a blackened wood wall tipped over like a playing card. The charred limbs of the big tree were covered in bubbling orange ooze from the chemicals in the firetruck's spray. They stood out against the background of the slowly lightening sky with smoke seething off them. Television crews showed up in vans, and newspaper journalists on motorbikes, to document the blaze as it razed the network of homes and melted mounds of collected material.

The place was well known as the Scavenger Village. Even the residents called it that, proudly. That's what they did: they scavenged garbage. That's who they were, it was their identity, they said. To the city authorities, they had no legitimate claims to property, and many of them didn't have identity cards. The media called a local politician for his thoughts, a man from the same office that built the half-empty, slowly decaying market. "I told them to get out. . . . they can't live there," he said. "I don't care where they go, that's their problem. It's not their land, it's a city-owned cemetery."

THE CEMETERY IS KNOWN as the Chinese cemetery. It lies across the road from the Dutch cemetery and the Muslim cemetery. In the 1940s and '50s, they were built on what was then the city limit. The Dutch cemetery holds the dead bodies of the Allies who fought the Japanese occupation. The Muslim and Christian cemeteries came shortly afterward, segregated in death as in life. Now roads and canals cut between the cemeteries, concrete tower blocks stand along their borders, and tight-knit, low-rise neighborhoods push right up to their edges.

The Dutch and Muslim cemeteries are both vast and have permanent guards and groundskeepers, but the Chinese cemetery, while still used by families, with new graves dug and bodies interred, sprouted a village after the city expanded. The exact date when the scavengers arrived is unclear, but it has existed at least since the Suharto regime in the 1960s, and Nazar claims to have been born there. I was told the current residents are ethnically Indonesian; though it is an unclear category, it usually means neither Chinese nor white. Nobody is certain how many people live there now. Figures range from three hundred to fifteen hundred people, according to different residents and media reports. But there is no census to check, because the residents don't officially exist, and they too fail to agree on how many they are. Residents told me that everyone originally comes from Java, but then I met a woman who immigrated from Sulawesi.

The village's main function is to intake, sort, and sell garbage from the surrounding neighborhoods. Some people fill wooden trollies with plastic lifted from the street and canal banks. Some work in the center of the settlement, where there is a giant, almost mountain-like deposit of compressed waste. One side was blackened and melted by the fire, which exposed layers of bottles, labels, bags, shoes, and other trash in bands, like geological strata. Black trucks from the neighborhood bring in loads of waste, which the scavengers break apart and separate. They cut the tops of plastic bottles from the bottoms, removing the lids and labels. Everything gets its own pile. The separated parts are then bagged and sold off to companies that bring the material to factories to incinerate or recycle. One pound of plastic is worth 500 rupiah, about three and a half US cents. What is not sold is burned on-site. In the evenings, it's normal to see smoldering fires smoking between the graves and cenotaphs. The fires are almost constant.

It would make sense that a settlement built of tightly packed, thin, scavenged wood planks, with fires constantly burning, would occasionally go up in flames. Mia, an activist in the local community center who lost her house in the fire, told me that someone came home late that night and started making coffee on the propane stove. They passed out, exhausted from work, before it was finished. Then everything went up in flames.

On the way into the village one day, I met Udin, who had come along the dirt path through the graves carrying a wooden cart filled with cardboard. His house had burned down too. He explained that the fire began with a spark from the electrical cables they hijacked from the surrounding neighborhood. Someone else told me that all the accounts were true: one thing leading to another had started the fire.

I began to wonder why no one could agree on the cause of the fire, and why some were ready to believe that two different sources could start it at the same time. It seemed intuitive that one would want to determine the cause, to locate the hazards within the village's precarious architecture and ensure a fire wouldn't happen again. But nobody seemed too concerned. Perhaps this was the condition of marginal people in Jakarta: exposure to physical danger was permanent. There was nothing that could be done about it, so why even bother with the cause of the fire? If this time it was a stove, next time it would be the electricity.

When I asked about Purnama and the recent election, Mia said people in the village didn't talk about city politics. "Your vote is your choice," she said. "It's private." She didn't know who voted for whom. I asked about Sandi, the guy who worked in the clubhouse for the Betawi Forum, which is an ethnic organization usually considered to be a criminal gang because it exacts vigilante justice. Mia said there were no relations between the cemetery's inhabitants and the gang—the scavengers keep everything peaceful. But Nazar had told me a few weeks earlier that the guys in the clubhouse were a bunch of thugs and extortionists and no one living in the cemetery wanted them there.

I went to the clubhouse a few days later. I was passed on to Ashoy, the 35-year-old director of program development for Sanggar Bilpin, who is a spokesperson for the village. As we sat on the green linoleum floor of the clubhouse drinking coffee, Ashoy explained that it was good that Purnama was no longer the mayor; he'd been evicting slums like theirs in the name of cleaning up the city. A few months ago, during Purnama's trial and the mayoral campaign, the local government had threatened to evict them again, a regular occurrence. But Ashoy went to the media: "The government became shy, scared, they backed off. I said we wouldn't leave until the government could guarantee a place in subsidized housing." There was a block currently under construction on the edge of the neighborhood; they wouldn't move until it was finished and promised to them. The person who eventually met their demands turned out to be the new mayor, Baswedan, who had defeated Purnama.

Ashoy showed me a photo on his phone and said coyly, "Look, a victim of the fire." It was him: Ashoy on his back, sunbathing on a cardboard mat in the black, burned-out remains. He swiped to a photo of himself kneeling in the same spot, with a man handing him a wad of cash. He zoomed in on the wad and said, "That is $10,000."

"Who is that?" I asked

"A donor," he said. I asked for details, but Ashoy was evasive.

"Where does he live?"

"Over there." He pointed vaguely south.

"Why did he give you money? What does he ask for in return?"

"He gives us money whenever there is a crisis, he doesn't ask for anything in return. We use the money to buy food and materials to rebuild the houses. Look, we used the money to buy cement and new wood," he said.

"He doesn't ask you for anything in return?" I asked again.

"No, it's just goodwill."

I asked if I could meet the donor, or at least be given a way to contact him, but Ashoy talked around me. He then showed me another photo, this time of him standing behind Baswedan at a dinner party during the campaign. "I was representing the village to Baswedan's team. I told him about us and that we wanted to move to the new apartment complex. Baswedan said they would help us out." After I left Ashoy, I noticed a Baswedan campaign banner hanging outside the clubhouse.

A few days later, in an empty Indian restaurant on the ground floor of one of Bakrieville's black towers, I told my friend Farid about the fire and how strange I found it. He said I was missing something: when things burn down in Jakarta and few people know why, money is involved. The police never resolved the fire that burned down the big market in January—also at four in the morning, before prayers. No cause found, no arsonist convicted, though the market was the size of a city block. It is quietly assumed that money tied to real estate changed hands. I remembered that the first time I came to Jakarta, in 2013, I watched from a thirty-second-floor balcony as a column of black smoke billowed from a skyscraper against the diffuse orange glow of the setting sun.

ABOUT A WEEK before I left the city, I came across another village on fire while walking through some new neighborhoods. There were hundreds of bystanders on the rail embankment, watching as villagers inside the smoldering buildings tossed buckets of water and firefighters used their hoses.

I was never able to uncover the identity of Ashoy's mysterious donor, but it's likely he was involved in Baswedan's campaign. The money he gave the slum dwellers led circuitously to support for Baswedan, perhaps in exchange for further favors down the line, including new housing. The village's reliance on trash scavenging was secure, because the city only controlled a small percentage of its processing. But if the city cleaned up the trash, the scavengers in the Chinese cemetery and thousands, or hundreds of thousands, elsewhere would be out of a livelihood, creating a reserve army of labor that could become politically dangerous.

But the scavengers are not conservative Muslims. Over the two months that I spent coming and going—taking regular lunchtime walks through the village, hanging out in the cafés late at night, and waiting out the nearby rush hour sitting on a tombstone with someone—I rarely saw a hijab. There is no mosque inside the village. Ashoy is openly queer. "I'm not embarrassed by who I am," he declared to me in the activist clubhouse one evening, lying on his back. His nascent potbelly protruded slighty through the opened buttons of his floral-patterned shirt. He told me about his hookups with various foreign men (usually Australian, he pointed out), and then, one afternoon, he introduced me to his pregnant wife. She knew Ashoy's preferences. But, as he explained, it made life easier to look pious from the outside. When necessary, he could perform the role of a working-class man in a traditional family.

The slum dwellers could sometimes use political figures like Baswedan to their advantage. This pattern seemed to be repeating itself across the city. More and more of them swelled the ranks of the Islamist parties, which would not fight the city's floods, would not clean it up, would not save it from sinking into the sea. +

SHANNON EBNER, *YES TOMORROW, NO TOMORROW*. 2006, C-PRINT. 32 1/16 × 40 5/8". COURTESY OF THE ARTIST AND ALTMAN SIEGEL, SAN FRANCISCO.

AN ACCOUNT OF MY HUT
Christina Nichol

IN 2017, THE WEATHER in California was the hottest in history. It was hotter than in 2016, which was also the hottest in history. The vineyard owners spoke nervously of how difficult it was to find people willing to pick grapes in this heat. The apple trees dropped all their apples. Over the summer the smoke from hundreds of wildfires burning throughout the state gave me a chronic cough, which turned into walking pneumonia. People began to talk about how illnesses are getting weirder these days. I decided to attend a climate change action meeting I had seen announced in the local newspaper.

It was an experimental prototype course founded on the ideas in George Marshall's book *Don't Even Think About It: Why Our Brains Are Wired to Ignore Climate Change.* After spending fifteen years studying climate change–denying microcultures, Marshall concluded that facts don't change people's minds; only stories do. We're so motivated by wanting to belong that we'd rather risk the dangers of climate change than the more immediate symbolic death of estrangement from our peers. In order to address climate change in our communities, Marshall suggests, we must appeal to the same desires that religion does: for belonging, consolation, and redemption.

For this reason, the purpose of the group—or "fellowship," as the organizers called it—was to borrow the most effective tools of religion to create a community of people who would work together when it was time to implement policy change, or even take to the streets. Their aim was to galvanize 3.5 percent of the local population—the number social scientists estimate is the tipping point for effecting social change.

You had to apply to the prototype course, so after the informational meeting I wrote the organizers the following email, thinking there'd be a lot of competition:

> I attended your Information Session last night at the Sonoma County Land Trust. I marked the sheet stating that I would like to take the course you are offering but I just want to reiterate how much. I grew up with a dad who would regale us with climate change statistics over the dinner table. If my brother said he was going to a Giants game, my dad would say that he better enjoy it now because there weren't going to be any Giants games in the future. Hanging on the wall was a color-coded map he created of what property values would be worth when ocean levels rose in the Bay Area. He terrorized all my friends by describing how the atmosphere would start to smell like rotten eggs as soon as the oceans warmed and started pluming carbon. In effect, I assumed that by 2020, life on Earth wouldn't exist anymore. I teach environmental studies and am looking for ways that I can bring hope to my students but also help motivate them (as well as myself). I found your session to be inspiring, especially in its emphasis on fellowship and taking concrete action, and I felt a newfound joy that I hadn't felt in a while. I feel ready to take on the commitment that this course asks for.

THE ORGANIZERS TRIED many methods for cultivating a feeling of fellowship. They'd start the session by banging a gong, or by reciting a poem by William Stafford or the former mayor. They encouraged us to discuss our vulnerabilities. But the most effective method was to scare the crap out of us with mini-lectures about the realities of climate change, which bonded us in common terror.

We were presented, at the beginning, with a self-proclaimed "humorless, brain-numbing deep dive into climate science." They told us it wasn't supposed to happen this quickly. Climate scientists had predicted that by 2017 we would be at 380 parts per million (ppm) of carbon dioxide in the atmosphere, but we were already past 410 ppm.

The man who presented this information was, like my father, a local architect. Scrunching up his face he said, "I don't want to depress you, but I want to tell it to you straight." He told us that when he designs a house he has to deal with very strict building codes, which are intended to prevent worst-case scenarios. By contrast, the Paris Agreement—whose purpose is to limit the temperature increase over the second half of the century to 1.5 to 2 degrees Celsius above preindustrial levels—doesn't address worst-case scenarios. "Would you put a loved one on an airplane if the airplane had a 50 percent chance of making it across the Atlantic?" he asked.

The most effective glue for bonding, our organizers said, was collaboration: we needed a goal we could all work toward. Our goal was to phase out the internal combustion engine in California by 2030. They gave us questionnaires so we could spend the next week testing the public's receptivity to this idea. Here are some of the responses we got:

What happens if the power goes out?

Where do the cars on the road go? Do we get a free car? What happens to the oil companies? Would you be punished for having a gas car?

Do I have to get rid of my brand-new car? How did we get into this mess? What can we do to ensure our children can understand so they know what is going on by the time they get through high school?

Why not just get everyone to stop eating meat instead? Agriculture creates as many greenhouse gases as automobiles. Haven't you seen *Cowspiracy*?

There are so many other issues. Why electric cars? We need to change our habits!

Our schools should feature human relationships and our relationship to the Earth. The 4 Rs: Reading, 'Riting, Rithmetic, Relationships.

Could I go to Nevada to buy a car?

Isn't solar production toxic?

What will I do with my beloved van that carries all my stuff day after day?

Would there be violent, emotional reactions to such a "radical" move? How do we deal with that reaction?

I like it. Get there!

Proud of you, Bill, for being involved. It's inspiring.

I'm not driving an electric car! I'm allergic to electricity and SMART meter rays!

2030 may be too late to avoid some of the most catastrophic climate & social issues.

> We have such a gas + car culture. Why do we let high schoolers drive to school? We need to change the consciousness. Only HS kids who work should have a car.

I asked my friend who works as a photographer for the Red Cross for her take on the electric-car issue. She said it was a good idea and invited me to help her install smoke alarms on houseboats in Sausalito.

"You should come," she said. "Get to know the houseboat community."

It's true that I was looking for community. I'd recently sent my friend an email about Russian House #1, a restaurant on the Sonoma coast where all the waiters have PhDs and the owners post a daily philosophical question diners are encouraged to discuss with one another. But I was also looking for a house to live in. I started wondering if a houseboat could be the solution to my housing dilemma.

I scanned Craigslist and called my boyfriend, Bongjun.

"Guess what? There's a way to live in the South Bay without paying a million dollars!" I said. "It's possible to live there for only a hundred thousand dollars. But actually, I researched it and it's *not* possible."

"What is it?" he asked.

"A houseboat. Three bedrooms for a hundred thousand."

"I saw a houseboat on Zillow last week," he said. "It was the kind of boat you discover the New World in. In the picture, the seller was hanging off the mast in a Renaissance costume."

"But these ones are actual houses. You get to know your neighbors."

"I don't want to live in a boat. I'd rather live in a bus."

"But you're always talking about how you love water, how you need to live near a river. We could go out in a kayak at night. Row to a restaurant."

"I don't like soggy socks."

"The water doesn't come *into* the boat."

"But I would have soggy socks in my subconscious."

Anyway, it didn't matter. It turned out that residents of Docktown, the houseboat community in Redwood City, were being evicted. All the houseboats without school-age children were required to vacate by February. That's why they were so cheap. But now I was back to negotiating with another person about a place to live in the midst of a housing crisis. "Maybe we could buy the houseboat and put it on some land," I said. "Then we'll be all set for when the oceans rise."

In California, the only people who own houses are people who bought them in the 1970s, work for tech companies, or were on the receiving end of a miracle. In Oakland, the blocks of homeless tarp housing continue to expand. In the grocery store you overhear people talking about the housing crisis. "It's called BYOH," the bagger says to the checker. "We buy a piece of land together and you Bring Your Own House."

In his book, George Marshall writes that people like to point to the Chinese pictogram *wēijī*, claiming that the character for "crisis" (*wēi*) is always paired with the character for "opportunity" (*jī*). But it turns out that *jī* doesn't actually mean "opportunity" at all. It means "a moment," "an airplane," and, sometimes, "organic chemistry." I started to wonder if there is a Chinese character that links "trying to solve climate change" with "trying to solve California's housing crisis."

THE DAY TRUMP WAS ELECTED, the first thing my mom said was, "Is today the day we can start smoking marijuana?" One of the consequences of California's legalization of marijuana is that industrial agriculture is appropriating the weed business. There are a number of reasonably cheap former pot farms for sale in the Santa Cruz Mountains.

Bongjun went to look at one to see if it was an appropriate place to build a sustainable community. Part of the road had been washed away by last winter's flood, so he had to park at the bottom of the hill. "We'd have to get four-wheel drive to get up there," he said. "You would really like the house, though. It has a grow room."

"But I'm not interested in growing marijuana."

"Oh, is *that* what *grow room* means?" he said. "I thought it was a place where Californians go to meditate, and, you know, *grow*."

I ONCE READ A STORY called "An Account of My Hut," by Kamo no Chōmei, a 12th-century Japanese hermit. Chōmei describes how after witnessing a fire, an earthquake, and a typhoon in Kyoto, he leaves society and goes to live in a hut.

Seven hundred years later, Basil Bunting, the Northumberland poet, wrote his own rendition of Chōmei's story:

> Oh! There's nothing to complain about.
> Buddha says: 'None of the world is good.'
> I am fond of my hut . . .

But even if I wanted to renounce the world, I wouldn't be able to afford a hut in California.

A FEW MONTHS AGO, Bongjun and I found a house in Oakland. The real estate agent said we were competing against twenty-eight other bids. She suggested that we write a love letter to accompany our offer.

"A *love* letter?" my former roommate from Florida said over the phone. "And everyone makes fun of people from *Florida*? They're all, 'That guy put his head in an alligator's mouth because he smelled licorice in there, but actually the licorice was on his face!' But that's nothing compared to having to write a *love* letter to a house!"

"Well, it's to the *owner* of the house," I told him. "I have to write something like, 'I will only use biodegradable detergents. I will only plant native plants in the garden. I will keep the bird feeder well stocked . . .'"

"Those people need to cut the cord," he said. "It's a *house* for god's sake."

We made an offer well over the asking price and tossed in our love letter, but got outbid by somebody who offered $400,000 over the asking price.

Another day we found a former sheet metal factory that we thought we could turn into a community performance space. It didn't have a sewage system, and it's possible that the previous owner had died from the black mold that encroached on all the surfaces. The factory needed a new roof, and if it burned down it couldn't be rebuilt because it was constructed in the 1940s, before the road got wider. We still got outbid by $150,000.

MY FRIEND FROM THE RED CROSS called to invite me to a pop-up house concert in Oakland called Songs of Resilience, a musical journey of sound healing, but I didn't feel like going. "Is it in a *community* house?" I asked. "Those people are going to look at me with that condescending look of pity that means they think I haven't set my willful intentions, that I haven't made that list of everything I want. But I made the list. It's just not working out."

"One of the problems is that Bongjun doesn't like to drive on curvy roads," I told my friend. "But the only cheap land available is at the end of a curvy road. There was one affordable place off Highway 17. It was more like an outhouse. The real estate agent was like, 'Oh, that one?

Well, it's hard to make the turnoff. I might miss the turnoff.' Instead, he drove us to a house way above what we could pay."

"It sounds like you're not enjoying this process," my Red Cross friend said. "Looking for a house together should be a journey of joy."

For a moment I believed her and felt a slow sinking feeling. Then I remembered that she's always insisting that I need to be more open-minded about the tech world, because Silicon Valley offers many opportunities for storytellers.

"Like what?" I asked once.

"Like Fitbit. You track the Fitbit family users. After they exercise, some guys go to the sports bar; their girlfriends go to the frozen yogurt shop. Which user consumes more calories?"

"That's a story?"

BONGJUN AND I FOUND a piece of land on top of a mountain, but it didn't have a single tree. "Why do you need a tree?" Bongjun asked. "There are plenty of neighbors' trees to look at." When I thought about it more, I realized that it wasn't really the top of a mountain so much as the side of a cliff. Maybe we could have put a yurt there.

The next time I talked to my friend from Florida I asked whether he thought I was doing something wrong because I wasn't on a journey of joy.

"Journey of joy? Ah hahahaha!"

I told him about the treeless mountaintop and the yurt. When he asked what a yurt was, I texted him a picture of the Lotus Belle yurt I'd found online.

"In California the only option is to live in a *smurf* house?" he asked. "A helicopter is going to be flying overhead and the pilot will look down and see this little puffball on the side of the cliff. 'What's that?' the pilot's gonna say. 'A giant Q-tip? No! It's a Journey of Joy!'"

ON OUR NEXT JOURNEY OF JOY, Bongjun and I visited a piece of land that turned out to be the receptacle for all the neighborhood runoff water. Black plastic pipes crisscrossed the marsh. Bring Your Own Boat. Here's where we could put the houseboat.

MEANWHILE, OUR CLIMATE CHANGE group provided a metastudy about the 97 percent scientific consensus on climate change. Because scientists never say that something is 100 percent true, and because scientists, by nature, are often poor at communicating on an emotional level and tend to resist alarmist scenarios, the climate change deniers have been able to point to that 1 to 3 percent of doubt. (Ninety-seven percent is also the proportion of scientists who support the theory of plate tectonics.)

We also learned that 61 percent of Americans say climate change is important to them, but they rarely or never discuss it with people they know. Our homework was to become climate change evangelists for a month. To prepare, we discussed how to raise the topic with a stranger. "Sure is hot these days," or "How often do *you* take the train? Trying to save on fossil fuels?" or "Do you *ever* remember it being ninety-seven degrees in October?"

I decided, as an experiment in humiliation, to discuss climate change everywhere I went. The following are methods I do not recommend.

1. Bumping into someone's shopping cart at Safeway. "Oh, sorry, I was just so distracted thinking about climate change." (Note to self: Try using the phrase "climate disruption," rather than "climate change." Or better yet, "global greenhouse gas chamber," the expression that Wallace Smith Broecker, the man who coined the term "global warming," wished he had come up with earlier.)

2. After complaining to my boss about the measly salary I make as an adjunct professor: "I apologize for expressing myself in such a heated manner about how impossible it is to live on this salary. I was just really distressed thinking about climate disruption."

3. During Hurricane Harvey, I was having dinner with my neighbor, whose car has bumper stickers like MY OTHER CAR IS A BROOM and NEVER FEAR, THE GODDESS IS HERE! So it was unsurprising to hear her say, "This hurricane is Earth Mama expressing her anger at the patriarchy!"

"Actually," I said, "I'm not sure if the hurricane has anything to do with the Earth getting angry. It might have more to do with greenhouse gases. I'm not saying that climate change is *causing* the hurricane. It acts more like a hormone, or an adverb, an intensification of the qualities already present. I'm afraid things are only going to get worse." She looked upset. "Wait, what's the matter?" I asked.

"You're triggering my PTSD!"

4. I went to my friend's *Blade Runner* party, which was filled with fortysomething guys who kept reciting all the lines and knew all the

trivia answers. During the pee break, one guy started talking about how we'd all be wearing Google Glass in ten years. "If the Earth doesn't burn up," I added.

"Right!" someone interjected. I thought we might be on our way to a useful discussion.

"This party just turned into a real downer," someone else said, so we went back to the movie.

Oh, no, I thought. I'm turning into my dad. He often told stories about how the heartbeat of the ocean might stop, which would affect the wind and freeze parts of the Midwest and Europe. For this reason I think of discussing climate change as a relaxing family activity. My father's second wife, on the other hand, got so tired of hearing about global warming that she considered getting a STOP GLOBAL DOOM-ING bumper sticker for her car. When my brother announced that his wife was pregnant, my dad told him he wouldn't need a college fund since there wouldn't be any college in the future. My brother, who was tenderly grilling ribs, threw down his barbecue fork and said, "For once I want to talk about life, and not always be focused on the end!" After that, climate change became a forbidden topic on holidays. Now I was rediscovering what I'd understood as a kid: people don't respond well to threats, to cajoling, to end-of-the-world scenarios, to dystopian futures, to hopelessness.

But as I watched the news about Hurricane Harvey, I was astonished that not a single anchor mentioned climate change. Instead they blamed the flooding on Houston's pavement. According to George Marshall, those who don't believe in climate change are *less* likely to believe in it *after* a climate disaster. Every single member of our group was confounded by this. "That makes no sense!" we said to one another.

If a person believes that weather fluctuates regardless of carbon dioxide in the atmosphere, or that catastrophes represent some kind of punishment from God, confirmation bias will lead him to view the latest climate disaster as proof. And after a climate disaster, people feel a heightened sense of community; they don't want to get into a politicized discussion with the neighbor who just saved their dog. Furthermore, Marshall writes, climate disasters operate according to the same psychological logic as lightning strikes. People who have been struck by lightning tend to believe they are statistically immune to it happening again, even as the actual odds remain the same. And if your house floods due to a changing climate, it is *more* likely it will flood again. If your house burns down, it is *more* likely it will burn again.

I WAS ALREADY MENTALLY and emotionally enfeebled from watching so much hurricane disaster news, but I still couldn't stop watching the hypnotic swirl of Irma. The way the news was reporting it, I thought for sure that *this* hurricane was going to be the end of America. I called up my friend in Florida. "I'm worried about you and that hurricane," I told him.

"Oh, really? I haven't been watching the news." A few hours later he texted, "Oh, shit!"

Later we exchanged emails. "Did I mention we are binge-watching our way through this hurricane with *Dexter*?" he wrote. "We didn't stock up on food so we are eating scrambled eggs and chicken potpies. But do you know what? I honestly *get* those guys who are shooting into the hurricane. I swear to god. It's not about shooting the hurricane. It's about blowing off steam. . . . I'd go outside and fire off a gun if I had one. . . . It's not my go-to move, but there is something about blowing a big ol' hole in something from a distance. I used to be a pretty good target shooter. OMG. A new food update from my fam. With a side of no concern for safety."

THE NIGHT THE FIRES STARTED in Northern California, Bongjun and I had an argument. Afterward, he took out the garbage. "Come here," he said when he opened the door. "Check out how hot it is outside." A little while later, the wind started to sound like airplane engines.

The following morning, my mom and my aunt both told me that they'd thought we were being attacked by North Korea.

THIS IS HOW Kamo no Chōmei describes the fire that broke out in Kyoto:

> It was, I believe, the twenty-eighth day of the fourth month of 1177, on a night when the wind blew fiercely without a moment of calm, that a fire broke out toward nine o'clock in the southeast of the capital and spread northwest. It finally reached the gates and buildings of the palace, and within the space of a single night all was reduced to ashes. The fire originated in a little hut where a sick man lodged.

The fire fanned out as the shifting wind spread it, first in one direction and then another. Houses far away from the conflagration were enveloped in the smoke, while the area nearby was a sea of flames. The ashes were blown up into the sky, which turned into a sheet of crimson from the reflected glare of the fire, and the flames, relentlessly whipped by the wind, seemed to fly over two or three streets at a time. Those who were caught in the midst could not believe it was actually happening: some collapsed, suffocated by the smoke, others surrounded by flames died on the spot. Still others barely managed to escape with their lives, but could not rescue any of their property: all their treasures turned into ashes. How much had been wasted on them!

Sixteen mansions belonging to the nobility were burnt, not to speak of innumerable other houses. In all, about a third of the capital was destroyed. Several thousand men and women lost their lives, as well as countless horses and oxen. Of all the follies of human endeavor, none is more pointless than expending treasures and spirit to build houses in so dangerous a place as the capital.

And this is Basil Bunting's rendition:

> On the twentyseventh May eleven hundred
> and seventyseven, eight p.m., fire broke out
> at the corner of Tomi and Higuchi streets.
> In a night
> palace, ministries, university, parliament
> were destroyed. As the wind veered
> flames spread out in the shape of an open fan.
> Tongues torn by gusts stretched and leapt.
> In the sky clouds of cinders lit red with the blaze.
> Some choked, some burned, some barely escaped.
> Sixteen great officials lost houses and
> very many poor. A third of the city burned;
> several thousands died; and of beasts,
> limitless numbers.
>
> Men are fools to invest in real estate.

Neither writer mentions the paper that falls from the sky.

o o o

O N THE EVENING OF the eighth of October, in the seventeenth year of this century, severe gusts of dry winds blew across desiccated grasses and diseased trees caused by years of excessive heat and drought. A great flood that year had fattened grasses into combustible fuel. The wind knocked down power lines that lit the trees on fire. The firestorm destroyed a thousand homes in a single neighborhood. Neighbors pounded on neighbors' doors, honking horns, trying to rescue one another. It took hours to leave town. Most people reported that drivers were calm, though a few resorted to the sidewalk, the median, and the opposite side of the road. One woman managed to stuff her pony in the back seat of her Honda Accord. Another woman had to choose between saving her car or her horse. She jumped on her horse in her pajamas and rode away from the flames. The fires burned for over a week, killed forty-four people, and destroyed more than ten thousand structures and 380 square miles of land. It was the most destructive fire in US history to date.

D URING THE FIRES I took walks, and I tried to read the paper falling from the sky. I wanted to collect the scattered notes, but they disintegrated when I picked them up, leaving the smell of poison on the tips of my fingers. The paper pieces lay curled like chocolate shavings. They were all the size of my palm. I was looking for stories, but I could only find information. Bible pages (sections from Genesis); cell phone bills; pieces of romance novels (so many of those); perfectly preserved letters so meticulously burned around the edges they looked the way letters do when you burn them in fourth grade to make them look romantic; gold-embossed stationery with someone's name written over and over in tiny letters at forty-five-degree angles; musical scores; Swedish vacation package-tour brochures; pieces of phone books (people still have phone books); a kid's homework (he did poorly); journal pages (so many pages of people talking to themselves); as well as tar paper and bits of insulation burned thin as paper. I walked and walked and tried not to breathe. Why was the sky directly above me blue, while everywhere else it was gunmetal gray flickering with particulate matter? Everyone spoke of particulate matter. In the hardware store all you needed to say was "Where are they?" and they'd point you to the pile of N95 masks. Someone passed me on the trail. I imagined he was judging me for not wearing a mask, but I couldn't read his expression because he was wearing one. I looked at the dun, shoulder-high grass; that explosive fuel, the color of pale grasshoppers, was all that stood between an out-of-control fire and me. The news never reported where the active fire was. We only knew that it was completely uncontained and that all effort was focused on rescuing people, evacuating the hospital, getting elderly people out of their homes. All we could do was hope the winds wouldn't change. I walked into the grasses to get away, to get away from the panic on people's faces.

There was no digesting this fire. There was no beginning, middle, end. I couldn't stop thinking about Sugarloaf Ridge State Park, which was now decimated. I hadn't walked on Sugarloaf Ridge in years, but whenever I used the words *poison oak*, or *gallop*, or *fog* my mind flashed femtosecond images of the park. Now it was ash. My old high school had burned down, as well as everything along the roads to get there.

Before the fires I'd been teaching a class on ecology. We were learning about systems theory and the interdependency of ecosystems, how trees communicate and send messages and medicines to other parts of the forest, how trees draw up water to share with other plants. We watched the Stevie Wonder video about his journey to the secret life of plants. We read a book about how to enter the imaginations of plants. We read stories of how bees know the location of every flower in a sixty-mile vicinity. We learned how butterflies make tinctures of nectar-soaked pollen grains and how elephants concoct forest booze and get drunk. We learned how a chimpanzee will fold a leaf like an accordion and swallow it so that it scrapes away the worms in his digestive tract.

We learned how insects can digest the compounds in eucalyptus and create poop that inhibits the growth of encroaching plants, like mustard. This is probably one reason why the eucalyptus has been so successful as an invasive species here. But why, in the 1850s, when the government planted eucalyptus throughout California at maniacal speed because its fast-growing wood was essential for railroad ties and fence posts, did these trees, unlike the old-growth groves in Australia, twist when they dried and become so hard they were no longer suitable for building? And now the volatile oils in their leaves turned out to be extremely combustible. In seasonally dry climates, native oaks are fire resistant, but with the introduction of eucalyptus we introduced an extreme fire hazard. I stared at the eucalyptus twisting in the heat.

THE WEEKEND BEFORE the fires I attended a grief workshop sponsored by the climate change group. They told us grief processed on one's own turns to despair, but grief processed communally becomes medicine. Now that we knew the reality of climate change, we would grieve the Earth. That way grief wouldn't hold us back when it was time to mobilize. To prepare us, they drew two circles on the board. YOUR COMFORT ZONE was written inside one circle. In the second circle, some distance from the first, they wrote, WHERE THE MAGIC HAPPENS.

The day before the workshop I had gone to the ocean to prepare but realized I wasn't yet ready to grieve the Earth. When I looked at the sea and the tangled seaweed on top, all I could think of was the word *holdfast*, the name for the dangly part of seaweed that clings to rock. Our climate group had read a poem about holdfast, and we had been encouraged to use it to steady ourselves when things got rough. Instead of reciting poems about the sea and cliffs and black rock as I used to while walking this beach, I now thought about how the oceans have been absorbing more than half of the CO_2 in the atmosphere, along with 90 percent of the excess heat. I thought of pH balances and dying plankton, and of how the last time the oceans were this acidic, 96 percent of ocean life went extinct.

At the grief workshop we drummed and journaled. The facilitator said that because we are continuously bombarded by bad news, we live in a state of chronic secondary trauma. It starts as soon as we are born with our cave-child DNA, expecting to see forty pairs of eyes looking toward us, asking us what we dreamed that night, if we want to help collect firewood, if we'll be at the ceremony tonight with the elders. Our psyches were never prepared to deal with the isolation of American culture, nor the sadness of the tragedies we see every day, nor the reality of our dying ecosystems. For hundreds of thousands of years grief rituals recalibrated the fields of trauma. These days there is no communal cup of sorrow; there is only psychotherapy, which colludes with the privatization of property, the privatization of consciousness, and the privatization of grief—with "own your sorrow." These days, the great fear we have about grief is that we have to face it alone. And so people avoid it and it settles like sediment over our psyches. There is personal grief, but since we are all connected, there is also the sorrow we feel for the world right now. And that cannot be processed alone. We cannot think our way through this mess. Nor can we moralize our way through it. Our workshop leader suggested that the thing that will save us may be our own broken hearts, for true action can only come through these deeper feelings.

THE NIGHT AFTER the workshop, I got into an argument with Bongjun. I was sitting on the floor because all the other flat surfaces were covered by lab equipment and mechanical parts. There were boxes of electronics, wires, sensors, laser parts, and, in the kitchen, an old dentist's light he'd accidentally bought on eBay. On shelves were laser-diode-current supplies, an oscilloscope probe, a function generator, a piezoelectric transducer driver, a microscope, boxes of lab snacks (just the boxes, not the snacks), a laser temperature controller, and, his favorite item, Marvin, the perpetually depressed robot from *The Hitchhiker's Guide to the Galaxy*.

"What is this?" I asked, pushing aside some sort of mechanical part.

"It's a transmission gear piece. They were getting rid of it at my work."

"You should get out of the Silicon Valley rat race and dedicate yourself to transitioning to a green economy," I heard myself saying. "You're a scientist. You can help develop technologies. This article says we have to treat climate change like we are fighting World War II. For example, we have to start movements where everyone paints their roofs white to try to dissipate the heat before it reaches a 2 degree Celsius rise. We have to cut carbon emissions now," I said. "Here's an article about what we can do to stay below a 2 degree rise. There are solutions. If you were to really *internalize* that we are the first generation to see the effects of climate change and the last generation to be able to do anything about it, would you change your life?" Even while I spoke I could hear myself sounding like a maniac. I kept reminding myself that people don't respond well to threats, to cajoling, to end-of-the-world scenarios. But I couldn't help it. I was in a bad mood because it was so hot outside.

Many years ago I lived in Korea. During the summers it would get so hot by eight in the morning that I'd have to stop at 7-Eleven on my way to the subway to buy honeydew-melon popsicles, or cold cans of pine-bud sodas, the drink invented by Korea's forest service. On the radio station inside the 7-Eleven, the announcers would warn everyone to be careful and avoid arguments in their work environments because the "uncomfort" index was high. Studies have shown that people's tempers flare in high heat.

"Yes, it's the right thing to do," Bongjun finally said calmly, in response to my grief workshop–induced rage. "But if it were really that bad, as bad as you say, don't you think Google would be doing something about it?"

ON THE FOURTH NIGHT of the fires, the humidity plummeted again, and anxiety peaked. A dry wind was expected to blow almost as strongly as on the night the fires started.

I packed a suitcase full of clothes and looked around my room. Should I pack the vase I bought in Turkey? How about the old Soviet tourist books about Tbilisi? How was it possible to choose between items of sentimental value? Better to leave it all.

"At least we have the public pool across the street," my mom said. We'd heard about the couple who took refuge in their neighbor's pool while their own house burned. They stayed in the water for six hours, covering their faces with wet shirts whenever they had to come up to breathe. "How long does it take for a house to burn?" the woman had wondered underwater.

My sister-in-law called and said, "Remember how when your brother and I first got married and your dad was always talking about global warming? Turns out he was *right*!" My dad called: "I've been needing Ambien to sleep. I'll forgo that tonight."

THE NEXT DAY, having survived the night and craving fresh air, I drove to the ocean. I was searching for clean air, but smoke covered the soot-colored sea all the way to the horizon. I could have felt guilty for driving a car with an internal combustion engine, but guilt goes on hold during fires. I sped on my way home, because the rule of law no longer applies during fires. This is the wildness that descends. This is the triggered reptilian brain. During the fires we craved sugar and fat and ordered take-out pizza and didn't mention that we usually never order pizza. During the fires my neighbor, the goddess, forgot she was gluten intolerant. During the fires all I could think of was the word *holdfast*.

WE MADE A PLAN. It seemed perfectly reasonable at the time. If the wind blew the fire this way we'd get in our cars and head to the ocean. If the fire kept following us, we would drive *into* the ocean.

MY FRIEND WHO HOSTED the *Blade Runner* party texted me: "I bought a fog maker for my upcoming Halloween party. But now with all the smoke outside I don't need it anymore."

A STUDENT OF MINE complained that he still had to work at the bank during the fires, since his branch was the only one open in the region. In one day customers deposited $600,000 in cash—a record—which they must have been keeping under their mattresses. My student said that all day his nerves were on edge because people kept walking into the bank wearing N95 masks. The firemen told us that the masks don't actually help much.

A FRIEND WHO WAS EVACUATED said he grabbed his two dogs and two banjos and hustled into his car. Driving away he realized he had forgotten to pack any clothes. During fires you hear, over and over, "I lost everything, but at least I have my life." A couple of people, after losing everything, knocked on the door of a man whose house was for sale. They said, "We've lost everything. Can we buy your house and everything in it?" He left everything he owned to them, including his toaster and bath towels.

MY FRIEND FROM THE RED CROSS described the evacuation center in Napa where she worked. There was face painting, acupuncture, aromatherapy, medicinal teas, massages, a whole Sikh temple feeding five hundred people with blessed food. "And Dreamers," she said, crying over the phone. "You know the Dreamers? Red Cross doesn't take donations, but there were so many donations we didn't know what to do with them. And then this woman, this random woman off the street, came in and said she would organize it all. She took it all out to the racquetball courts, arranged care packages of shoes—different sizes—and food, put it in backpacks. And for three days cars would pull in, ten at a time, and these Dreamers, behind the scenes, afraid for their lives, distributed all these packages."

THE SONGS ON THE LOCAL radio stations were especially upbeat during the fires. They interspersed Tom Petty's "I Won't Back Down" with quotes from locals who had lost their houses. "Fires are burning in eight

California counties," the news announcer said with the Tom Petty beat in the background. A woman's voice: "I came out to get my dog and looked down the ridge and saw a glow and I looked at the wind and I told my parents that they might want to pack up something just in case, and my mom said that the fire was already at the bottom of the hill . . . *No I won't back down, no I won't back down. You can stand me up at the gates of hell but I won't back down . . .*" Another woman: "I just want to thank all of you first responders. I love you all from the bottom of my heart. I thank you all for being there. For being away from your families, to help everyone else out there . . . *Hey baby, there ain't no easy way out. Hey . . .* we are Sonoma County strong . . ."

I cried when the song came on, though I'd already heard it five times. I cried while driving, and when I saw the banners on every highway overpass: THANKS, FIRST RESPONDERS. THANK YOU, FIREFIGHTERS. Or the signs in front of the cafés: FIREFIGHTERS EAT FOR FREE. Even as the fire raged on.

ALL THE MEXICAN RESTAURANTS were closed except one. I went in to get a burrito and found it full of evacuees. "Sure is busy here," people kept saying. One man said to the cashier, "It'll have to be bulldozed. Totally demolished. How was yours?"

"We're OK."

MY FAMILY DECIDED to go for a picnic. When we called the Point Reyes ranger station to check the weather and the recording said "Smoke," we stayed home instead. But still had a picnic. Outside. In the smoke.

Over the beet salad, I brought up the need to join together to find climate change solutions to a young relative who works in tech. He said, "Evolutionary theory says that diverse species never collaborate. People only want to take care of their families."

"But humans have never encountered the reality of climate change," I said. "Maybe this will rearrange our biology."

He shrugged. "Why worry? Technology will take care of everything. If the Earth goes, we'll just live in spaceships. We'll have 3D printers to print our food. We'll be eating lab meat. One cow will feed us all. We'll just rearrange atoms to create water or oxygen. Elon Musk."

"But I don't *want* to live in a spaceship."

He looked genuinely surprised. In his line of work, he'd never met anyone who didn't want to live in a spaceship.

WHEN I TOLD MY AUNT that in my class we were trying to read the minds of plants, she said, "Can you teach *me* how to read the mind of a plant?"

"I haven't really figured it out yet, but according to the book, you first have to *believe* that you can do it."

Bongjun said, "The only way you'll be able to read the mind of a plant is if you slow your metabolism *way* down. Humans can't slow their metabolisms to the rhythm of a plant. Plant thoughts are too slow for humans to understand."

But I'd been practicing the long, slow view. Nature's metabolism works much more sluggishly than ours; the cumulative effects of CO_2 are slow but steady, like a tortoise, or a bionic woman in slow motion. I tried to listen. I took a rock and used it as a clock. I started thinking in geologic time. Started thinking one thousand years into the future, *after* the great extinction. Started thinking about the time after the age of heat and darkness when that other version of humanity would need solar and wind technology.

IN 2004, MICHAEL CRICHTON, the author of *Jurassic Park*, wrote *State of Fear*, one of the few novels about climate change. Crichton's book is about a group of "eco-terrorists" from the Environmental Liberation Front who set out to trigger natural disasters in order to foment mass panic about climate change and install a "green" dictatorship. It includes a dense technical appendix to "prove" climate change is a myth. George W. Bush spent an hour with Crichton in the Oval Office and then presented the novel as "scientific" evidence to the US Senate that climate change was a hoax.

In his book *The Great Derangement*, the novelist Amitav Ghosh writes that not too long ago, everyone who lived in the Sundarbans, the dense jungle along the Bay of Bengal, had a family member who had been killed by a tiger. Those who escaped would describe the weird, uncanny look of mutual recognition when they met the tiger's gaze: an expression of preternatural wildness and intimate communication with the nonhuman. Ghosh says that now, in the age of anthropogenic climate change, we will confront that wildness again, this time in the eye of the hurricane, the tongue of a flame. Stories will become more alien, less human, more strange. The stranger the stories, the more we will recognize them and be recognized in them. They will speak, in his words, of the "interconnectedness of the transformations that are now under way."

AFTER THE FIRES we watched Josh Fox's documentary *How to Let Go of the World and Love All the Things Climate Can't Change*. We realized that indigenous movements are the most active in facing climate change. And every one of them knows how to dance. We realized that if we want to save the planet, we have to learn how to dance.

Bongjun finally read the peer-reviewed articles by climate scientists. He spent a long time studying the graphs, in the same way he once studied the medley of eight prescription medicines his mother had accidentally mixed together, and finally announced about the square-shaped ones, "Actually, these are chewing gum."

"It's scary," he said, pointing at the West Coast on the map. "The West Coast will burn up. Korea, and the rest of Asia, will go through a famine. The only problem with solar is storage capacity. I could try to get a job in a national lab experimenting with hydrogen fusion. But I don't know if they've made much progress on that since I was in the seventh grade."

It was still hot: ninety-five degrees in late October. We wondered if winter would ever come again. You can't get into a pumpkin-carving mood when it's so hot. On Halloween a few kids came looking for candy, but it seemed like everyone else went to the movies. The parking lot at the theater was full.

I had a dream that I had to evacuate, and the only thing I grabbed was the leftover bag of Halloween candy. I handed out Kit Kats to people as we ran from the fire.

After the fires people posted the most random item they grabbed when they evacuated.

>   daughter's piggy bank with $2.35 in coins in it
>   Grandmother's Christmas cactus
>   a wetsuit
>   an avocado
>   the cat-scratcher tree

a Hermione wand
the cookie cutters
tarot cards
all the beer
kids' pinewood derby trophies
the sewing machine
dog's ashes
the spice rack
Norton Anthology
son's Darth Vader alarm clock
husband's Hawaiian shirt collection
jury duty notice for the next day
the cat-litter box and all the cat litter
combat-ready lightsabers
a toothbrush (even though the man who grabbed this one was evacuating to a dentist's office)
a jar of Miracle Whip (because they were evacuating to a mayo-heavy household)

BONGJUN AND I FINALLY found a hut in the Santa Cruz Mountains. It was part of a co-op with twenty other little houses. Maybe this was it! Maybe this was our sustainable community. The day we were set to drive down there, the whole region caught on fire. It burned for a while. "I can't take much more of this," I thought.

THE FIRES DIDN'T DISCRIMINATE between the houses of the rich and the poor. Everyone's pearls melted, no matter how large. Nor did they discriminate between the houses of the "realists" and the "idealists." After the fires, the realists wanted to rebuild as fast as possible with the same footprint. The original developers of Santa Rosa's Coffey Park, which was destroyed by the fires, offered to use updated versions of their old floor plans in rebuilding efforts. Homeowners were upset to learn that they were now required to rebuild in adherence with the 2016 California Green Building Standards Code. They argued that they shouldn't have to.

Before the fires, the builders who showed up to city council meetings were the same people every time—they all seemed to be on a first-name basis. But after the fires, something changed. People began presenting ideas to install rain-catchment and gray-water systems, community gardens, and bike paths. They wanted to revamp the land-use laws, change the zoning for tiny houses, use fire-resistant straw-bale construction and concrete and foam. The city council was inundated with people wanting to rebuild with green roofs and walls, to rebuild in a way that would promote bees and carbon-capturing methods, even permaculture methods and composting plants. City officials looked a little frightened as they listened to a large group of people talk about a town in Kansas that rebuilt with renewable energy after getting hit by a tornado. More than seven hundred people showed up for a breakfast sponsored by Daily Acts, an organization that builds community by working with neighborhoods to turn lawns into drought-tolerant gardens. A farmer who had lost his farm and all of his bees spoke at the podium: "Why can't Sonoma County *always* be able to feed its poor?" My neighbors started talking about "agrihoods," a new trend in which affluent, slow-foodie millennials move to neighborhoods surrounding a farm, instead of to the golf-course communities of their parents' generation. My dad even wrote an op-ed about it.

AFTER THE FIRES, I started reading a book by Alejandro Jodorowsky, the Chilean French filmmaker/poet/therapist who maintains an unusual psychotherapy practice. If someone feels poor in spirit, or even in material wealth, he'll prescribe that they glue coins to the bottoms of their shoes so that they feel like they are always walking on money. He describes how Chile, being "a poetic country," graciously accepted his poetic acts. He and a friend once decided to walk in a straight line across the city, disregarding any obstacles they encountered. Sometimes this would mean having to walk through people's houses. This is how he describes it:

> Having rung the bell of a house and having explained to the lady of the house that we were poets in action and that our mission required us to cross her house in a straight line—she understood perfectly and had us leave through the back door. For us, this crossing of the city in a straight line was a grand experience, the way we managed to avoid all the obstacles. Little by little, we went about inventing more extreme acts. . . . Another day, we put a large quantity of coins in a bag full of holes and traveled to the center of the city. . . .
>
> Also, we dedicated ourselves to very innocent acts that were no less powerful, like putting a beautiful shell in the hand of the conductor when he came to

take our bus tickets. The man stood there stupefied for a long time without saying anything.

He goes on to say,

Life is like that, you understand? Totally unpredictable. You think things will happen this way or that way and, in reality, while standing on the corner talking to a friend, you can be run over by a truck; you can run into an old lover and go to a hotel to make love; or the roof can fall on your head while you work. The telephone can ring to announce the best or the worst of news. Our acts as young poets were performed to prove this, to swim against my parents' rigid world. . . .

My father practiced Psychomagic without knowing it: He was convinced that the more merchandise he had, the more he would sell. He had to give shoppers the image of superabundance. . . .

What is generally called "reality" is just a part, an aspect of a much greater order. +

ETIENNE COURTOIS, *UNTITLED*. 2014, ARCHIVAL INKJET PRINT. 33½ × 42". COURTESY OF THE ARTIST. © ETIENNE COURTOIS.

SUPERKING SON SCORES AGAIN

Anthony Veasna So

SUPERKING SON WAS AN ARTIST lost in the politics of normal, assimilated life. Sure, his talents were often sidelined, as the store forced him to worry about importing enough spiky-looking fruits every month. (There were only so many Mings he could recruit to carry suitcases filled with jackfruit, bras padded with lychees, and panties stuffed with we-don't-want-to-know through customs.) Sure, he reeked of raw chicken, raw chicken feet, raw cow, raw cow tongue, raw fish, raw squid, raw crab, raw pig, raw pig intestine, and raw—like really raw—pig blood, all jellied, cubed, and stored in buckets before it was thrown into everyone's noodle soup on Sunday mornings. When we walked into the barely air-conditioned store, we pinched our noses to stop from vomiting all over aisle six, which would ruin the only aisle with American products, the one with Cokes and Red Bulls and ten-year-old Lunchables no one ate. (Though the Mas would shove their shopping carts through the vomit without blinking an eye—they've seen much worse.) And sure, Superking Son wasn't nice. He could be cruel, incredibly so. Kevin won't talk to him anymore, and Kevin was our best smasher last season.

Still, even with this in mind (and up our nostrils), even with it creeping through our common sense, and even with our aspirations for something more, we idolized Superking Son. He was a regular Magic Johnson of badminton, if such a thing could exist; a legend, that is, for the young men of this Cambo hood (a niche fan base, admittedly). The arcs of his lobs, the gentle drifts of his drops, and the lines of his smashes could be thought of, if rendered visible, as the very edge between known and unknown. He could smash a birdie so hard, make it fly so fast, we swore when the birdie zipped by it shattered the force field suffocating us, the one comprising our parents' unreasonable expectations, their paranoia that our world could crumble at a moment's notice and send us back to where we started, starving and poor and subject to a genocidal dictator. Word has it when Superking Son was young, he was an even better player, with a full head of hair.

Yes, to us, Superking Son was our badminton coach, our shuttlecock king. That's who he would always be. But what was he for everyone else? Well, it's simple—he was the goddamn grocery-store boy.

WE LOOKED TO SUPERKING SON for guidance—on how to deal with our semiracist teachers, who simultaneously thought we were enterprising hoodlums and math nerds that no speak *Engrish* right; on whether wearing tees big enough to cover our asses was as dope as we hoped. And every time we had exciting news, some game-changing gossip we heard from our Mas, like when Gong Sook went crazy from tending to his crop of reefer before he could even sell one bushel, we headed for Superking Grocery Store. So when Kyle informed us about the new transfer kid—Justin—who he spotted smashing birdies and doing insane lunges across the court, being all Kobe Bryant at the local open gym, we dropped our skateboards and rushed to find Superking Son.

We ran from our usual spot, the park where our peddling aunts never set up shop, the one next to the middle school that shut down from gang violence, and we ran because we couldn't skate fast. (Our baggy shirts went down to our knees, covering our asses and compromising our mobility, but who cares about mobility when you look as fly as this?) It was February, and as chilly as a rainless California winter ever got, but we worked up a sweat doing all that running. By the time we found Superking Son in his back storeroom, we dripped beads of salty-ass water from head to toe. We were a crew of yellow-brown boys collapsed onto the floor, exhausted from excitement.

Superking Son greeted us by raising his palm against our faces. "You fools need to shut the fuck up so I can concentrate," he said, even though we hadn't uttered a word. He was talking to Cha Quai Factory zSon about how many Khmer donuts he wanted to order that week. Superking Son stared intently at a clipboard, as if he could peer into its soul, his constant pen chewing the only sound we could hear.

"Come on, man, what's taking you so long?" Cha Quai Factory Son grabbed the clipboard away from Superking Son. "Just go with the usual! Why do this song and dance every week?" He pulled out his own unchewed pen and signed the invoice before anyone could let out a whimper about merchandizing fraud. "Stop second-guessing yourself," he continued while shaking his head. "God, I've aged ten years waiting for you to make a decision."

"Stop giving me shit for being a good businessman. You can't do things without thinking," Superking Son said.

"This guy takes one business class at comm and he thinks he's the CEO of Cambo grocery stores. Like he's Steve Jobs and those spoiled Chinese sausages are MacBook Airs," Cha Quai Factory Son joked as he waved the clipboard around. "I was in that class with him, and all we ever learned was that mo' money is better than no money."

Superking Son crossed his arms over his semipudgy chest—over that layer of fat that seemed to have grown at a steady rate since he took over the store. "All right, everyone out of my storeroom. Y'all are sweating all over and I don't want this asswipe smell clinging to my inventory. I sell food people put in their mouths, dammit."

We urged Superking Son to wait, each of us frantic for approval. We raved about Justin, how he could replace Kevin as our team's number-one player, how Kyle swore he was the best player who'd set foot in open gym all year.

"The open gym at the community college?" he said, sarcasm stretching his every syllable into one of those diphthongs we learned about in sophomore English. An entire Shakespearean monologue nestled in the gaps between his words. "That's not saying much. At that open gym, I've seen players smack their doubles partners in the face with their rackets."

We only wanted to make the team better, so Superking Son's reaction disheartened us. Yet it wasn't different from what we had grown to expect from Superking Son. It wasn't worse than that time a pregnant, morning-sick Ming threw up in the frozen tuna bin and ruined a month's worth of fishy profits, which inspired him to assign us two hundred burpees every day for a week. And it was nowhere close to that time his mom, while sweeping, slipped in the produce section and broke her hip, next to the bok choy of all places. (We're pretty sure this was the moment he started balding. By his fifth medical payment, he looked like Bruce Willis in yellow-brown face.) We told ourselves Superking Son was simply stressed out. Everyone, including our own parents, relied on him to supply their food. He needed to restock his shelves for next month or mayhem would commence, we told ourselves, as if the store didn't require restocking every month.

"Bring the kid to conditioning, and we'll see how quickly one of you bastards gets whacked in the head." He stepped over us, grabbed the door, and turned to look down on us. "I'm serious. Get out or I'm locking you guys in here." His biceps flexed, even that small part of his body begging to be bigger than it was.

Cha Quai Factory Son started to leave first, but as he approached the door, he slid behind Superking Son and grabbed him by the shoulders. He massaged him, digging his big, dough-kneading hands into the perpetually tense tissue. We watched as Superking Son's eyebrows furrowed in revolt while his mouth formed silent moans of pleasure. "Okay, let's leave this big boy alone so he can think about BUSINESS," Cha Quai Factory Son said. Then he patted Superking Son on the stomach and jolted out the door.

Superking Son reached out to grab him, almost falling over in the process. He missed, by more than he would admit. And as he leaned forward into the gaping hole of the doorway, watching Cha Quai Factory Son flee from his grasp, we could tell he wanted to scream out some last remark. But he didn't. He probably couldn't decide on anything to say.

THERE ARE STORIES OF SUPERKING SON you wouldn't believe. Epic stories, stories that are downright implausible given the laws of physics, gravity, the limitations of the human body. There's the one where Superking Son's doubles partner sprained his ankle during the final match of sectionals. The kid dropped to the ground, right in the middle of the court, and Superking Son fended off the smashes of Edison's two best varsity players by lunging over his partner's injured body. He kept this up for ten minutes, until one of the Edison players also slipped and sprained his ankle, resulting in a historic win for our high school's badminton team. (They later learned the floor had been polished by the janitors, who neglected to tell the badminton coaches. The guys who sprained their ankles sued the school, won a huge settlement, and now both have their own houses in Sacramento. Three bedrooms, two and a half bathrooms, everything you could possibly want.) Then there are the many times he's beaten Cha Quai Factory Son in a singles match, often without letting him score a single point. Once, Superking Son bet Cha Quai Factory Son a hundred dollars he could beat him while eating a Big Mac, one hand gripped around his racket, the other around a juicy burger. Cha Quai Factory Son agreed, but wanted to triple the bet on the stipulation that Superking Son couldn't spill even a shred of lettuce. Halfway through, Superking Son had played so well, he got his friend to throw him another Big Mac, then a box of ten McNuggets. At the end of the match, the gym floor remained spotless. Cha Quai Factory Son refused to eat at McDonald's for ten years.

We didn't believe the stories at first. We thought, Superking Son's talking out of his ass. He wants to talk himself up to kids more than a decade younger than him. That was why he let us practice skating tricks in the parking lot and gave us free Gatorades (albeit the neon-green flavor no one bought, never light blue). Then when we started high school, Superking Son took over as coach of our badminton team. Just as he'd carried the team on his back as a class-ditching player in the '90s, he coached us to two regional championships. (There weren't opportunities to go to state or nationals, no D1 recruiters scouting matches with athletic scholarships in their butt pockets. This was badminton, for god's sake.) Superking Son launched our team to the top of the California Central Valley standings—the first time we called ourselves number one at anything. But more than that, it was from the little gestures—the fluid flair of Superking Son's wrists when demonstrating how to hit, the way he picked up birdies and sent them flying across the gym to any player he chose, the way he tapped into rallies, held his racket with his left hand so as not to annihilate the player he was coaching—that we realized the stories were true.

JUSTIN WAS NOT IMPRESSED. He was the new kid who showed up driving a brand-new Mustang and parked it next to Kyle's minivan, one of those beat-up machines abandoned at the local car shop and then flipped and sold to Cambo ladies like Kyle's mom, who were praying for the day their eldest children could start driving around the youngest. (The Mustang didn't have flames on it, but we could tell from the way Justin spiked his jet-black hair into pointy peaks that he had the clearest intentions to paint red, yellow, and blue flames on its side.) So no, Justin was not impressed with the abandoned parking lots we hung out in, the pop-up restaurants located in Cambo-rented apartments where we ate steaming cups of noodle soup in clean but still roach-infested kitchens, the mall that did so badly Old Navy closed down, and he definitely did not see what we saw in Superking Son.

But Justin, despite the pretensions, was a damn good badminton player. Plus after school he bought us rounds of dollar-menu chicken sandwiches, giving us rides in his Mustang while we inhaled that mystery meat. And we saw where he was coming from, because this year Superking Son was indeed off.

Conditioning was a shit show. Two weeks of Superking Son showing up late, his shirt pits stained with sweat (we hoped it was sweat), fish guts and pig intestines stuck in his hair and stinking up the joint. Two weeks of him never knowing what exercises he wanted us to do, miscounting lunges and crunches and not stopping us from planking until we fell to the ground in pain—he was constantly checking his phone instead of keeping track of what we were doing. And he kept forgetting Kyle's name, Kyle whose dad went into Superking Grocery Store every week to buy lottery tickets and fish-oil pills ("Gotta be healthy for when I'm rich," Kyle's dad often said, kissing both his ticket and pills for good luck), Kyle who Superking Son practically watched grow up, as Superking Son's Ma used to babysit Kyle when he was a baby. (Babysitting for her meant pushing a naked Kyle in a shopping cart through every aisle of the store.)

"What's up with your coach?" Justin asked one day while driving a couple of us home after practice. "I don't mean to be a hater, but I could get better conditioning doing tai chi with the old Asian ladies in the park. Only the left half of my body is getting a workout, man, like if I kept doing this, my muscles will get all imbalanced and I'll topple over."

Not sure of ourselves, we told him there was nothing to worry about because sometimes Superking Son got caught up with the store. Sometimes Superking Son was so stressed out he didn't think straight.

"It's amazing that store makes money looking the way it does. It's such a dump. I hope you guys are right, though. My mom is getting on my case about college applications. She wants me to quit badminton and join Model UN, but I keep telling her that the coach is supposed to be this legend and the team can win a bunch of tournaments. Don't get me wrong, I wanna keep playing badminton, but . . . I mean, Model UN does have some cute girls . . . girls that wear cute blazers . . . and know stuff about the world . . ."

As Justin trailed off, thinking about all the girls he could woo with his faux diplomacy and political strategy, we saw him slowly slipping away from our world. We saw this college-bound city kid, this Mustang-driving badminton player, how he might be too good for our team, our school, our community of Cambos. Sure, Justin was Cambodian, but he seemed so different. That's what happens when your dad is a pharmacist, we thought, you can just whip out Model UN skills whenever you want.

WE HAD THE MIND TO THROW an intervention for Superking Son. We needed to do something to keep Justin around. For a week, we met as a team—sans Superking Son—to discuss intervention strategies, talking points, and counterarguments, who would say what and in what order and where each of us would stand to demonstrate the appropriate amount of solidarity. We even made contingency plans, which detailed what to do if Superking Son freaked out and threw produce at our heads to chase us from the premises (it happened more often than not). But when we got to the store, ready for a confrontation, we found Superking Son in the back storeroom surrounded by what looked like a militia, minus the rifles and bulletproof vests. We saw our Hennessy-drenched uncles, the older half-siblings no one talked about, and those cousins who attended our school but never seemed to be present at roll call.

We hid behind the stacked crates and spied on them. Superking Son was in the center of the circle, staring intently at the floor. His hand seemed stuck to his chin. Some ghostly vision played out in front of his eyes, and it shocked the color out of him. Cha Quai Factory Son was there too, his hands on Superking Son's shoulders, like he was both consoling him and holding him back from doing something stupid. A wave of money flashed around the circle, only stopping to be counted and recounted, probably to make sure no one had slipped any bills into his pocket. We spied on them, each of us brainstorming reasons for this meeting that were innocent and harmless, not doomed by the laws of faux-Buddhist karmic retribution. If we're being honest with ourselves, none of us figured out a reason worth a damn.

BADMINTON PRACTICE ONLY GOT WORSE. Superking Son coached everyone who wasn't Justin and hardly acknowledged Justin's existence, not even to reprimand him. Yet when we crowded around a Justin match and cheered as he nailed smash after smash, we swore we saw Superking Son in awe of his talent, analyzing Justin's form and failing to find any faults. Sometimes we saw something darker, something seething, within his stares, some envy-fueled plot being calculated in his expression, but then he would break his gaze from Justin. He'd checked his phone for the thousandth time and let anxiety about his father's store overtake, yet again, his love for badminton.

Justin reciprocated Superking Son's snubs. He ignored Superking Son's directions and went through practice entirely on his own agenda. That first week, Superking Son and Justin interacted only through overriding each other's instructions to Ken, Justin's hitting partner. Every practice, Superking Son told Ken to practice drop shots, Justin said smashes, Superking Son yelled at Ken for not doing drop shots, Justin still refused to change drills, Superking Son made Ken do laps around the court for undermining his authority, and so on until Ken bailed on practice, hid in the locker room, and smoked a cigarette for his anxiety. (He stole packs from his dad, who bought them wholesale from Costco. His dad gave them out to relatives in Cambodia like candy, in an effort to pretend he was some hotshot American business tycoon.)

Shit escalated one day when Superking Son was so late that Justin, fed up with waiting, assumed the role of the coach and started practice. We knew that Superking Son would be pissed. We'd seen him fire cashiers for not abiding by his no-double-bagging policy, butchers for using his personal office bathroom and getting pig blood on his fake granite tile. (Of course, he always rehired them because his mom heard from so-and-so's Ming about so-and-so's kids needing food on the table and braces to fix their messed-up teeth, because they couldn't eat said food on the table with crooked-ass incisors.) At the same time, we were with Justin. We felt his exasperation. We looked like a gang of little assholes on the floor of the gym, sitting in our butterfly stretches, acting like we were doing something substantial so the janitors wouldn't kick us out and start cleaning.

Justin had charisma, which allowed him to take charge of a group of teens his age without sounding like a douche. For once, practice was going smoothly, no kinks, delays, or conflicting instructions jamming the flow between our hitting drills. We became a well-oiled machine of flying birdies and perfect wrist technique. Not a single one of us smacked another in the head with a racket.

"What the hell is going on here?" Superking Son yelled. He was standing at the double doors, sweating like the pig whose blood had stained the clothes he wore. His phone seemed permanently attached to his hand, he was gripping it so hard. Muffled voices, all sinister and incomprehensible, issued from the speakers.

"You weren't here, so I started everyone on drills," Justin replied, without turning toward Superking Son. He resumed correcting the position of Kyle's legs and arms, while Superking Son stormed across the gym, stepping on birdies. Soon they were standing within inches of each other, their eyes locked. Superking Son's were fiery. Justin's stayed cold.

"You want to repeat that, boy," Superking Son said, straightening his posture and locking his shoulders back. He sounded like he was competing in a who-can-breathe-more-heavily contest. We noticed how much taller Justin was than Superking Son.

"We waited for almost an hour. Did you expect us to sit around doing nothing until you got here?" Justin didn't let a whiff of emotion undercut his statements. Superking Son puffed up his chest. He was red in the face, the color rushing to his hairless scalp. We braced ourselves for Superking Son to power up into fire-breathing-angry-uncle mode, for Justin's even-toned facade to disintegrate in the face of decades of pent-up refugee shit and the frustration of premature balding. We thought this was the last of Justin the effective team captain, the stand-in coach, or at least that this confrontation would make practices even more awkward, straight up drive Ken to become a full-blown, black-lungs kind of smoker.

Superking Son sucked in a deep breath, and just when it seemed like he was going to exhale some grade-A-beef insults, hesitation rippled through his expression. Maybe he'd realized it was petty for a business owner to pick fights with a baby-faced high school badminton player. He could've become the level-headed coach we knew he could be. After all, Superking Son was one of the good Cambo dudes. He didn't belong to that long legacy of guys who spent adulthood sleeping on their moms' couches and eating their moms' cooking. (Kevin's older brother, for instance, literally had a full-time job at the DMV and lived with his mom, paid her jack shit in rent, and never did chores because he was too busy playing video games. One day she snapped, set his PlayStation on fire in the middle of a *Call of Duty* campaign, and switched the TV channel to her favorite show—*Family Feud*.) By taking over the grocery store, Superking Son had done right by his father's life. He had sustained his father's hard work—his empire of raw meat and imported fruits and baked goods baked in random Cambo apartments—and made sure his lifetime of suffering didn't go to waste. We looked up to Superking Son. We wanted to keep it that way.

The hesitation in his face directed his sight to the phone in his hand. A dial tone emitted from the speaker, and its dull beat gradually subdued Superking Son. "Everyone go back to what you were doing," he yelled. We watched him scramble out of the gym. He frantically called back the person he was afraid of snubbing on the phone. He disappeared into the dark hallway. We heard him chant *sorry, sorry, sorry* off into the distance.

THE NEXT WEEK Superking Son posted the roster for our first meet of the season. We crowded around the sheet of paper, excited to see who would play what, ready to be disappointed or excited by our ranking, if we had made JV or varsity or—god help us, humble Buddha bless us—if we'd been cast out into exhibition matches to rot away with the freshmen. We knew Justin would be varsity rank one for singles. We had joked for weeks how he would destroy other rank-one players, even that smug kid from Edison with the thousand-dollar racket (joke's on him, he'd been scammed into buying a counterfeit racket by Kyle's cousin). Justin didn't look at the roster. He just stood behind us with his arms crossed.

"Come on guys, hurry up. I wanna get some food from the gas station before practice," he said. Each of us turned back to look at him. "What's the deal? You know I like my steak-and-cheese taquitos."

The revelation that Justin was not rank one, not rank two, but rank three on the varsity team stunned us. Our mouths dropped to the floor. Ken, who was rank one and unprepared to take on that burden, was breathing so heavily he was basically hyperventilating (the cigarettes didn't help). Justin stood there, silent, staring toward the roster, though there was so much space between him and that sheet of paper, who knows where he was looking.

Justin could have thought of confronting Superking Son. He could raise hell the way his mom did when Mr. White had the gall to give him a B– on his Civil War paper. He could also quit, call it a day, and take his taquitos home to eat. Looking at his face, we couldn't tell exactly what he was thinking. What we did see was not so much anger as pity. It was sad for Superking Son to stoop this low and fuck over a teenager half his age. Maybe we saw in Justin's expression what we all thought ourselves.

T HIS TIME WE CONFRONTED Superking Son for real. We found him sitting on a footstool in the aisle at the edge of the building, where customers hardly ever went. Surrounding him were pots and pans, cheap Asian supermarket dishes, and the prayer kits Mas bought to convert their bedrooms into DIY spiritual mausoleums for those who died in the genocide.

We squinted to see him because the store lights didn't reach this aisle, and we looked down on him because he was basically squatting on the ground. You gotta reconsider the team rankings, we said.

"Don't you fools get tired of coming to this shithole?" he asked in a daze. He was looking through us, either at his life or at the spilled rice behind us he would need to sweep sooner or later.

We appealed that we were being serious, that it didn't make sense for Justin to be rank three, not even in terms of stacking our roster against other teams. We would lose all our rank-one and -two matches, we argued. Superking Son sighed, not really registering our words. His face wore that mugshot look our dads got when, instead of getting bowls of noodle soup, we dragged them to eat unlimited salad, soup, and breadsticks at Olive Garden—the look of unresisting contempt.

"Badminton," he said. "It was the only thing I was good at. My body was made for it. Never had to think, make decisions, be all stressed out when I played a match. I just, you know, did it. I used to think something about the hood, the way Cambos like me grew up, made for good badminton. We didn't have it as good as you guys do now. We dealt with a fuckload of bullshit." He spread his arms wide, signaling to us that the store was just that, a fuckload of bullshit. Or maybe he was referring to us, our issue with his decisions as a coach, how we looked up to him, and the pressure of living up to that, as he said, bullshit.

He continued talking, and a couple of us peeled off to grab Gatorades and snacks. We needed sustenance to keep listening to Superking Son's tirade on the ethics of badminton. "You motherfuckers will never really get what we went through, just like how fuckers my age will never understand all that Pol Pot crap."

Stuffing Funyuns wrapped in dry seaweed into our mouths, we asked him what this had to do with Justin's ranking.

"How many times do I have to hammer this into your dense heads?" he asked us. "Badminton is a balancing act. You gotta have both strength and grace. You need to smash the shuttlecock with just the flick of your wrist. None of this tennis swing, use-your-whole-arm nonsense. And to create the gentle tap of a drop shot, you use the force of your entire body to lunge across the court. Then you halt your momentum right before impact and make the hit. You think your all-star is good, but I've seen him driving around in his fancy Mustang." For a second, we thought he would call us out for getting rides from Justin, for buying into his richness.

"He's a spoiled dipshit," Superking Son continued. "His dad walks around like his fancy pharmacy degree makes him better than the rest of us. And his mom doesn't shop here, you know. She thinks the store is beneath her. His parents are always bragging about how smart he is and how hard he studies and how he's gonna go to a real university. You should hear the way his parents talk about him at my mom's parties, like he's slaving away reading SAT books. Badminton takes work—real work. You gotta practice until your wrist feels like it's on fire. When I was your age, I used to curl every item my dad made me stock on these shelves. Ten reps each, using only my wrist, curling boxes of those fucking chips you're eating."

We had no response to Superking Son, partly because of his crazed logic, but mostly because we didn't agree with him. It was real work to do well in school. And weren't we supposed to want what Justin's family had? Weren't we supposed to go to college and become pharmacists? Wasn't that what our parents worked for? But we couldn't think of how to express this, how to reason against someone who carried so much emotional baggage we almost wanted to tip him for his labor.

"Shit." Superking Son dropped his face into his palms. "Badminton was the only thing that made me happy. What a fucking joke." He swung his arms in exasperation and knocked over a stack of dishes. "This place is so fucked."

We looked around the store—at the meat counter lined with blood and guts, at the sacks of rice piled to the ceiling, at the oily Khmer donuts Cha Quai Factory Son supplied, the ones that tasted so good it was hard not to eat yourself sick. All of a sudden, the building looked paler, sparser, empty, like the walls had caught the flu. Were the fluorescent lights dying above us and messing with our vision? Had we simply never looked at the store from this last aisle? We asked Superking Son why he didn't take a break from coaching, just for a couple of weeks. We urged him to focus on the store, assured him that we could run practices on our own in the meantime. We had Justin to watch over our drills and give us pointers. Something about the store seemed off, and we needed him to fix it.

"I can't stay here all day. There's no reason for me to anymore." We watched Superking Son slowly rise to his feet. He prepared himself to face whatever had driven him to this aisle in the first place. "This store disgusts me," he said, mostly to himself. "It always has." He brushed his shirt off, like he saw what disgusted him crawling over his torso, like the store's literal essence had laid claim to his body.

IT WAS QUIET the next few days. Superking Son canceled a week of practices, told us to stay at home and rest. Something strange was happening at the store, and no one, not even our gossipy Mings and Mas, knew what it was—why Superking Son closed the store randomly in the middle of the day, why he failed to appear at Kevin's second cousin's engagement party. Justin, too, was a mystery. He walked the halls in silence, calculating his next move against Superking Son. At lunch he talked our ears off about how canceling practice was an affront to his manhood.

The afternoon practice resumed, Justin bought us bean-and-cheese burritos from the gas station and splurged on a forty-four-ounce mango Slurpee we passed around. He didn't mention Superking Son once the entire day. Something seemed off, but we weren't about to turn down free food. We hadn't received a break since Kyle's oldest half-sister's other half-brother was promoted to assistant store manager at the nice Walmart and every Cambo in the hood got the hookup with a 10 percent discount.

Stretching and warm-up went as smoothly as ever, in the sense that Superking Son was typically late and not present. Justin offered to lead us through some drills. We were hesitant at first. "It'll be chill," he said, too eager in his expressions and voice to sell us on the "chill" factor. "What's the worst that could happen?"

Of course, shit went down when Superking Son walked in, looked up from his text messages, and found himself amid a shuttlecock tornado before getting whacked in the head with a racket by a freshman.

"What the fucking shit is going on here?" he yelled, after grabbing the freshman's racket and throwing it to the ground. In response, Justin began laughing—either hysterically or fake hysterically. His body hunched over, his arms wrapped across his stomach, it seemed like he wanted to piss off Superking Son. Superking Son pointed at him. "You wanna start something, don't ya? You're just trying to get me riled up."

"As a matter of fact, I am." Everyone turned to look at Justin. He walked through the crowd of players up to Superking Son, stepping on fallen birdies on the way. "I challenge you to a match."

Ken gasped for air, but that was probably his developing smoker's lung.

"Oh yeah?" Superking Son said, imparting to his words as much condescension as possible.

"Yes, and if I win, you have to make me rank one." Justin's posture was completely upright to emphasize his height over Superking Son.

"What's gonna happen when you lose?" Superking Son asked.

"Then I'll quit. As simple as that. You won't have to deal with me undermining your whole I'm-the-coach-and-I-demand-respect routine."

"That's boring," Superking Son said. "You're not offering any real stakes."

"Fine, if I lose, I'll not only stay at my ranking, but I'll also serve as designated birdie collector for every single practice and meet." Our ears pricked up at this proposal—cleaning up the mess of white feathering nubs was easily the worst thing about playing badminton.

"Deal." Superking Son grabbed a racket out of Kyle's hands.

We crowded around the centermost court, the only spot in the gym well lit by the crappy ceiling lights. Superking Son offered Justin the first shot, saying, "Show me what you got," as he handed over the birdie—and when Justin served, Superking Son charged. He smashed the birdie so hard it ricocheted off the ground and whacked Ken in the face, leaving a red welt. *Damn*s and *Ooooohhhhh*s came from the crowd as Ken yelled, "My face! My fucking face!"

For thirty minutes, Superking Son and Justin became dance partners. Their moves fed off each other with the intensity of two Mas shit-talking their grandchildren. Superking Son lobbed, Justin drove the birdie back. Justin lunged forward for a drop shot, Superking Son sprang forward in anticipation. Superking Son jumped for a smash, Justin crouched to retrieve it. Neither gained more than a two-point lead. Both were so effortless in their playing, so in tune with their own and each other's bodies they seemed half asleep, steered by some master puppeteer.

The most beautiful badminton unfolded before our eyes. Birdies flew impossibly close to the net. Feet glided across the court, bouncing, lunging, leaping. Racket strings trembled. We exclaimed at every point and every unthinkable shot. We rooted until their sheer athleticism became routine, until all the incredible smashes averaged out into the same shot. Our voices fatigued and our eyes stopped caring.

The second half of the match turned downright boring. Instead of paying attention, some of us opened our textbooks and studied. Ken lay down on the bleachers with an ice pack on his swollen face. Others busted out a deck of cards and started a round of big two. (If anything, the big two game became more riveting. Kyle squandered his ace of hearts, lost ten bucks, and completely upended his weekend plans—the bet required the loser to drive the other players' Mas to the temple, the one in the boonies next to the bad Walmart.) Superking Son and Justin were too good. They predicted each other too well. There was no drama, no tension or grit, no underdog who could bounce back and surprise us. And when Superking Son scored that final, winning shot, no one really gave a shit. Even Justin seemed apathetic.

But Superking Son gave tons of shits. He pranced around his side of the court, ran victory laps, and stomped his feet so hard we're pretty sure our half-deaf, half-dead, he-should-retire-but-tenure-is-cushy English teacher (it's no wonder kids barely make it to community college) heard him from across campus. He yelled, "Fuck yes!" over and over, like winning this badminton match against a high schooler was better than all the sex he'd ever had (which was probably true). He shifted into older-Cambo taunt mode, donning the same antagonism our moms did when we try to buy shoes not on sale, our dads when we prioritize our homework over the family business, our Mas and Gongs when they hear our shameful Khmer accents, and our older siblings when we complain about responsibilities they previously shouldered, about enduring what could never match what had already happened to everyone we know.

"Who else wants a piece of this shit!" Superking Son yelled, beating his chest with his racket-free hand. He traversed half the gym to direct his taunts not only at Justin but at every guy in the room. "None of you have what it takes. None!" He seemed blinded with misguided passion, the bulging veins in his fat neck pumping blood straight to his eyeballs. "Get out of my fucking face!" We felt spit fly from his slobbering mouth and into our faces.

Our memories go out around the time Superking Son began challenging us to matches, even the poor freshmen on the exhibition team, pointing with his racket at kid after kid and repeating, "Come on! Show me what you got!" like a robot stuck in an infinite loop. The next thing we remember is this: the shock of watching Superking Son's ego spurt all over the gym began to fade. Our bodies settled into pity. We looked at our coach, an overgrown son fed up with his place and his inheritance, perpetually made irritated and disgusted and paranoid by his own being, and we looked at each other. Right there in the gym, Superking Son screaming in our faces, we made the collective decision, silently, almost telepathically, that one, Superking Son was an asshole—a tragic one, but still an asshole; two, we had too many assholes in our shitty lives; and three, we didn't have enough asswipes to deal.

LOOK, WHAT CAN WE SAY? We were busy. We had our own lives full of responsibilities and expectations we were always on the verge of failing. Sure, there were signs, tons of them. It's not like Superking Grocery Store was packed with customers. There were no lines of people throwing cash into the registers. Superking Son wasn't driving around a new Porsche. He wasn't decked out in Rolex watches and Ralph Lauren polos.

First our Mas started complaining about the lack of fresh vegetables, about papayas as old as their concentration-camp-surviving hands decaying on the shelves of the produce section. Then shadowy Cambos started rolling into the store, not to shop for rotting papayas, that's for sure. They rushed to the backroom, sometimes with loads of packages, sometimes in the middle of the afternoon, sometimes at closing, never to be seen leaving the premises. After a while, Superking Son stopped letting us into the backroom. That giant bulky guy, the ex-army Cambo who took Kevin's sister to the prom, guarded the door. Superking Son barely trekked back there himself, not even to play solitaire on his ancient HP computer.

We'd seen it happen to Cambo businesses before. We'd seen it when Angkor Noodles Lady hired a new cook who made soggy-ass noodles. (The old cook pulled a classic drunk dad move—he went on a bender for a week. When they finally found him, he was passed out at a roulette table in Reno and had gambled away his kids' college fund.) Angkor Noodles Lady borrowed more and more money from the higher-up Cambos. Each month she promised to pay them back with full interest once business picked up. Business never picked up (the new noodles were gross), and the restaurant floated on Cambo community money until Angkor Noodles Lady ditched town. She ended up nursing a boxed-wine addiction from her niece's guest room in Bakersfield until she died of liver failure.

Now Superking Son isn't dead, don't worry. We see him out all the time, usually at the good pho place, usually with Cha Quai Factory Son, who has been ranting about the same far-fetched business plan for years. (It involves mass-producing in neon party colors those weird suction cups that make Cambo moms look like they're getting abused to people with white savior complexes.) When the store closed and Superking Son couldn't even offer the higher-up Cambos his back storeroom to use as their headquarters, Superking Son's mom saved his skin by selling her house and paying back his debts.

We don't know how Superking Son makes a living anymore, but sometimes, if you're lucky, Superking Son will appear at an open gym. He'll play a match or two, give some pointers on form. His lunges and smashes will strike you as impressive for someone his age, someone who probably has knee and wrist pain. Halfway through the session, he'll leave the player queue and sit on the bleachers. He'll watch a crew of younger Cambos play the game that, according to him, was the only thing that made him worthwhile as a person. When open gym is over, you'll drive home, and if you're taking Pershing Avenue to Manchester Street, you'll pass what remains of Superking Grocery Store. And even though the building has been empty for years, gathering dust and gang signs like flies to a pile of bloody meat, even though the community has moved on to bigger and better things, like college degrees and Costco bulk food, you'll swear, on the graves of all those murdered Cambos, on every cupping bruise your mom self-inflicts to rid her body of trauma, we promise you'll swear that the lingering smell of raw fish never left the air. Trust us. +

KIM DORLAND, *ALL IDEAS ARE WRONG*. 2018, OIL ON LINEN. 96 × 72". COURTESY OF THE ARTIST.

MISSING TIME

Marissa Brostoff

S. WAS THE ONE WHO usually wrote our fanfic. It's all there in my files, packed into the box my mom sends me from the Valley when I decide to write about the show. It tends to be in screenplay form and leans toward the carnivalesque. It's 1970s night at the Haunted Mansion and we are all together: Mulder and Scully, me and S.; their nemesis the Cigarette Smoking Man, a deep-state puppeteer responsible for countless acts of terror, and our nemesis Ms. Simonds, an English teacher at Gaspar de Portola Middle School whose crimes I cannot recall. Exene Cervenka of the legendary LA punk band X makes a cameo appearance. After a few tequila-and-opiums, our gang throws open the gold-plated doors at a members-only club hidden in Disneyland's New Orleans Square and discovers we've passed through a portal to the Life Café, where everyone hangs out in *RENT*. We order soy dogs and sing.

My stuff sounds stilted and self-conscious by comparison. My one real contribution to the genre was a naive first attempt, a fanfic that could not yet speak its name, which appears as a notebook entry from the beginning of seventh grade.

9/22/97

Dear B.,

God, we have a lot of catching up to do. Well, first of all, between now and maybe a month ago or so, I became an obsessive *X-Files* fan. Call it hanging out with S. too much, but it is seriously the best show ever made. I even have a completely screwed up, totally bogus theory about it. This is it:

> The X-Files is not a Fox 11 TV show as commonly thought by a vast majority of sane people in the world. It is instead written and produced by the secret government. Now, Marissa, you may ask, what the hell are you talking about? Well, according to my theory, this Secret Government began around the time of World War II. What they intended was to gradually build suspicion about their existence until people began rebelling. Then they could declare the rebels, who would be the majority of the American people, a threat to society, and have them vaporized. (Am I starting to sound just a wee bit like a militia member here?) Unfortunately for them, the cold war and McCarthyist policies and stuff started. So people got their attention off the Secret Government, and vented their anger at the Russians instead. OK, skip to the '80s. The cold war is almost over, and the SG (you figure it out) guys are thinking, OK, now we can get down to business. So they create fictitious people like George Bush and Bill Clinton to lure the people into a false sense of security. But all the while, they're dropping hints to get people neurotic. So there should be a surge of UFO sightings soon (which, of course, are just planted by the SG) and that's how *The X-Files* started!!!!! Don't you just love my logic?!?
>
> Anyway. I started the coolest club. It's called the Messed Up People Club.

Things continue in this vein.

Sixth grade had not gone well. Around the beginning of the school year, I had become an ardent communist. I knew about communism from musicals and Jewish historical fiction and the night of the big earthquake when I was 8, when everyone left their houses at four in the morning to loop past the palms on March Avenue in silent procession because the location of safety had moved outside. A few months later, a big tacky house that only appeared to have cracked in a few places went on sale nearby, in the foothills at the far edge of the Valley, and we moved in. My mom spoke glowingly of our proximity to nature. Rabbits ate the lawn, and sometimes coyotes ate the rabbits. My parents hired a gardener to replace the grass with AstroTurf. It was the mid-1990s, but like a lot of people, we lived outside historical time.

As for the ardency, who can say? Like everything I started wanting in the months before my first period, the desire for communism seemed both endogenous and alien, secret and self-evident. To me it seemed to explain a lot of things, but I tried to keep quiet about it because it was, as we said at the time, very random. I found a Marxist reader in the den among my father's college books; it was too hard for me, but I buried it like a fetish under my bed. It had always been my custom to hide the media that could hurt me, like novels with bees or Nazis, around the house. The philosopher Ernst Bloch distinguished between two currents of Marxism, one warm and one cold. The cold current—"the detective glance at history"—was about where capitalism came from, how it worked, and ways it could be overthrown, and about all this I knew very little. My current was the warm one, all strikes and hammers and bread and roses, a child's communism. Sometimes, if I started having too much fun being with other people, I laughed so hard I peed in my pants, and a warm current froze into a cold one down my legs.

People think that only adults felt groggy and homesick after the end of history, but children were sad, too. In the Valley, you could dress up as any decade. Kids were covered in meaning. Or, I thought we were. Obviously I was bullied. Every day after school I sat at my desk drawing automated rows of smiling girls and tried to divine who would eat whom, just from looking. My only friends, B. and the other fuzzy glowworms who lived in my stomach, formed a council to address the crisis but schismed. At the end of the school year, I addressed them sternly in my notebook.

6/5/97

A Letter to B.:

I am writing this because I don't think you should be a communist any more. In that Marxist book or whatever it is that Daddy has it says that the main idea in communism is to abolish private property. Well, obviously, that has to do with economics and all that. I think when we grow up we should focus on something less extreme and something that will actually be paid attention to by regular people. Here's a list of practical causes and stuff that I can protest/advocate at some point in time:

Fur
Abortion
Gun control
Death penalty
Drugs (but not heavy ones)
Assisted suicide

love,
marissa

The following entry, from August, concerns a birthday party to which I was not invited. By September there was S., and *The X-Files.*

S OMETHING HAD HAPPENED, and we could not remember what it was. In *Missing Time*, a 1981 best seller that helped establish the conventions of the alien abduction memoir, ufologist Budd Hopkins explained that evidence of an extraterrestrial visitation often took the form of precisely this sort of mysterious gap in experience. Abduction was a way of describing rupture in its purest form, a literal wrinkle in time. I could relate: it wasn't like I had a better excuse for being such an old-fashioned girl. But I was not alone. In the 1990s, anyone could be abducted, though the aliens seemed to have a thing for white girls, and a way of making men feel like white girls even though they weren't. Weird syndromes coagulated everywhere. The deeper in the suburbs they appeared, the more mysterious they seemed, like signs from another world. A postwar infrastructure of office buildings and tract homes designed to cordon off the white middle class from the contagious city turned out to be built from noxious materials that made people sick. Asbestos, formaldehyde, and 4-phenylcyclohexene, or "new carpet smell," dewed up in moldy corners beneath the level of perception. Veterans returning from Iraq reported a rash of problems—memory loss, respiratory trouble—that they attributed to chemical exposure. When no physical marker could be found for Gulf War syndrome, mass psychogenic illness, a new term for hysteria, was extended for the first time to men.*

The X-Files was born into this biosphere in 1993 on Fox, an upstart network trying to figure out how to undercut its more established rivals with niche programming like *The Simpsons* (1989 to present) and the Fox News Channel (1996 to the end of the world). A seriously ambitious program, *The X-Files* "made TV cinematic," as critic Theresa Geller put it in a recent monograph, inspiring waves of cerebral genre programming and launching the careers of showrunners like Vince Gilligan (*Breaking Bad*) and Frank Spotnitz (*The Man in the High Castle*). But the show was also a quasi-respectable cousin of *Jerry Springer* at a time when reality, too, was remaking TV. In this sense the series wasn't science fictional at all, but took place in a world just like our own, where women being poisoned by their microwaves floated around with Lyndon LaRouche

---

*See Michelle Murphy, *Sick Building Syndrome and the Problem of Uncertainty: Environmental Politics, Technoscience, and Women Workers*. Durham: Duke University Press, 2006. p. 3, 81, 93.

supporters and AIDS denialists and 12-year-old ex-communists in dubious pursuit of a history of the present. There they were, serially archived on a single flashing screen, from the Loch Ness monster and the chupacabra to the JFK assassination and the defamation of Anita Hill. In the last years of the 20th century, this solar system of conspiratorial thinking was where the postmodern condition lived its best life. You could find yourself in cozy exile there, social theorists said, if you'd tried too hard to picture technoscientific global capitalism and your brain broke. I'd barely begun to try, and mine already had.

On *The X-Files*, the United States government was a shell company for extraterrestrial interests in our GDP of biopolitical slop: neurons and wombs, oil fields and cornfields, radio towers and internet cables, Nazis and bees. The cold war wasn't really over, but it had also never really begun, the whole thing having been, as Thomas Pynchon put it in *Gravity's Rainbow* twenty years earlier, a front for the war of multinational technology cartels against everyone else. Now, in the Nineties, world-historical conflict farted in its fresh grave as hoax and scandal filled the deregulated airwaves. Cable news proved such a deadly carrier of "subliminal messages" that in one episode, people in a DC suburb watch TV pundits weigh in on Bosnia and are hypnotized into homicidal rage against their loved ones. In other words, paranormal activity caused by US–alien collusion manifested on a day-to-day basis as unaccountable violent symptoms bugging out the collective sensorium. In the parlance of the show, this sort of thing was an X-file, a local mystery with national implications that the federal government didn't *want* to solve. Such cases fell to an odd couple of FBI agents: Fox Mulder (doofy, irreproachable David Duchovny), a believer bent on avenging a government cover-up of his sister's abduction, and Dana Scully (acute, deadpan Gillian Anderson), a medically trained skeptic assigned to spy on him. Mulder and Scully spend the series investigating strange phenomena, from a 120-year-old serial killer who hibernates between meals of human liver to an American luxury liner perpetually invaded by Germans because it's always 1939 in the Bermuda Triangle, on behalf of a regime that wants to snort their brains. *The X-Files* may not have been the best postmodern novel ever written, but it was, despite stiff competition, perhaps the longest.

The show ran until a few months after September 11, 2001. It spawned two forgettable feature films and started up again as a series in

2016 in a painful nostalgia exercise; this spring, it was ostensibly laid to rest for good. *The X-Files'* creator, Chris Carter—a SoCal boy who spent thirteen years at *Surfing Magazine* before he started the show—shot episodes like small movies where the sublime architecture of conspiracy in the post-Watergate thriller entered the orbit of Lynchian Americana: *All the President's Men Meet the Log Lady*. Some episodes layered one aesthetic atop the other: in countless scenes, girls in white nightgowns run barefoot through the woods illuminated by the glare of spacecrafts or SWAT teams. Others seemed located halfway in between, in endless gray suburbs where Washington and Main Street alike flicker in between commercials on a half-watched screen before a working mom is gobbled up by a swarm of irradiated cockroaches. Either way, everything looks like Vancouver, where the show was shot through its fifth season, creating the uncanny impression that, in the Nineties, the entire country was a Northwestern logging town haunted by industry. The show's devotees created an online subculture largely populated by female X-philes, who debated the relationship between its conspiracy-driven "mythology" arc and its less sweeping but often more satisfying "Monster of the Week" one-offs, as well as the persistent question of whether Mulder and Scully should bang. ("Shippers" said yes, "no-romos" said it would ruin the show.) At a time when being obsessed with stuff on the internet was still the province of freaks and geeks, the show's producers winked back, turning losers into collaborators.

Teetering between police procedural and science fiction, *The X-Files*, Geller notes, forgoes the positivistic comforts of a regular forensic drama, in which truth can be discovered and justice served in the space of a single episode. The show's collision of genres, she writes, conscripts Mulder and Scully into the role of social detective—Fredric Jameson's term for a sleuth, sometimes a policeman or a journalist, but sometimes a Jane Q. Public or even a whole community—who, motivated by forces beyond the need to file a report, approaches "society as a whole" as "the mystery to be solved." As such, our heroes stumble through each X-file in a state of epistemological crisis. Halfway through the pilot episode, driving one stormy night down a back road in an Oregon town zapped with extraterrestrial enterprise, the agents are enveloped by a halo of light, and their car goes dead. When the light subsides, Mulder checks his watch and squeals that nine minutes have vanished into thin air. "Time can't just disappear!" Scully, panicked for the first time, stammers through the rain at her giddy partner. "It's a universal invariant!" Mulder, riveted beyond gloating, pants back, "Not in this zip code."

By granting impressive measures of scientific reasoning to one and gestalt interpretation to the other, the show gives its leads a basic measure of dramatic and intellectual equality. Neither agent is Sherlock to the other's Watson, and each contends with the harassment that befalls women who do autopsies and men who read tea leaves. Both are smart, stubborn, lonely, and brave. At the same time, a persistent sleight of hand gives *ontological* priority to Mulder: it's his world we're visiting, and in the final instance, his research methods tend to be the ones that work. (Not coincidentally, Anderson is a serious, thoughtful actress who would go on to play Lily Bart and Nora Helmer. Duchovny, at his best, just kind of *is* Fox Mulder. Had he not dropped out of Yale to play gender-bending roles in *Twin Peaks* and porny indie films, he might have finished his dissertation on Pynchon and his peers, "Magic and Technology in Contemporary Fiction and Poetry.")

To be Scully—or, in a more archetypal sense, to be "a Scully"—is to insist on the laws of physics even as the aliens stretch you out on board their ship. It's to begin a sentence, as she does in "Die Hand Die Verletzt" (The One Where Devil Worshippers Run the School Board), "I mean, there's nothing odd about—" only to be cut off by toads falling from the sky. It's to climb the rungs of an institution that seeks to push you off the ladder, to stoically salute your authoritarian father's coffin, to relax by studying the DSM-IV on a Friday night over a glass of wine, and still to somehow find yourself among mutants, the odd girl in a different boys' club than the one you'd intended to join. As with her predecessor Clarice Starling, Jodie Foster's dogged young criminologist in *The Silence of the Lambs*, Scully dares to look into the hearts of the coldest killers, and they alone dare to look back.

To be a Mulder, on the other hand, means your ears buzz with white noise but your sacred duty is to keep it Real. Because you're obsessed with getting outside, you take a job way on the inside, put on the gray suit you were born in, and work both for and against the (Cigarette Smoking) Man, who considers vaping you every eighth episode but then just maims you again like a favorite broken toy. Your basement office under the panopticon is so close to where the maps are made, it's off the map. You're a polonium-tipped dart's throw from knowledge but so far from power that they don't even bother harassing you half the time. So you curl up in the belly of your own surveillance, eat sunflower seeds out of the bag, and jerk off at your desk beneath your iconic poster of a grainy UFO with its block-lettered caption, I WANT TO BELIEVE. "It's interesting," a shape-shifting rapist tells him in an episode called "Small Potatoes" (The One Where Mulder Gets Impersonated by a Man with a Tail). "I was born a loser. But you're one by choice." To be a Mulder is to be a kind of idiot, and to be right. In many episodes, he crumples to the ground as though literally stricken by the force of terrible knowledge. I did that too, I bragged to my journal. And I liked to watch.

IN OUR BOOK, even in the late section titled "The Great List of Differences," S. and I never quite come out and say that she is a Scully and I a Mulder. This might appear in retrospect like a correction for the show's own bias, a critique of how contemporary metaphysics still estranges science from magic after all these years, or a mature recognition that Mulder and Scully aren't *real*. In fact, I think S. was happy to acknowledge her own allegiance to the latter, while I was too uneasy to admit to such a fundamental split.

I had known S. since the second grade. We liked each other because we were both serious, but for the same reason didn't play together much. Once I borrowed an armload of her books, then forgot about them for so long that we had outgrown them by the time I brought them back. In middle school we became part of the same carpool, and at the start of seventh grade she became what, had we been paranormal investigators, I would have called my partner. It was 1997. Earlier that year, the thirty-eight remaining members of Heaven's Gate, a UFO cult that started in the '70s, washed down phenobarbital with vodka for the same reason everyone did what we did in those days: the millennium was coming.

My mom, a special-ed teacher, only diagnosed me with autism spectrum disorders when I was getting on her nerves, which in those days I usually was. S. presented her with a complicated case. At school, most kids on the spectrum had trouble getting along, or only hung out with each other. S. gravitated in their direction, but she was as cool as an algorithm, or a brand, and could sense the same quality in the objects around us as disinterestedly as a nurse checking for fever. Later, when there were more of us, we spent years trying to account for her unaccountability, as though she had joined us from another planet. In retrospect, though, she was simply from a feminist cyberpunk future that never quite happened. She was a tiny child, pale with freckles and acne, who wore a spiked dog collar and soft bright T-shirts from babyhood and who seemed to have more processing power available to her than anyone anyone had ever met. She learned programming languages and, like the girls who took Korean lessons after school, turned her handwriting into a font. At one point she tried to make pocket protectors happen and almost succeeded; if we'd had more internet in those days, she might have. She was mean to boys and they fell in love with her; if we'd had more internet in those days, she might have become one herself. When she wrote about middle school as an adult, her alter ego was a secret robot.

To her great frustration, S. had to share a small room with her sister, but in my mind her house was, if not a portal to the Life Café, at least a peephole. Through it could be glimpsed a full-spectrum pastiche of cultural politics: her aunts and uncles on one side included Marxist art historians and a regional leader of the Objectivist society; on the other, a Sonic Youth producer with a bathtub full of records. It was her father, who drank wine and watched baseball and read John Barth, who informed me one day in our carpool, "Work is hell." S. and I silently agreed that I would come as close as possible to taking on her tastes, habits, and Myers-Briggs classification (INTP: the Logician) and use the results to establish our superiority to the normies around us. Throughout my files from this time, our belief in the typological power of codes we had made up ourselves appears with a conspiracist's selective rigor. ("I've finally figured out why my mom and I don't get along," I wrote. "She's an ESFP!") In the notebooks I manically maintained in the fall of seventh grade, I claimed that we had become so close, we seemed to be merging into one.

I kept, for those months, not one but two journals. In my regular journal, I fantasized about making a suicide pact with a boy in a Pearl Jam shirt and global annihilation as an antidote to slow violence. I copied S. I complained about my mom, who compared me during one fight, I reported indignantly, to another young woman lacking in "fundamental values": Squeaky Fromme, the Manson girl who'd plotted murder from Spahn Ranch just a few miles up the canyon from our house. In my *X-Files* journal, which opens with an apology for "my ever-insistent urges to write even *more* rambling pages" about the show, I traced David Duchovny's face out of *Us Weekly*, hit critical walls (what was the proper level of detail to include in an episode recap for which I was the only reader?), and tried to suck a political education out of my television.

History, we were told in the 1990s, was something that happened to other people. The recent past was littered with code-named police actions that, rendered pointless by the evaporation of the cold war, no longer even had the dignity of the unmentionable. Conservatives kept building monuments to the death of communism that no one wanted to visit. Liberals wanted to forget the whole messy business and gave themselves endless Oscars for movies about World War II. Only fools with sheaves of xeroxed newsletters thought they were smart enough to construct a narrative out of a deafening drone. The more distant past, upon inspection, turned out to be much the same, leading some to suspect that history had never happened at all. There were, however, exceptions to the rule: events taken to be unique in their world-shattering horror and exceptional people who had come near them and gotten away no longer quite themselves. We, too, could be exceptional: if we were good and listened hard, history could become something that happened, though only by proxy, to us. Every year on the Day of Remembrance, survivors came to Hebrew school and asked us to feel on our skin the licks of the Shoah's eternal flame and to guard with our lives its redemption in the birth of a handsome nation. In history class in regular school, we learned nothing at all. And yet the past kept ghosting through like reruns.

Reruns were the form in which I watched the show, already five seasons in and beginning its long decline by the time I got on board. Seeing its baffling conspiracy arc unfold out of order saved me the hassle of getting fully invested in a plot that often made no sense. True to its times, *The X-Files* lacked a show bible, the reference guide typically used to maintain consistency over the course of a series. Yet even at its most labyrinthine the program imparted the crucial thesis that cataclysmic violence was not merely the stuff of historical memory, but an ongoing process of natural history still ravaging lands and bodies zoned for continuous extraction. "Something just clicked about the whole Holocaust," I wrote, shaken, after watching season two's searing "Anasazi" trilogy (The Ones Where Mulder Gets Decolonized), in which we learn that the Kissinger-era State Department collaborated with ex-Nazi scientists on the production of human-alien hybrids, using tribal populations as test subjects. When Mulder finds evidence, the government destroys the tape, but Navajo code talkers have already memorized its contents. The Final Solution, the episodes suggested, emerged not from the depths of an unfathomable hell but had a *logic* that preceded the camps and survived their dismantling; maybe it was even right at home in the United States. Here, if memory stood a chance at enduring through the body, it was lodged in throats intubated by colonial force.

Did I get all that, or did it go over my head entirely? Was it even there to begin with? *The X-Files*, a show whose social detectives are at the end of the day still cops, occupied a cunningly ambiguous slot in the ideological lineup of its equivocating era: symptomology without diagnosis, conspiracy without collectivity, paranoia for its own sake, a bossa nova accelerationism for a rainy evening with an eclectic drug collection and nowhere to go all night. Critics spanning the political spectrum loved it, especially those concentrated at its weirdo ends like S.'s aunts and uncles. The appeal to academics on the left of a series about intrepid hauntologists trapped in an institutional maze run by evil overlords perhaps goes without saying. The show was like Duchovny: if it hadn't landed on Fox, it would have just taught cultural studies. Many of its most poignant, sophisticated episodes are seminars on the power, and the limits, of Mulder's methods for patiently sifting through piles of cultural detritus on the lookout for connections between dubious Monsters of the Week and tortuous conspiracy arcs. On the dust jacket of her excellent cultural history of ufology, *Aliens in America: Conspiracy Cultures from Outerspace to Cyberspace*, the Marxist political theorist Jodi Dean broke the fourth wall of scholarly detachment entirely, posing in front of an I WANT TO BELIEVE poster and appearing to suppress a giggle. But the libertarian right boasted hard-core fans as well, and for similar reasons. The show represented resistance to neoliberal governmentality in the form of clandestine cells: hacker collectives, militias, cults practicing archaic magics bright and dark. In doing so, it seemed to beckon its own cult following, wrote the libertarian scholar Paul Cantor, who has devoted hundreds of admiring pages to *The X-Files*, "as if the program were trying to replicate in its audience what it shows in the world at large."

For me, too, *The X-Files* held out the promise of subculture, the meaning of style. I studied Mulder's methods—suspend disbelief when doing fieldwork, wink at your interview subjects—and tried to make them my own. But because I was twelve and had never heard of anything, the show functioned even more literally as a dictionary of esoteric knowledge from which America could be inferred. The secrets made me giddy and desperate, like hearing an incredible bit of gossip over a wiretap. S. and I got on the phone every Sunday night after the show ended and talked for hours.

Fandom was a way of organizing knowledge and desire, a kind of epidemiology. You learned from the cluster of objects that drew near you what kind of person you were. The internet was like that, too: it sorted. S. loved it there and from it brought back news of our cult. From her I learned of the epic online battles between shippers and no-romos, and S. and I took up the cause of the latter with the passion of hardheaded agents who thought romance was for little girls. Around the beginning of seventh grade, men from the phone company had come to my house, too, and installed our own beeping, flashing modem. My journal makes no mention of the internet's installation, but by the end of the year, it's there in every entry, a thrilling, ugly hassle. I went through the motions of fury with my parents for limiting my access to its catacombs, but even S. knew I basically agreed with them: I wanted it to leave us, and hoped it still might.

Sometimes, through the entropy of perversion, curiosity, a hunch, I found myself in bad company. "I finally managed to subscribe to the INTJ page, and they're all Ayn Rand freaks!" I griped to my journal. "'Mercy is a trait that only an F can possess'!" And yet my diary itself, in the moments it draws most clearly from my *X-Files* notebook, sounds unnervingly like the adolescent fascism of 4chan. There is a short story about the Pentagon "vaporizing" rebels in Montana, a state my mother often used to illustrate the point that even in the Nineties, a Jew could not go everywhere. There is a poem called "Awaken" in which the speaker steps into reality, "where bureaucrats are not cheerful pink bunnies / And dreamers do not rule the world." It wasn't that I'd switched sides in my private political pantomime, where communists and fascists were still at war. If anything, I probably rested too easy in the assumption that I never could. It was simply that my enemies had the advantage of actually existing, at least in larval form, filling the web with paeans to the intellectual superiority of white men who liked to code. I dabbled in their language because, as far as I knew, I did not.

On New Year's Day, I described a fight with my parents in which I lost access to language and became "a dead circuit." Chunks of the recent past had gone missing, and the cloud of absence threatened the borders of the present. The visitors had landed, Jodi Dean wrote that year: the internet was changing people; it had gotten into our blood, scrambling codes. Just as Budd Hopkins, the ufologist, had promised, we were no longer the watchers but the ones being watched. I still have information sickness. I don't know what it's really called.

On January 2, though, I had better news. I took out what amounted to full-page ads in both my regular and *X-Files* journals, indicating in giant purple letters that something had changed in my house, something that meant I would now be able to watch the show every night:

WE

GOT

FX!!!

And then, for months, I barely wrote at all.

WHEN MY JOURNAL picks up again around the start of eighth grade, a new kid has emerged, kind of hyper, in the midst of a determined cultural discovery process. I loved Sylvia Plath and the Violent Femmes and "anarchists" and my JNCOs. My mapping had become more focused; there were fewer global conspiracies and more genealogies of punk. An *X-Files* soundtrack had introduced me to Nick Cave, and a Nick Cave CD had a cover of "All Tomorrow's Parties," and "All Tomorrow's Parties" led me down the stairs to the Velvet Underground. At some point in the process I no longer needed the show: I could read lots of things now. It was 1998. In Calabasas, where the rich girls from Hebrew school lived behind locked gates, a new outdoor mall was built in the shape of a fake Umbrian plaza. They called it the Commons.

By the time S. and I graduated from middle school, we had built a world together. *M. and S.'s Book*, made one long weekend after graduation in the summer of 1999, catalogued that world before it was destroyed, as we knew it would be, by our departure for different high schools: a math-and-science magnet for her, a humanities one for me. Like an eponymous first album, it did not have another name. Its cover is adorned with cutouts and stickers—a Lisa Frank palm tree, Beck, the Ayatollah Khomeini, a potato. Its handwritten pages are filled with song lyrics and comics and fanfic and assessments of our friends and endless inventories of our universe.

Things We Want (in S.'s writing), No. 41: No tongue so I can sound like the Sex Pistols (M. thought of this first).

Stuff That Scares Us (S. again), No. 31: Obsessive fans-turned-assassins. Where the hell is your brain, I'm talking to you, Mark David Chapman.

Things That Depress Me (my writing), No. 14: How Columbine made all these shitty laws happen and now you can't wear trench coats and stuff.

___ No. 15: How my dad fucked my computer and I can't get in.

___ No. 16: How communism didn't work.

We wanted to distribute our book widely, but my mom read it, noted that it was, among other things, a burn book—"Oh, and her choreography sucks," S. wrote of one friend—and forbade this, instead driving us to Staples to print the only two copies in existence. "It's just me and S. again," I wrote in my journal at the end of that summer, "and god we had the most depressing conversation tonight. About how we're so worried about *everything*: high school, college, life. How this era totally sucks and even our parents admit they had it easy, but at the same time we are so lame cuz all our music is old and we act like it came out yesterday. We are obsessed with old dead people. Everyone is fuckin dead or they own stores in places like Silver Lake." On bad days, I admitted, "I completely lose myself in time."

MULDER AND SCULLY'S partnership could not survive the turn of the millennium and neither could mine and S.'s. In the show's final seasons, the agents finally seem to be sleeping together, ruining an important source of dramatic tension exactly as we knew it would. Both leads had pulled back from the series and were partially replaced by generic opposite-gendered investigators. George W. Bush was elected, the twin towers fell, and the national appetite for conspiratorial fantasy was sated, for a while, by the nightly news.

By that time I had stopped watching. S. stuck with the original series until the end; I quit when the going got tough. She wanted to remain an extraordinary child and I was trying to become a more ordinary miserable teenager. Neither of us could keep up with the other, and we suffered and quarreled. For S., computing offered safe passage to wonder; the beauty of form was on the inside. I remained locked out; computers break when I come near. At Armenian church camp one summer, she welcomed Jesus into her heart and kept him there for a few years, and I discovered my own bewilderment in the face of belief. She was celibate; I just couldn't get laid. We both loved other girls but not quite, we decided, each other. Later, she would study engineering, and I would study its critiques. Later still, she would move to the Pacific Northwest, build brains for a big company, and fill a mansion with marvelous toys and then children to play with them. I moved across the country to my city, where I wander around staring uncomprehendingly at objects and waiting for them to stare back. I still have my I WANT TO BELIEVE poster over my desk. It was the first thing I ever bought online.

What is easier to see with greater distance is that the epistemological tension that had held the show together—the coy flirtation between magic and science—had been consummated, just like the relationship between Mulder and Scully or between conspiratorial fantasy and political reality. We had been literalized into a strange new lifeworld entirely saturated by computer technology. *The X-Files* filled its characters with alien-manufactured microchips, but it never really caught up to a world with smartphones. Detective work on *The X-Files* had happened under the cover of darkness, the agents' flashlights casting single beams across a blackened screen. But by the turn of the millennium, the night was fading. In Russia, a space company made plans to dot the sky with satellites that would reflect sunshine back to earth at all hours, creating "daylight all night long."* The satellites never launched, but it didn't matter: the new order of things had eliminated shadows, and with them, an entire methodology for seeing in the dark.

The *X-Files* reboot first aired in the early months of 2016, when the air was humid with denial. Fittingly, the real problem is the lighting. Anderson has a self-help book out; Duchovny, back from rehab for sex addiction, wrote a novel in which farm animals representing Israel and Palestine make friends, and has a Twitter account for his dog. In the new episodes, they uncannily seemed to be playing themselves—her with sharpened cheekbones, him with an open top button on a crisp white shirt—like they'd just come from brunch in Santa Monica. But an influx of daylight created a problem for the series on another level,

---

*See Jonathan Crary, 24/7: *Late Capitalism and the Ends of Sleep*. New York: Verso, 2014. p. 4.

too. In "My Struggle" and its sequels (The Ones That Felt Longer Than a Knausgaard Novel), the show's updated myth arc revolves around our protagonists' attempt to deal with a strange new bedfellow, a popular right-wing conspiracy peddler on the model of Alex Jones, who is both clearly odious and possibly onto something. For all the original program's storied self-reflexivity, the new show could not figure out how to live up to its twist, both jaw-dropping and enragingly inevitable, on the old one: *Fox Mulder Meets Fox News*. The call is coming, all too obviously, from inside the house.

The reboot rebooted again in early 2018, its problems further magnified by everything we've learned in the past two years. Season eleven, does, however, include one all-time great episode, "The Lost Art of Forehead Sweat" (The One Where an Alien Does a Trump Monologue), a bittersweet film essay on the impossibility of *The X-Files* in a "postconspiracy" age when power refuses to go through the motions of concealing its most brutal machinations. In one montage that spans the Reagan through Obama years, a nebbishy paper pusher evolves from a bored postal clerk to a napping Securities and Exchange Commission operative to a CIA agent casually waterboarding a bound man to a drone operator accidentally bombing a far-off wedding, all from the comfort of the same cubicle. At the episode's end, Mulder and Scully meet a bedazzled extraterrestrial ambassador who has arrived in a flying saucer to inform them that the aliens' study of Earth is complete; the intergalactic confederation no longer wants anything to do with us. "We are building a wall," he intones cordially but firmly. As a parting gesture, he gives Mulder a trim, leather-bound book called *All the Answers*, "in case you have any questions remaining."

"It's okay, Mulder," Scully reassures her stunned partner when the spaceship has whizzed off. "There will always be more X-files." "No! It's not true!" Mulder howls, hurling the book and crumpling to the ground.

The *New York Times* recently reported that the Pentagon has spent millions of dollars on UFO research in the past decade. Weird objects are appearing in the sky again, or maybe they're just Teslas. It's all been met with a collective shrug.

As usual, Mulder was right.

IN THE MONTHS BEFORE the election, I lost my method, too. I was trying to write my own dissertation about magic and technology in contemporary literature, and left my city to be alone with my devices. Keeping myself safe from stories and refusing to stumble on mysteries, my information sickness spread until I could not know things at all. A dead circuit. Instead of a map, Trump's giant face.

That November, the earth opened and we fell through the cracks, picking up speed. It wasn't one big hole but endless small ones, like gas coming up through the tundra, or like our house in the Valley with its network of hidden fissures that opened up one day twenty years after the earthquake. Broken clocks floated by. They were melted but no longer missing. I am a communist again, like lots of kids. As I write this, children across the country are marching out of their schools together because the location of safety has moved outside. The rich are planning missions to the stars.

The world felt strange in the late 20th century when politics congealed into fandom, like being haunted by ghosts. Now that fandom on the right has melted back into politics, it feels psychotic, like being stalked by monsters or chased by cartoon frogs. When we get accustomed to the political unconscious becoming conscious, the imperceptible perceptible, we say we are woke; the Nazis say red-pilled. It is uncanny to remember a time when we spoke only through the things we liked and wore, like looking back at cultists who think they have outgrown the swaddling of history, but in fact simply will not speak the names of their devils and gods. When alt-right thinkers complain about a specter they call postmodernism, I wonder if they miss it.

It's hard to say whether the new show we are living in is a sequel to the old one, or just its reboot. We were in the park at night: a different friend and I, a different time. I'd tangled myself in a swing and was spinning round and round when he told me about Roko's basilisk. The basilisk, born on an internet chat forum for the philosophical wing of the new tide of fascism, is a super-powerful artificial intelligence from the future. He wants you, earthling, to work toward his establishment as a supreme being ruling a neofeudal order. He will not bug you if you do not know his name, but once you do, you're in or you're out, and if you're out he will fuck you up, even if he has to rebuild your consciousness out of machine dust in order to do it. The basilisk is a folktale of our time. In him, we meet the ultimate conspirator in the shape of a chintzy Monster of the Week. Like a bit of malware in your head, he insists his story be passed on.

"Let him come," I said to my friend. "If we refuse to speak of him, we give him the power of our childhood phantasms. The enemy has revealed himself. Now we can fight."

"You are a white girl in the park on acid," he said. "On the border, they are building camps."

I put my foot out sharply and stopped spinning. One looks at one's friends and neighbors and wonders who will turn. One turns to oneself.

I do not know if we can organize from a place this disorganized. But I want to believe. +

WENTRCEK ZEBULON
POWER IN THE 2
REPORTING NEW GAINS
Increased Lineage 69

NEW! NEW!

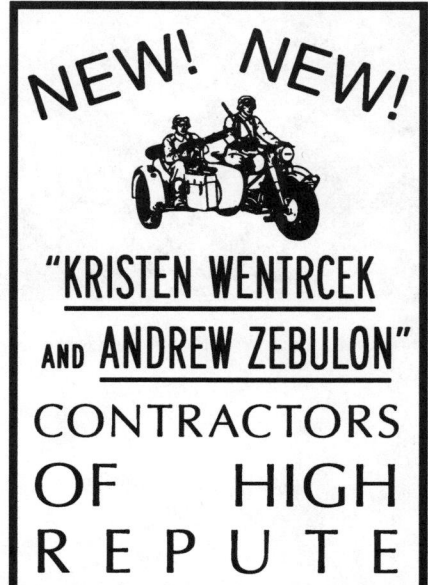

"KRISTEN WENTRCEK AND ANDREW ZEBULON"

CONTRACTORS OF HIGH REPUTE

WWW.WENTRCEKZEBULON.COM   NEW YORK, U.S.A.

NOW IS THE TIME TO SUBSCRIBE TO
@wentrcek_zebulon

For Health & Strength

冬のチェックゼブロン

SUPER ENERGY FORMULA
スーパーエンジェル COMPANY

La Familia Bros. "It's a beautiful day outside today."   www.bros.family

FAMILY BROS.
CUSTOM DUALS · TURBO · GLASS PACKS
ORIGINAL EXHAUST · EMISSIONS
TESTING · THOROUGHLY RESEARCHED

*U.S. News & World Report
#1 Ranked Office Sign
Company*

@BROSDOTBZ

BEES COIN
Take control of your currency,
take control of your data –
that's when you're going to
have true freedom.

eric bees

Invest now in BeesCoin™
561-3068

CAITLIN KEOGH, *UNTITLED*. 2016, ACRYLIC ON CANVAS. 81 × 108". COURTESY THE ARTIST AND BORTOLAMI, NEW YORK.

TWO STORIES

Helen DeWitt

Written in 1985, these stories are a portal into a not-quite past that nearly became a future for Anglo-American literature. This is a way of saying they were "ahead of their time." But that overused phrase, beloved of introducers, is also nonsense. Nothing is ahead of its time.

"Famous Last Words," the latter of the two, is a snapshot of academic life among a rare but very real subset of people who felt the charge of poststructuralism as an intellectual and erotic force, a way of being in, understanding, and shaping their world, not merely positioning themselves in the job market or exercising "cynical reason." In most literary portrayals of academics from the 1980s and 1990s, Realism gets its revenge on Theory, the old ideas of human nature assert themselves against newfangled culture, and Theory is satirically synonymous with self-deception. The conversations and scenarios depicted here, however, have a rare, almost unheard-of fidelity to the people who lived theory as their truth in ways that escaped even highly observant novelists like David Lodge, Zadie Smith, and Philip Roth. What looks on the surface like a conventional theory-as-gateway-to-seduction story gets turned on its head. As much as one character wants to break the code and play the typical academic louche, the narrator won't let him. Sometimes you win in life and lose in theory—and vice versa, and that's what happens here.

Saying that something was "ahead of its time" is also a way of signaling that you've probably never come across it. Certainly nothing in these stories fits with our culture's current nostalgia for the 1980s. Who, back then, would have published a philosophical parable about two academics in conversation that also has so much fun with its own status as a work of would-be literature, in a story that's also dispassionately observant of gender roles and performance? Obscure or marginal writings often start out obscure because their authors sought obscurity or immersion in a subculture. In both these stories, however, one can sense a fierce yearning for an absolute clarity. That desire to reach the truth through the fiction, to tell truths about fiction in fiction—so inconveniencing, like all overwhelming desires—animates all Helen DeWitt's writing, and that's no less the case now than when she was starting out. The truth is always right on time, and also perpetually just ahead of it.

—Marco Roth

IMPROVISATION IS THE HEART OF MUSIC

"THE REST WAS PURE *Arabian Nights*. Gazelle-eyed maidens with perfumed robes brought inlaid boxes of Turkish delight and roast hummingbirds and sugared grapes and honeyed wine—ghastly stuff—and tiny cups of sludgy coffee. Silks kissed the earth. Our host raised his hands and clapped—once—twice—three times, and on the third the strains of a harp wafted in from the wings.

"'But my dear chaps! You're not eating!' he cried. 'Try the hummingbirds, I assure you they are excellent. Or a morsel of lamb? And you must, you positively must sample the mare's-milk cheese, it is a speciality of my people, a great delicacy. Fatima! See that the gentlemen have some cheese!'

"He went on in this way for some time, and after I suppose half an hour or so said—'But come! I shall order them to prepare us a hookah, and my companions shall entertain you. Which did you favour among those who served you?'

"Now, I was prepared to see what the hookah was like, and even—dare I confess it?—be entertained by one of the companions, at least up to a point. But Angus is a true Scot; his Presbyterian blood curdled at the sound of this.

"'Of course I'll not touch his filthy hookah,' he whispered to me in tones just loud enough not to be tactful.

"Our host went on with the utmost urbanity, as though nothing had been said, urging us to express a preference for one of the girls. Angus preserved the silence of outraged virtue. I murmured something non-committal, all extremely attractive, impossible to choose one above the rest. This, it turned out, was a bad move.

"'My dear fellow'—he cut me short—'I understand perfectly—to tell the truth I'm not, myself, entirely in the mood—as your friend's tastes, it seems, are not in that direction' (he smiled rather maliciously at poor Angus, who went bright red as only a rufus can) 'you shall have them all!' A barrage of claps, and a bevy (it really is the only word for it, echt B-movie stuff) of beautiful girls surrounded me, urging me to recline on a sort of divan strewn with silk rugs and shawls dripping with fringe.

"Mahmet excused himself with a profound bow, leaving me, I took it, to disport myself with the company provided. If this was his object the ruse failed dismally, since he neglected to take Angus with him. Angus continued to sit bolt upright on his cushion, pulled out his pocket copy of Thompson's *Making of the English Working Class* in a battered old blue-and-white Pelican edition and buried himself in its pages, the picture of dour intellectual respectability. It effectively cast a damper on the debaucheries in which I was supposed to be rejoicing at the other end of the tent. After a little laboured banter with the beauties I sent them off, pulled out my Edmund Crispin, and started reading—it was the final humiliation to have nothing better to show than a humble green-and-white Penguin.

"We turned in soon after. We never saw our host again: in the morning the Nubian appeared with a message on a tray. I took it, and he disappeared without a word. It was from Mahmet:

My dear chaps,

Business calls me away unexpectedly. So sorry to interrupt our larks together! Please avail yourselves of the yacht for as long as convenient. What a story for your grandchildren! You can tell them you were once shipwrecked with

Sindbad the Sailor"

Edward paused dramatically before the name; after pronouncing it he fell silent, ending the story with a resounding close. He leant back into the corner of the sofa with a little expectant smile. The silence stretched out, a little awkwardly. As always with Edward's stories, a round of applause seemed the most fitting response, but this is seldom used other than ironically in private conversation. Maria had not yet worked out an acceptable substitute, though she had had plenty of opportunity to practice: Edward was a gifted raconteur. Edward and Maria were engaged, but without the ease this implies—Maria still found herself struggling to keep up with a companion of such wonderfully polished conversational skills. What *was* the appropriate response to narrative tours de force? Should one praise the performance? Aim for intelligent comment? Laugh? Counter with a story of one's own? "That reminds me of the time I—" But Maria's life offered little in the way of anecdotal material; none of Edward's stories had any connection with the sort of thing that happened to her.

"What a story!" she exclaimed. "I've always wanted to hear a genuine traveller's tale; you don't happen to have a bit of roc's egg lying about, I suppose?"

"Nary a one—I did think the least our host could do was leave us each a ruby the size of an orange, but Sindbad seems to be a bit of a Thatcherite these days."

Maria laughed heartily.

EDWARD AND MARIA had a big wedding. Maria had a very pretty dress (lace over satin); she decided to have a *long* veil. The men wore morning suits. She had a little going-away suit in nubbly pink silk, with binding, just the least bit Chanel, and a little hat. How can you have that kind of wedding and not be just the tiniest bit camp? Edward and Maria got in the limo amid showers of rice and confetti. Edward laughed and kissed her. "You look lovely, my dear."

THEY WERE TAKING a real old-fashioned honeymoon! They would go to Paris by boat train, spend a week there, then go south to the Riviera. They would spend two weeks on a cruise ship, stopping first at various Italian ports, then at the Greek islands. They sat side by side in their compartment, holding hands—it was not something they had done often.

"Y'know, I hope I have better luck this time than the last time I went sailing," said Edward.

"Why is that?" asked Maria.

"The last time I went sailing I got shipwrecked! Have I ever told you the story? It was when Angus McBride and I went island hopping after finals. Altogether a fantastic tale! We'd booked onto something that sounded perfectly respectable—the *Hellenic Swan* or some such thing—but turned out to be a great tub of a Victorian yacht that had been restored and put to work for the tourist trade. Amazing boat! Someone had clearly done it up to the nines about eighty years ago. Plush upholstery—swags of gold rope—thick Turkey carpets—vast numbers of cut-glass chandeliers—and a lot of brass and mahogany woodwork. It was all rather the worse for wear by the time it crossed our path, and its owners hadn't had much luck in luring tourists aboard—the only other passenger was a mysterious Turk! Well, we'd only just started to make his acquaintance by the tarnished grandeur of the bar when we ran into a bit of rough weather in the Adriatic, and the bloody boat started to go down!

"Mahmet got us rather briskly into one of the lifeboats and winched us down. Then Angus and I started rowing like blazes! We saw the crew pulling off in another boat. We'd got perhaps a couple of hundred yards away when we saw the ship go under. I don't suppose I've ever seen such a terrifying sight. One moment rather a lot of the bow and a fair bit of cabin roof were still above water; then an enormous swell rose above it, and the whole shebang was sucked under in a couple of seconds. A few flecks of foam and a stray life preserver were left floating on the surface where just a few minutes earlier there'd been a twelve-ton yacht.

"We were at sea in the lifeboat until noon the next day. Angus and I had already started wondering whether it might be prudent to ration supplies, but Mahmet was superbly unconcerned. In the event we could have gorged on the water biscuits and tinned luncheon meats in the hold: we were picked up by a magnificent yacht, which turned out to belong to Mahmet. He'd been on his way south to meet it at Genoa, but its captain had had the sense to head north when he heard of the disaster which had befallen the *Swan*. We were shown to a cabin, where we slept heavily all the afternoon—we hadn't got much sleep the night before. When we woke we found we were at anchor off an unidentifiable bit of coast. A gigantic Nubian told us we were to join Mahmet on shore for dinner, and saw us into a small motorboat. We were taken ashore and escorted into a vast tent which had been set up on the sand.

"The rest was pure *Arabian Nights*. Gazelle-eyed maidens with perfumed robes brought Turkish delight in inlaid boxes and roast hummingbirds and sugared grapes and honeyed wine—ghastly stuff—and tiny cups of sludgy coffee. Silks kissed the earth. Our host raised his hands and clapped—once—twice—three times, and on the third the strains of a harp wafted in from the wings."

Edward raised his hands and clapped; paused; clapped; paused; clapped again; and then caressed, gracefully, the air with his right hand in a wavy glide suggestive of the delicate notes of the harp.

"'But my dear chaps! You're not eating!' he cried. 'Try the hummingbirds, I assure you they are excellent. Or a morsel of lamb? And you must, you positively must sample the mare's-milk cheese, it is a speciality of my people, a great delicacy. Fatima! See that the gentlemen have some cheese!'"

Maria crossed her legs, shifted on her seat, held her elbows. She had been, from time to time, slightly put out by Edward's habit of modulating out of dialogue into anecdote, but she had supposed it to be, at least, a matter of spontaneous impulse. This mechanical repetition was something quite other and alarming.

"We turned in soon after. We never saw our host again: in the morning the Nubian appeared with a message on a tray. I took it, and he disappeared without a word. It was from Mahmet:

My dear chaps,

Business calls me away unexpectedly. So sorry to interrupt our larks together! Please avail yourselves of the yacht for as long as convenient. What a story for your grandchildren! You can tell them you were once shipwrecked with

Sindbad the Sailor"

Edward paused dramatically before the name, and after pronouncing it fell silent, ending the story with a resounding close. He leant back into the corner of the compartment with a little expectant smile. Maria smiled back nervously. So well rehearsed a performance seemed to call more than ever for applause. What conversational alternatives were there? Would it be acceptable to repeat her comments of last time? Would Edward recognise them, and realise that he had told her the story before? Maria felt that this would be hideously embarrassing. She must come up with something new. At the same time it seemed unfair: *she* must improvise because he had rehearsed.

Perhaps it was a matter of rehearsing conversations until one got them right. Perhaps she had not responded well enough last time, so that Edward had had a niggling sense that a proper performance of story and reception had not taken place; perhaps this was her chance to improve. This was an alarming thought: if she did not rise to the occasion, the story might be brought out again and again until she perfected her reply.

"What a marvelous story!" she exclaimed hastily. "I've always adored *The Count of Monte Cristo*—there's a wonderful Dumasian quality about this, isn't there, the European swept suddenly from the midst of the working-day, technological world into the fantastic improbabilities of the Orient!"

"Yes," said Edward, smiling agreeably, "one did rather feel that one had been catapulted into a big baggy monster of romantic French historicism. Thoroughly enjoyable for someone with low tastes like me, but a terrible trial for poor Angus, who felt he'd done nothing to deserve it. He stalked off the yacht at the earliest possible opportunity, injured innocence writ large on his brow."

THE *RAPIDE* HURTLED through France. It was night; the windows of the compartment showed Edward and Maria only themselves surrounded by the paraphernalia of travel: the *Spectator*, some paperback mysteries, one of the Lucia books (Maria was not yet enough at ease to buy herself *Vogue*); a partially eaten Cadbury Fruit & Nut bar, a packet of Jaffa cakes, a couple of oranges; a thermos flask of tea. The hours of travel had been punctuated by the recounting of anecdotes, many of them familiar to Maria. After each story Maria would pick up a theme for comment in the counterpoint that must follow; Edward would develop it briefly, then silence would fall. Sometimes Maria would bring out a new subject, which would be canvassed for a few moments before it reminded Edward of another story. Sometimes they turned to each other and smiled, and kissed, abandoning the struggle to converse.

THE MORNING BROUGHT other pleasures. They sat in the dining car, looking at each other brightly across a table with a cloth. A waiter brought croissants and a pot of very strong coffee. They reached eagerly for croissants, for jam, drank coffee, set their cups down with a little sigh.

"Why is it, do you suppose," said Edward, "that the continental breakfast has only to cross the Channel to be so damp and depressing. It *seems* simple enough—why does it travel so badly? In England one wonders whether it is really meant to be eaten. Here it is invariably ambrosial."

"It is the tyranny of the toast rack," said Maria. "No self-respecting bed-and-breakfast can be without them; and once you've invested in the technology, you're *committed* to sliced white. But if you offer croissants and pastries of course no one will touch the white toast, so no one ever does offer anything else. They feel they must get a return on their investment."

"There is something in what you say," said Edward. "But that doesn't account for everything. Why are croissants in England so awful? You never mind not having them because they taste like limp cardboard anyway."

The subject of food is like "Chopsticks": almost anyone can improvise on it. Two people who devise variations on something simple and silly end of course by collapsing into laughter: Edward and Maria smiled at each other in relief.

THE YACHT WAS COMFORTABLE, nothing remarkable. The islands, of course, were enchanting. They'd go for walks in the morning, not *too* early, taking a picnic lunch; stop at the beach, spread towels, eat brown olives and feta and yellow tomatoes and funny bread, drink retsina or local plonk; spend the afternoons swimming in the limpid water.

Edward had been there before and had lots of stories: about German tourists solemnly pacing through an olive grove at Mistra, heads popping up and down as they consulted an archaeological guide, sneering at the merely Byzantine and poking about for a few dusty stones of Sparta; of Americans looking haplessly round the local taverna, speaking wistfully of McDonald's; of the plausible scoundrel who'd wanted only to open a high-class tourist shop in Rhodes, to sell genuine local handicrafts made in Taiwan.

Maria smiled and laughed. Everything was new to her.

"Oh, look!" she cried; it was a fat old woman in black with a mule and a CD Walkman; it was a gnarled old man in Nikes with a sheep round his neck; it was a couple of very beautiful young men in very tight Calvin Klein jeans, "and they say there's no such thing as platonic love! Alive and well and on the strut in the agora, wouldn't you say?"

But it was hard to be perfectly at ease.

Novelty disturbed Edward; he made an awkward remark or two about the old woman, was only happy when he had been reminded of one he saw years ago and could supply a polished little story for the occasion. Repetition disturbed Maria; it was like trying to play jazz with someone who has the sheet music for "Ain't Misbehavin'" and works it in whenever he can.

They met a couple of college pals of Edward's in Lesbos and took them back to the yacht for dinner.

"Not very grand, but perfectly seaworthy," Edward said agreeably, leaping to the deck from the pier. "One learns to appreciate these things. Did I ever tell you of the time I was shipwrecked?"

If he had no one would admit to it.

"Oh, it was yonks ago, when Angus McBride and I went island hoping after finals," said Edward, leading the way to the bar. "What can I get you? I think we've got all the usual. Altogether a fantastic tale! We'd booked onto something that sounded perfectly respectable—the *Hellenic Swan* or some such thing—but turned out to be a great tub of a Victorian yacht which had been restored and put to work for the tourist trade..."

EDWARD AND MARIA return to the little house they have bought in Leckford Road, Maria trailing the past behind her. Every conversation she has had, every story she has heard, is on record in her phonographic memory, and on record also are the responses made by all the people she has ever known, and the records of her friendships are the most complete. Perhaps friendships are a matter of similar collections: you have the original, the friend has a backup. Her conversations with Edward are all on record, but hers is the only copy.

Edward bounds gaily into the house, the happy wanderer with his little light backpack of essentials, and she follows him slowly, carrying the luggage.

"Shall we have some people to dinner for a housewarming?" she asks, and sees her words thin into the air like vapour off early morning water.

"Oh, yes, we must," says Edward, and they do.

EDWARD AND MARIA sit at opposite ends of the dining room table, and between them are six or seven friends. They fill glasses, urge seconds, swap honeymoon anecdotes—the friends are married, they have their share.

"A yacht," says Sarah. "Crumbs. George and I went Eurail! You must have felt frightfully grand."

Edward opens his mouth.

"Oh," says Maria, "Edward was sickeningly blasé. One really felt it was an awful comedown for him. Have you ever told them about the splendour amidst which you were shipwrecked, darling?"

EVERYONE HAS GONE, and Edward and Maria repair to the kitchen to tackle the washing up. Edward scrapes and stacks; Maria fills the basin with Fairy Liquid and steaming water. As she lets the first stack of dishes sink beneath the suds she begins to sing softly.

"o when the saints, o when the saints, o when the saints come marching in."

"how i long to be in that number," sings Edward, "when the saints come marching in."

"O WHEN THE SAINTS. O WHEN THE SAINTS. O WHEN THE SAINTS COME MARCHING IN! HOW I LONG—TO—BE—IN THAT NUMBER, O WHEN THE SAINTS COME MARCHING IN."

o when the saints (o when the saints) come marching in (come marching in) o when the saints come marching (marching in), how I long to be in that nu-u-mber. When the saints come marching in.

FAMOUS LAST WORDS

"STRUCTURALISM IS OUT OF FASHION anyway," says Brian, who likes to be a kind of thinking man's philistine. He slides a spoon into raspberry sorbet.

"Poststructuralism is out of fashion," says Jane. They're married, it isn't really surprising.

"Fashion is out of fashion," says X, in the tone of voice that makes you think "quipped."

"Fashion is out of structuralism," say I. It's nice when they leave you the best line. X doesn't like it, though. Didn't see it coming.

"I liked that pasta alla Gorgonzola," I say to Jane. "Is it really so easy? How do you do it?"

Cross looks round the table. I blush, as so often. It was an *intellectual* conversation. Jane doesn't want to answer, she resents being dragged down to this level.

"Oh, you improvise like mad," she says airily. "Gorgonzola and sheep's yogurt are the only essentials."

This is not very helpful, but I don't like to press her. Brian starts telling stories about Derrida: perfectly happy, it seems, to accept all the privileges of the author. Theories of authorial absence, says Brian, tend to leave out the curious circumstance that the author is always there to pick up his cheque.

X does not seem to resent this. X says as a matter of fact Derrida is a stickler about copyright.

I've finished my sorbet. I finish my coffee. I start thinking about the death of Voltaire.

X AND I HAVE A LONG WAY to walk home afterward—X lives up the Abingdon Road, I live in Osney. It's about midnight when we leave, and the Woodstock Road is deserted but well lit: the road is pocked and blackened like a battered sheet of gold, the chestnut trees are brassy.

"Brian is such a wanker," says X. "blaBLAblaBLAblaBLA—gossip gossip gossip."

"Lucky Brian," say I. I scoop up a handful of dust from a driveway and let it sift through my fingers on the wind. "The streets are paved with gold."

X cheers up suddenly. "Still, I think I made a good impression. You can't ignore politics."

We cross Leckford Road.

"I was thinking about the death of the author," I say. "People use '*la mort de l'auteur*' like '*la mort de Dieu*.' I mean, to describe the disintegration—no, the devaluation—the *discrediting* of a concept. It's metaphysical. Nobody thinks God actually died: they think it was never alive in the first place. I think Barthes actually says somewhere '*l'Auteur, lorsqu'on y croit*'! Putting it that way is a paradox—how does a universal die, anyway?"

"Dunno," says X. "Kind of obvious, innit?" X sometimes likes to be a philistine's philistine.

"The life of the author in Barthes is a matter of being paid too much attention. Death would just be being ignored. No more *Paris Review* interviews—no more of those weird questions. 'Do you write on the typewriter?' 'Do you write to a schedule?' 'When did you start to write?' 'Does it come easily?' 'Was it hard for you to write about oral sex?' Leon Edel—Leslie Marchand—André Maurois—Gordon Haight will languish unread on the shelves."

"Kind of a Berkeleian nonexistence," says X, going along with it. "There's no one to think of the author but God, and God's dead."

"But," I say, "that leaves you with the death of the author. There are what we could call, for the sake of argument, impostors—people who have deathbeds. There is a sense in which the death of the author is incompatible with '*la mort de l'auteur.*' Think of somebody like Voltaire. There's something strangely fascinating about the way everyone tried to write his death."

X holds up a finger and says in a strong Cockney accent:

> An orphan's curse would drag to hell
> A spirit from on high;
> But oh! more horrible than that
> Is the curse in a dead man's eye!
> Seven days, seven nights, I saw that curse,
> And yet I could not die.

"Your basic author," says X, "is transfixed by the eye of the dead God. What you're talking about," says X, "is the night of the Living Dead."

I think this is clever, but, allowing for the accent, it's the kind of thing Brian might have said.

"But it's interesting," say I. "It's a different slant on the question of sincerity. Not 'What did you really mean?' but 'Would you still say it?' Recantation . . ." I say it emphatically, it's a word I expect to appeal to X.

"Authority . . . ," X says thoughtfully.

"Exactly. This idea of getting the one who said it first to take it back—or stick to it! More words from the same source. It's this business of validation, or invalidation, coming from a particular direction—"

"Parsifal!" says X. "'*Die Wunde schließt der Speer nur, der sie schlug.*'"

"Eh?" (I can read German, but it never seems to sound the way it looks.)

"The wound must be healed by the spear that made it."

"*Yes*. And I think there's something very striking about the candidates for deathbed conversions: intensely rational, articulate, revolutionary people—Voltaire and Hume. As if no one could be sure of their own arguments unless they could get Voltaire or Hume to repeat them. All these deathbed confessions of Voltaire—it's hard to say what's more interesting, the multiple last statements or the endless arguments about them. Which was genuine? Why did he refuse the sacrament? I've got this book at home, *La religion de Voltaire*, that gets incredibly anxious about it."

"Sounds interesting," says X.

"Oh, it is. Pomeau thinks the confessions are tongue in cheek—he goes through them word by word. Which of course simply shows the futility of the exercise—the very problems of sincerity, of interpretative validity, which were to be settled at last without possibility of revision, are all to be settled again for the 'final words.'"

"I wouldn't mind having a look at that," says X.

"I'll have to show it to you sometime," say I.

"It's not that late," says X. "I can come by your place."

"Oh," say I. "Oh, OK."

MY PLACE IS VERY SMALL. I have use of the kitchen, and a room on the second floor with a narrow view of the canal and swans. X and I sit at the kitchen table, surrounded by books about deaths of authors. I have Noyes's biography of Voltaire, and Pomeau, both with extensive discussions of the death of Voltaire. Noyes also includes a description of a visit to Voltaire by Boswell. Besides these I have the volume of Boswell's journals that includes his interview with the dying Hume. I say that I think I once read something somewhere about the death of Foucault, but I can't remember where.

"The thing that interests me," I say. "One of the things that interest me is the way there is this emphasis on inserting the body of the writer into the scene, as if making a connection between this physical presence and the *derniers mots* will somehow make these specially valid. Look at Noyes." I pick up the book.

"'We must obviously not picture him here with the "eternal grin" of Mr. Lytton Strachey, but with the bloodstained rag at his lips, and eyes that had been looking into the face of Death. Those eyes are turned for a moment, with the curious wonder which is a sick man's only way of reproach, upon a secretary who is trying to defeat a purpose definitely decided upon before this illness occurred.'"

"The bloodstained rag," I say, "says this is real and true. The document is genuine. Its statements may be *attached* to Voltaire."

X is flipping through Pomeau.

I start rehearsing facts and dates. On February 26, 1778, Voltaire took confession and signed a statement: *"Je meurs dans la religion catholique où je suis né, espérant de la miséricorde divine, qu'elle daignera pardonner toutes mes fautes, et que si j'avais jamais scandalisé l'eglise, j'en demande pardon à Dieu et à elle."* He refused to take the Sacrament because he was spitting up blood and might "spit up something else" (the exact words are disputed). On February 28 he issued the following statement: *"Je meurs en adorant Dieu, en aimant mes amis, en ne haïssant mes ennemis, et en détestant la superstition."* At the time of his death, he was attended by the curé of Saint-Sulpice, La Harpe, and Prince Bariatinsky. The curé asked whether he recognised the divinity of Jesus Christ. Voltaire replied, *"Laissez-moi mourir en paix."*

X has found Pomeau's analysis of the confession. "Wouldn't take the Sacrament—says he dies in the church, not a member of it—second statement the real Voltaire—whew! *'Il était mort en théiste, non en chrétien.'*"

"Whereas Noyes," say I, "says Voltaire's early religious training gave him a strong sense of the sanctity of the host."

X puts a hand on my knee.

"Boswell sounded Voltaire out on immortality," I say. "Boswell wore his flowered velvet at the interview. Noyes smiles up his sleeve at this: if the bloody rag is the mark of intellectual commitment, the flowered velvet is that of silly Scottish dilettantism. Boswell asks whether immortality is not a noble idea. Voltaire agrees, but thinks it more desirable than likely. *'Potius optandum quam probandum'*—isn't that a great line? On Voltaire's authority, Boswell goes to see Voltaire's doctor for confirmation that Voltaire had never been afraid of death."

I look for this in Noyes and read: "'Had he any horror of it?' 'No! The more seriously ill he is, the better Deist he becomes . . .' 'Ah, well,' says Boswell, 'I can say all that, then, on the best authority. M. de Voltaire bade me ask you whether he feared death, as ministers of religion had affirmed.'"

X and I are smiling. We are both charmed by the flowered velvet. X's hand moves up my thigh. I have noticed this tendency to reductionism in X before. The text is infinitely variegated, the subtext always the same. I tried once to resist this by accusing X of believing in final causes—that for the sake of which the rest is there—but it didn't work. X said I took everything personally. X takes nothing personally: X discussed the deconstruction of teleology and put a hand on my knee.

What is a subtext? You may think of it as a movement in the circumambient language whose presence you divine by distortions and ripples in the text; what lies between the lines is as invisible, as plain to the eye as the breeze that stirs the leaves of the copper beech in the quadrangle, the high wind that toppled trees in Hyde Park. And we know that the disruption is not in one direction only: the text is a kind of windbreak.

One walks quicker with the wind at one's back. I feel the subtext pushing us forward, and I am rather afraid it will outstrip the text altogether, before I have got to Boswell and Hume, so that—although I could say a good deal more about the "solemn and singular conversation"—I hasten to open *Boswell in Extremes, 1776–78*, and bring to X's attention Boswell's recollections of the day when he was too late for church, and went to see David Hume, who was a-dying.

"'I found him alone, in a reclining posture in his drawing room. He was lean, ghastly, and quite of an earthy appearance. He was dressed in a suit of gray cloth with white metal buttons, and a kind of scratch wig. He was quite different from the plump figure which he used to present.'"

"You see what I mean," I say, "the physical presence, with its marks of imminent dissolution, guarantees the seriousness of the speaker—at the same time that it threatens permanent absence of the speaker. This, it says, is your last chance to find out what he really thought."

"Yeh," says X. "Basically it's your capitalist perspective on meaning as property: authorial presence can be bequeathed to some textual children—others may be disinherited. Boswell's hoping for a bit of melodrama—a deathbed scene where the *Treatise* and *Enquiry* are cut out of the will." X squeezes my thigh.

I read rapidly:

"'I had a strong curiosity to be satisfied if he persisted in disbelieving in a future state even when he had death before his eyes. I was persuaded from what he now said, and from his manner of saying it, that he did persist. I asked him if it was not possible that there might be a future state. He answered it was possible that a piece of coal put upon the fire would not burn.'"

"Straight out of the *Enquiry*," says X. "If Hume had had a Pomeau he'd have been cheering. *Il était mort en athéiste non en théiste*."

"The bulk of my estate," say I, "I leave to my beloved son, *An Enquiry Concerning Human Understanding*."

"Boswell writes Hume very well, doesn't he," says X. X puts an arm round my shoulders and looks down at the book in my lap.

We read together:

"'Well,' said I, 'Mr. Hume, I hope to triumph over you when I meet you in a future state; and remember you are not to pretend that you was joking with all this infidelity.' 'No, no,' said he. 'But I shall have been so long there before you come that it will be nothing new.' In this style of good humour and levity did I conduct the conversation. Perhaps it was wrong on so awful a subject. But as nobody was present, I thought it could have no bad effect. I however felt a degree of horror, mixed with a sort of wild, strange, hurrying recollection of my excellent mother's pious instructions, of Dr. Johnson's noble lessons, and of my religious sentiments and affections through the course of my life. I was like a man in sudden danger eagerly seeking his defensive arms; and I could not but be assailed by momentary doubts while I had actually before me a man of such strong abilities and extensive inquiry in the persuasion of being annihilated. But I maintained my faith."

"Oh ho!" says X. "*La mort de l'auteur c'est la naissance du lecteur.* Happy birthday, Bozzy."

"The author really is like God," say I. "Dead? Not dead? Opinion is divided. The Barthesian texts, meanwhile, are like the witty, iconoclastic works of Hume and Voltaire. You remember, in '*La mort de l'auteur*'? Refusing to assign a single sense to a text releases activity which is '*contre-théologique, proprement révolutionnaire, car refuser d'arrêter le sens, c'est finalement refuser Dieu et ses hypostases, la raison, la science, la loi.*' Boswell would have gone to the deathbed of Barthes."

"The author can't die yet," says X. "*S'il n'y avait pas d'auteur, il aurait fallu l'inventer*—capitalism requires the existence of someone to pick up the cheque."

"I know what Barthes would have said to Boswell," say I. "'*On n'a donc rien écrit?*'" I am proud of the *on*, and wait for applause. Then it occurs to me that this is cheating. I have wilfully revived the author, or rather "*l'auteur*," constructing "characteristic" remarks to be uttered by the collector of royalties in extremis. I could have said this at dinner. X will have something to say about it.

"Oh, you!" says X. X kisses me. "Let's go upstairs," says X.

THERE IS A TEXT I could insert at this point that begins "I'm not in the mood," but the reader who has had occasion to consult it will know that, though open to many variations, there is one form that is, as Voltaire would say, *Potius optandum quam probandum*, and that is the one which runs "I'm not in the mood," "Oh, OK." My own experience has shown this to be a text particularly susceptible to discursive and recursive operations, one that circles back on itself through several iterations and recapitulations, one that ends pretty invariably in "Oh, OK," but only about half the time as the contribution of my co-*scripteur*. I think for a moment about giving the thing a whirl, but finally settle on the curtailed version, which leaves out "I'm not in the mood" and goes directly to "Oh, OK." X and I go upstairs.

X AND I SIT ON THE BED. The subtext is suddenly too much with us, and it is clear it will soon push us into what is not spoken. X begins to move oddly: a hand traverses space but makes no gesture. X's movements, my movements must become the thing meant; X cannot approach this. The words have slipped away, the distance between signifier and signified is no doubt not very great—but the threshold of silence is daunting. X begins to talk about construction and deconstruction of gender, and succeeds again in "placing a hand on my knee." "What is woman?" says X. "Is this the mark of woman?" X puts a hand on my breast, cannily pursuing *sous-texte sous prétexte*.

X talks about clothes, which gesture at the difference they conceal. Or don't. X begins to undress. Each signifier, says X, signifies a further signifier. Each difference is meant and meaning. Difference gestures beyond itself. I begin to undress. X is talking very fast while unfastening all fastenings: buttons fly from holes, zips unzip, clothes fly from skin to the floor. My clothes fall to my feet. And X, who has been taking this road very fast, goes into a skid on the slippage of meaning and smashes up against silence. It is as if we have accidentally removed, with our clothes, all signs of desire and desirability, as if we have sloughed off tits cunt prick with bra skirt trousers and find ourselves, stripped of language, indifferent featherless bipeds, trying to put it all back—but we are to each other as pale and lumpish and uninteresting as Cranach's Adam and Eve. We catch each other's eyes; after all, we always understand each other.

"Blue, not-blue," say I.

X shows a flicker of interest at the Edenic language: his cock lifts its head.

"Blue and not-blue," he replies. He thinks a moment. He holds up crossed fingers. "*Bleu*," he says grinning. He pulls me over onto the bed, and starts kissing my breast.

WE PLUNGE AT LAST into silence. No. Silenced, beneath X, my text goes *sous-texte* and presents the question: is it then the physical that makes sense of my story? Is it here that you find the array of possible meanings contracted—does this compel you to take things a certain way? Must X be a man? It seems inescapable to me.

It is as if I am lying on the bottom of a lake looking up through clear water at the sky: I see ripples across the surface at the meeting of water and air. I wonder how this looks to X. X sees, perhaps, a single body of water across which Hume, the scratch wig, that pleasing notion immortality skim and skitter like watermen. I close my eyes. I see a vast slate-coloured ocean with an immense and wrinkled skin.

I think of one of the *fragments d'un discours amoureux*. "This cannot go on." I think: "This could go on all night."

I OPEN MY EYES. X rolls over on his back. He begins to sing softly:

"Well it ainno use ta sit an wonder hwhy babe, iffen you dont know by now. An it ainno use ta sit an wonder hwhy babe. It'll never do somehow." X likes songs that hug the vernacular. He dwells on whatever is most untranslatable to pen and paper, whatever written language can only hint at, what written language must be distorted even to acknowledge: hoarseness—nasality—drawing out of syllables—chromatic scales through the diphthongs. X does not, of course, admit that anything could be irredeemably unwritable, his position is that all these marks of the spoken are repeatable and therefore written. But X cannot sing and state his position at the same time. Singing, X indulges in illicit joys—he will restate the position after the song.

"Well it ainno use in turnin on yer light babe. The light i—never knowed. An it ainno use in turnin on yer light babe. i'm on the dark side of the road." X catches my eye. "Well i wish there was sumpn you would—do er say—Ta tryen make me change m'minden stay—We never did teuu much talkin anyway—But don think twice it's all right."

X likes songs that gesture at inarticulacy. He is drawn to the poignancy of a world in which the unspoken is two-thirds of the iceberg. He is drawn to lovers who take things for granted. There are lovers, says the song, who do not include in their writing of *la situation amoureuse* the texts that play around the theme "I'm not in the mood"—that must pare down discourse quite considerably. I myself am strangely drawn to a form of closure that leaves things so largely unsaid. X and I face a very long and wearisome collaboration on the end of the affair. Having written so much it seems we must continue: language squeezes an author like an orange. X and I are not in a position to walk away; we can part but not leave. Face to face some things are impossible to say. It'll never do somehow.

I think of telling X that we think too much alike. I imagine writing down a song and handing it to X in a note:

You say either and I say either
You say neither and I say neither
Either Either Neither Neither
Let's call the whole thing off.

You say tomato and I say tomato
You say potato and I say potato
Tomato Tomato Potato Potato
Let's call the whole thing off.

I AM IN THE COMMON ROOM looking through the paper. x is reading a book in a dark blue cloth binding. I stand by x's shoulder, the *TLS* in my hand, and look down at the page. In a frame that consists of the angle of x's neck and shoulder, x's right forearm, x's left knee, I read:

In the Euclidean space R_n the Cauchy–Bunyakovsky inequality has the form

$$\left| \sum_{j=1}^{n} \xi_j \eta_j \right| \leq \sqrt{\sum_{j=1}^{n} \xi_j^2} \sqrt{\sum_{j=1}^{n} \eta_j}$$

it holds for any pair of vectors x = (ξ₁, . . . , ξₙ), y = (η₁, . . . , ηₙ), or what is the same thing, for any two systems of real numbers ξ₁, ξ₂, . . . , ξₙ and η₁, η₂, . . . , ηₙ. (This inequality was discovered by Cauchy in 1821.)

The frame is very simple: x's checked flannel shirt, with an open neck and short sleeves, has a Wittgensteinian innocence. The dark blue trousers are just trousers. The arm is long and bony. I am looking at the score of the music of the spheres. I gaze at this silent material for some time. The harmonies I see represented remain perfectly inaudible to me, but I see from the repose and concentration of x that x can hear them.

I have mastered subjects and failed to love them. I have looked at the sun and not been blinded; I have dimmed the sun. I will be a lover of the moon.

I lie on a bed with x. It is covered with a spread of purple chenille. The room is filled with humble objects lent dignity by the light of the moon: an electric kettle that does not switch off automatically; a mug with a picture of Miss Piggy; a box of Brooks PG Tips, a jar of coffee powder; a packet of My Mum's digestives; a skimpy blue-and-red-striped towel thrown over a chair; a shiny orange anorak.

On the desk are a pad of graph paper, four or five medium-point blue Bic biros, two or three stubby pencils, a calculator. Ranged along the back against the wall are books: *Diophantine Inequalities*, I read on a spine. *Bauer Trees of Sporadic Groups. Amenable Banach algebras. Singular Perturbation Theory.* I suppose that these books map out truth, or at any rate truths. I believe that mathematical truths are eternal, or rather timeless; but it is comforting rather than not to have so many of these truths allied to names and dates. I have not forgotten that the Cauchy-Bunyakovsky inequality was discovered by Cauchy in 1821! x has thrown a few library books on a chair by the door: *Volterra integrodifferential equations in Banach spaces and applications. The Penrose Transform. Classical Fourier Transforms. Automorphic Forms, Shimura Varieties, and L-functions.* These names commemorate persons who heard, wrote down snatches of the piece. I am happy for them. At the same time it is sheer accident that one rather than another happened to do so—x sometimes tells me stories of simultaneous discovery. x can't see why these delight me. Sometimes I ask x "Who was Banach?" "What about Shimura?" "Just who was Penrose, anyway?" just for the pleasure of hearing x's confessions of ignorance, or professions of knowledge—the answer, when x has one, is always of the form "A was someone who discovered that B."

X, who had views on everything, would not have stood for it. What was his line? "The truth is that counting has proved to pay." "It can't be said of the series of natural numbers that it is true, but: that it is usable, and, above all, it is used." This sounds familiar—I'm sure I remember X quoting it—but whether pro or con I can't recall. Certainly mathematics were not to have the privilege of referential semantics, but the ins and outs of the arguments for levelling escape me now. I look at the face of x, calmly intent upon a book: the light must come from somewhere.

x sometimes has a book propped open against a knee. I look over x's shoulder at *Probability Approximations via the Poisson Clumping Heuristic*; my eyes wander restfully across a page of Greek letters and brackets. x holds, sometimes, a small spiral pad, one of the blue Bic biros, from time to time x scrawls a note, pursues a line of thought in strings of symbols that modulate down the page. x's wrist lies along the edge of the pad. I see the articulation of the joint, thin delicate bones jut out beneath thin pale freckled skin; x's large knuckles clamp round the pen, bitten fingers press into the palm. How close they look! I am seeing the moon through a telescope. It is not the smooth flat surface you imagine, seeing that disk suspended in the sky; but there is a kind of wonder in seeing the rocky cratered plain which nevertheless disperses light—in seeing how, even at closer range, the line between black and brilliant white is absolute.

I PUT MY ARM AROUND X. x's forehead is very high and pale, the skin stretched tight over the sleek pure curve of the skull. I lay my forehead against it and close my eyes. I do not strain my ears to pierce the silence; I know that within that bone and blood, a few centimetres away, plays the music of the spheres.

LOST IN INTERTEXTUALITY

Author's Note: "Famous Last Words" is alluded to in the unpublished novella Paper Pool, *which offers this helpful elucidation:*

I never show my story to Simon. I show my story to Nick (not his real name), who says:

"Is this about you? Who's X, one of your boyfriends?"

"Of course not," I say. "It's a variable."

"It's a natural thing to think."

"It is *not* a natural thing to think," I say. "The whole point is that it could be anybody. It works like a pronoun, only it gives less information, we don't even know if the character's M or F."

"Of course he's a guy," says Nick. "It says so."

"It does *not* say so," I say. "It says X."

"But he's *obviously* a guy. All that talk about politics."

"Exactly," I say. "So we see how far the reader goes beyond what's actually there, you know how much is constructed, so that introducing *corporeal* properties seems to tell us something we already know." It occurs to me that this is a trick with all the conceptual sophistication and avant-gardist chic of *The Mysterious Affair at Styles*.

"I still maintain he's a guy," says Nick. "And how come he changes from a capital X to a small x at the end? You have to admit that's *deliberately* obscure."

"It's *not* obscure, it's a totally different variable," I say. "You might as well say it was confusing to have a character named David and another one called Dave. And you see we never do know what little x is. The dark blue trousers are just trousers—what a great line. And so true."

"Hmmm," says Nick. +

ISSUE 16 | SPRING 2018

what are intellectuals for?

Subscribe for 20% off with the code INTELLECTUALS:
thepointmag.com/subscribe

SIGNE PIERCE, *OPTICAL DELUSIONS*. 2017, C-TYPE PRINT AND FRAME. 20 × 16". COURTESY OF THE ARTIST AND ANNKA KULTYS GALLERY.

TWO STOPS

Natasha Stagg

NOVEMBER 6, 2017

THE AFTER-PARTY FOR the Calvin Klein Underwear exhibition was held on one of the piers, I forget which one. I couldn't even tell if we were in Brooklyn or Manhattan, because we'd been driven to the venue in a bus with tinted windows. The party's centerpiece was a performance by Kesha, but she canceled last minute. Now that we didn't have to watch her perform, we had an excuse to say we were fans.

There were free drinks at the bar, and waiters kept coming by with hors d'oeuvres. My date, B., was an intern I'd met a few months earlier at another sponsored party. Since then I'd learned that he was into threesomes, didn't work in fashion or PR, and didn't have Instagram. He was from Switzerland and new to America and refused to tell me his age. Whenever we were together it was hard to tell what would happen between us: nothing, something, or something crazy. I wondered if my friends thought I looked too old for him.

I knew B. liked to flirt at parties, but that night, every time he shook someone's hand he put his arm around me and held me closer. He kissed me softly on the cheek, a more tender gesture than I was used to.

I watched as he flirted with gay men while making sure they knew he was joking—he would never! Especially not that night, when he was with me. This was offensive, the way B. would always tell men he'd make exceptions for each of them, except that he wouldn't. Would he?

I talked to my old coworkers about their new jobs and about our old boss, an awful man who would never get called out for his misconduct.

Some of us had seen him on dates with the male models he brought around to the office, but we didn't know for sure that he'd slept with them.

We talked about other editors we knew who were cruel and sleazy, about fashion photographers who should have been jailed long ago. A couple of weeks earlier, Condé Nast had announced they were no longer working with Terry Richardson, but by that point the allegations against him were many years old. One editor at the party seemed uncomfortable talking about any of it, maybe because his magazine featured Terry's work all the time.

B. handed me a champagne flute.

"We're talking about sexual misconduct," said the editor.

"My favorite topic," B. said with a wink.

There was a giant, glowing CK set up in front of a window overlooking the river. We walked through a selfie room, where classic Calvin Klein Underwear ads were projected onto a wall. I'd heard rumors that the *Times* was working on a story about Bruce Weber, who had taken many of these iconic photos. It was still early, but B. wanted to leave.

"Two stops," he told the driver.

I asked B. why. He said that he was tired and had to work in the morning. I was drunk and mad about a lot of things in my life. I hated my job and all the other guys I'd been going on dates with, and I wasn't over my recent breakup. It was clear that B. had started dating someone. That he'd used me to get into the party, flirted with my friends, flaunted his connection to me, and always planned on meeting up with someone else later. Maybe he was planning on bringing her back to the pier. Did he want her to see that same scene, with him as the protagonist?

My voice was rising, and B. was gesturing with his hands that I needed to lower it. So I got louder and told him to get out at the next light. I didn't really mean it when I said I didn't want to speak to him again, but that's what ended up happening. Later I found out he was 21—ten years younger than me.

NOVEMBER 7, 2017

CHINA CHALET FOR AN ART AUCTION. A friend, C., had just found out that her boyfriend, the director of a gallery, was cheating on her.

C.'s editor was also at China Chalet. He'd brought along D., an intern from their magazine. The editor left, but D. stuck around and joined us at a table.

"I can't look at Facebook anymore," D. announced. "I'm too triggered by all this '#MeToo' stuff. I just don't want to read every single person's trauma story right now."

I'd read a good op-ed in the *Times* by Lupita Nyong'o, I said, about the way professional and personal boundaries were often blurred in filmmaking. "Our business is complicated because intimacy is part and parcel of our profession; as actors we are paid to do very intimate things in public," Nyong'o wrote. She demonized the perpetrators while tearing a little hole in the sheet that separated the people in power from their victims. This was why these cases fascinated me. It was like learning we were all part of a cult. Maybe there was a way out. But maybe there wasn't.

"Isn't Lupita Nyong'o transphobic?" D. asked. The lights came on before I had a chance to respond.

Outside the party, I saw E., a man I'd slept with once, years ago.

C. and I got into a cab, and D. followed us inside. "Am I overstepping?" he asked.

"No, of course not," C. said. We told the driver to take us to Clandestino. C. had noticed the weird moment between E. and me on the sidewalk. "You know him, don't you?" she asked.

Around when I'd first moved to New York, I said, I'd gone home with E. after a party and was so drunk I'd almost passed out in the car. We had sex on a sandy mattress on the floor of what counted as a room in his curtained-off loft, and I blacked out. I walked home in the morning thinking I'd never see him again, since he was a messy punk who lived with like ten roommates. But at a gallery opening a few weeks later, a friend introduced me to E. as an old classmate from a prestigious art school. I smiled and said "Nice to meet you" and shook E.'s hand before I recognized him. He looked hurt and confused, and I turned bright red. But shouldn't I be the one who's upset? I said in the cab. He shouldn't have taken me home in that state.

"Yeah," C. said. "I mean, '#MeToo.'"

"But who hasn't been in that situation?" D. asked.

At Clandestino all the barstools and tables were taken, so we each got a cocktail and stood in a circle. We started talking about skin-care treatments. C. and I were the same age and terrified of every line or acne scar we spotted while washing the mud masks off our faces every Sunday, hungover. D. said he wanted an alternative hair removal treatment because lasers wouldn't be able to detect his blond follicles.

"What hair do you want removed?" asked C.

"All of it except my head hair," he said, eyes wide and suddenly very serious. "I identify as hairless. But the treatment is really expensive," he added mournfully.

"You identify as hairless?" I asked.

"I don't necessarily want a constructed vagina," he said, clarifying. "I just want this hair removal procedure."

This felt like a non sequitur, and it took me a few minutes to understand what D. was saying: he was claiming hairlessness as his identity; hairlessness would free him from the constraints of his cisgendered condition. It wasn't until the next day that I made the connection—his connection—between hairlessness and femininity. Did I also identify as hairless, or was it simply expected of me?

NOVEMBER 8, 2017

SOME FRIENDS AND I stood in line for champagne at an after-party for an arts gala at Halston's old town house.

A famous young artist kissed both my cheeks. "Did you know that the guy who used to live here, he was this guy who hung out with Andy Warhol?" he said. A blond socialite wearing a high fake ponytail and Ray-Bans told me she liked my look. She wore a new Gucci dress with a sequined cape, and I had on the three-seasons-old JW Anderson sweater I'd worn to work that day over a wool skirt and black tights. She talked to me about what New York used to be, when she was out getting into trouble. She looked about my age. I learned that she'd been married once and engaged again, but the recent fiancé had gotten "heavy into drugs" and was now in rehab.

"That was all back in Malibu, you remember," she started saying to a friend, a giant man I recognized from last week's Halloween party at the Brooklyn Museum. She introduced him to me as F. He didn't seem to recognize me. On Halloween, F. had fed me bump after bump of coke from the wing of his hand in line for the bathroom and then asked me to come into a stall with him. His girlfriend was waiting downstairs, he said. In the stall we played a game of truth or dare. I'd picked dare.

"I dare you to show me any body part I want to see," F. said, preparing another small pile. I hesitated, and he quickly said "Tits." I was wearing a sexy costume and felt like a different person, like I was in New York before it sucked, which is how I always felt at big parties full of drag queens and drugs. I pulled down my top for a half second.

"Truth or dare," I said. F. picked dare.

"I dare you to give me more drugs," I said. F. asked me to make out with him, and I left the stall. The friend I was with, a girl from another magazine, said we should go with F. to the Boom Boom Room. "Something bad happened in there," I said, pointing to the bathroom.

"Yeah," she said, "before you got in line, I made out with him. He's a big art dealer, or curator, I forget."

At the Halston house, F. was telling me about his wife and about old New York, spitting in my face with every sentence. I hated him, he was so ugly and uncool, and yet I didn't tell him he was spitting on me, or that he had called his wife his "girlfriend" when we'd met before, or that we'd met before. Then he started telling the socialite about the party on Halloween: "I was at the museum, and then I ended up at a warehouse party in god knows where, I really have no idea, and then at about six in the morning, I press a button and I'm in a car on my way home. Still have no clue where I was or what way the car took me to get back, but that's the future, isn't it? We're living in the future. I'm telling you, I'm having the best time I've ever had in New York. It's only getting better here."

Even the socialite looked confused by this. "Now?" she asked, frowning.

We were supposed to meet Rose McGowan at Café d'Alsace after the party, but she canceled at the last minute. I saw on Twitter that she had been hit with a drug possession charge, which she insisted was a scheme to keep her Weinstein dirt quiet. I hadn't even read her Weinstein story. I'd read Asia Argento's, Gwyneth Paltrow's, and Lupita Nyong'o's, and then I'd stopped. The stories were so familiar and dark, but also loaded—I wanted to ignore their details. It was an instinctual reaction.

I still wanted to know that the articles were being published, and in large quantities, but reading stories of abuse and humiliation, like the big Bill Cosby exposé from a few years back, was as stupefying as a hangover. I didn't feel empowered; I only felt more hopeless. I wanted to watch the patriarchy go up in flames, but I wasn't excited about what was being pitched to replace it. If we got all of it out in the open, what would we have left? My fear was that guilt would destroy the classics and there'd be no one left to fuck. All movies would be as low-budget and puritanical as the stuff they play on Lifetime, all of New York would look like a Target ad, every book or article would be a cathartic tell-all, and I'd be sexually frustrated but too ashamed to hook up with assholes, or even to watch porn.

NOVEMBER 9, 2017

I LEFT WORK EARLY and went to my intake session at the city counseling center. I told an old woman very briefly about my family and my childhood and the man who broke my heart in grad school by cheating on me and the man who scandalized me just months ago by cheating on me with a lot of women in our shared field. I was happy with my career, I said. That was one thing I had under control. I'd initially wanted to go to therapy because I had writer's block. Now there were so many other reasons. My eyes clouded over but I didn't let any tears fall. I wanted to seem strong, so I would be assigned a good, smart therapist.

The *Times* was keeping a running list of men who experienced professional fallout following accusations of sexual misconduct. Along the edge of the list were photos of guys with pale, drooping jowls, rosacea, male pattern baldness, glasses, bulbous noses, squat or too-narrow heads, and puffy bags under beady eyes set too close together.

I wasn't immune to finding power sexy. I'd gone out with men because I was impressed by their jobs, thought about leaving men and then remembered their jobs. I told myself that this wasn't a shallow train of thought, it was actually a tribute to a man's character: the position he held said something about him, something I was supposed to like. But now it was clear that the jobs, especially the impressive ones, were the parts I hated most about the men. The cheating happened at the office. Maybe it stemmed from the atmosphere there.

Later, I went to a performance that combined opera, modern dance, pornographic sex, and a stage play about modern technology and its effect on relationships. Afterward, a group of us took the train into Manhattan and tried several Lower East Side bars until we found a bearable one. I tried to tell a story about the extreme behavior of certain young millennials, but either it came out wrong or there was no right way to tell it. "He identified as hairless," I said. No one said anything in response.

We went to the park so some of us could smoke a joint, but it was cold out, and there were too many rats scurrying around. I shared a ride home with a comedian who had been very serious the entire night. In the cab she told me a story about a man she'd been seeing while she lived in Amsterdam. He was the lead singer in a band, and now a lot of the women he'd slept with on tour were speaking out about him possibly date-raping them after shows. She was still in love with him, but she didn't seem emotional or bitter at all.

"I tend to believe the victims," she said quietly. "It takes a lot of bravery to say something like that. People always say that victims come out of the woodwork to get attention, but really, how many women want that kind of attention? They're still interested in dating men, right? And they're going to have a much harder time doing that once they're known for calling out a rock star for misbehaving—oh, right here is fine," she told the driver.

NOVEMBER 10, 2017

I WENT TO THE GYM and started sobbing on the treadmill. I texted my ex. I told him he had ruined my life and that I was so depressed I couldn't function. I told him I was crying at the gym, thinking this would provide him with a clarifying mental image. I thought about texting him other things, like how earlier that day I'd seen the neighbor's cat we used to play with together on my fire escape. The cat would come inside through the bathroom window and let us brush him. Alone that afternoon, I ran a comb through his thick fur, picking up a mass of gray undercoat while he purred. After a few minutes, he crawled back out the window, down the fire escape, and into my downstairs neighbor's bathroom window, where another cat who looked exactly like him was waiting. They hissed at each other and then both stepped inside. I wanted to tell him that it might have been two cats the whole time. Instead I texted him that he was a monster. He apologized again, and said that apologizing was all he could do.

NOVEMBER 11, 2017

I WENT TO SEE SOME FRIENDS do stand-up. I laughed a lot, and then got anxious thinking about what I could contribute to this crowd. I wasn't funny at all. I hardly talked after the show, but my friends kept making sure I was involved in the conversation by bringing up things they knew about me. The whole experience made me emotional, which made me get even quieter. The bar closed, so we went to another bar. Someone did lines off a table. At one point everyone was in agreement about Kevin Spacey—it was totally normal, they said, to hit on a minor drunkenly in your twenties.

"Gay teens have sex with old men," someone said. "There's a movie out about it right now. It's getting Oscar buzz!"

NOVEMBER 12, 2017

I STAYED IN MY BEDROOM all day. When it got dark out I turned on the lights and went to the gym. At nine I went to a dinner party that honored the winner of an annual fashion fund. Everyone was happy and telling one another how happy they were. This was the most deserving recipient in the history of the award, we all said. An older man with one pearl earring walked in, and my friend and I talked about how great he looked.

Later on, he grabbed our asses at the same time and whispered into the space between our heads, "I'm not here. I have no name."

Another friend I hadn't seen in a while asked me about my boyfriend, and I had to tell him we'd broken up. Usually, people change the subject when I tell them, but he said, "He seemed like such a nice guy," so I had to fake a laugh and say, "Well, turns out he wasn't." After the ceremony, everyone else went to a karaoke bar, but I put my headphones in and walked alone to West 4th.

The long, sloping passageway that led to the platforms was covered in ads for a grocery delivery app. SPECIAL INSTRUCTIONS: NO DRESS-ING, one said. It showed a cartoon man sitting on his couch, wearing only boxers. WHAT DO YOU KNOW? SALMON DOES TRAVEL UPTOWN, said another. On the lower train platform, another set of ads, this one for a phone with an improved selfie camera: DOES LOVING

YOURSELF HAVE A LIMIT? The train charged in, blocking images of a duck-lipped woman in deep focus. I sat on an empty bench and looked up. Along the seams of the subway car's ceiling, a set of ads for a bedding company said, GET DRESSED NEVER, 500 MORE MINUTES, and LET'S NOT RUN AWAY TOGETHER. I turned to read the vertical ads mounted behind me. They were for an apartment listing app and said things like, SEARCH: SEPARATE ENTRANCE FOR ROOMMATE, and SEARCH: CRAZY CAT LADY–FRIENDLY. There was a poster-size ad further down on the train for something medical. The only part of a Spanish phrase I could translate was YOU ARE NOT ALONE.

NOVEMBER 13, 2017

I GOT UP AND READ THE NEWS of another public figure being accused of sexual harassment, like I did every day. At work, I went to a bathroom stall to either cry or get lost in a sexual fantasy about a man I was messaging via Tinder, or both, at different times. The days were getting shorter and darker and everyone was talking about bleakness and cuffing.

NOVEMBER 14, 2017

I MET G. AT HER APARTMENT after work so we could go to a techno show we'd bought tickets to weeks earlier. She poured us two huge glasses of white wine. In the Lyft, I realized she was very drunk. We got to the venue in Gowanus and she stumbled out of the car. She stayed for a few minutes and tried to pull herself together, but she had to leave before eleven. I stayed there, dancing alone.

The DJ I liked finally went on at one in the morning. I was very drunk. I felt hands on my thighs and turned around to face a girl with long blond hair, a lacy cleavage-baring bodysuit, and tight black jeans. She danced with me for a while and then danced with a girl with long black hair and a mesh top over a black bra. Then she came back to me and got closer and closer until we kissed. She yelled into my ear that the girl with black hair was her girlfriend, and then took my hand and led me to the back of the dance floor. We danced in circles and made out for what felt like hours. She had perfect teeth when she smiled. Eventually, she asked me how old I was, and I lied and said 30. I should have said 29. Thirty is just as bad as 31. She laughed and said she was 22. She kissed me again to show me she didn't mind. She asked me where I lived, but the music was too loud for us to understand each other anymore, and she said she didn't know English well. When the girlfriend found us, the blonde started talking to her quickly in Spanish and laughing. They both laughed. I went to the bathroom and was glad to see that they were not in the same spot when I came out. It was almost three. I got in a cab that took me in a huge loop before the driver realized his mistake and then blamed it on me. I didn't argue.

NOVEMBER 15, 2017

THE STORIES ABOUT LOUIS C.K. came out and I was devastated. The way he wrote about sex felt necessary to me. There were perverts everywhere, and we should understand them because we should understand the world we live in. It was easy to imagine that Louis thought what he was doing was attractive to the women he assaulted, even if it was traumatizing: when he did it on TV, people loved it. His new movie was canceled, and everyone insinuated that he was a sicko who deserved to never work again. Maybe they were right, I don't know. But I wasn't ready to live in a world that censored a pervert honest enough to say he was perverted. It was his fault—he shouldn't have done those things. It was my fault, too. Maybe I shouldn't have loved his comedy. I shouldn't have shown that art dealer my tits on Halloween. Sometimes I felt guilty about loving the recklessness that came with being a woman.

Most days, I felt exhilarated when I read about men getting fired. I thought about my ex-boyfriend, who had cheated on me with women who were trying to advance their careers. This was an imbalance that was being abused. But he disagreed with me that his behavior was inappropriate, beyond the fact of his cheating. And yet I didn't want to start a campaign against him. I was afraid of looking petty, or, worse, like a victim. I'd rather erase the memory, not explode it. Because if I hadn't been cheated on, I would have gone on thinking that I never could have been, which would have been preferable. Maybe if I didn't know about any of it, I would be able to read about other women being humiliated.

Every time I broke up with someone I'd go back to the gym. It was a different gym each time, because new gyms kept opening closer and closer to my apartment. My roommate, H., went to many gyms, too, but with greater consistency. He was dense and angular; he drank protein shakes and carb loads or whatever. Whereas I spent my time stretching and hunching in the mirror, trying to see more concave areas, more negative space between hips and ribs. No matter what, my weight read the same on the scale. I looked thinner and felt lighter, but the numbers didn't get smaller. I wanted to take up so little space that my coworkers would look at my chair, assess the amount of room left on either side of me, and not be able to mask their envy.

It was easier for me to give up eating than it was for me to give up drinking. I didn't stop eating, though, because then I'd have to stop going to the gym, and then I'd start smoking again.

NOVEMBER 16, 2017

AFTER WORK I ATTENDED A LAUNCH for a new smartphone and a new R&B album. The launch concluded with a pink neon-lit party, during which my friends and I took pictures of our new free phones with our old ones, drank free cocktails, and ate hors d'oeuvres you had to work for. From a back door came a procession of wooden planks strapped to smiling waiters that held anise-spiked dark chocolate that had to be chiseled off a bar, whole bunches of baby bananas, persimmons with the stem attached, skewers of shell-on shrimp, and white radishes that looked like they'd just been pulled from a field. G. said she was keeping her old phone and her new one: one for personal use and one for sponsored posting. "It has a really good camera," she said.

Later, I met up with a brand consultant for a second date. I started telling him about other Tinder dates I'd been on. I lied and said that they'd all happened before our first date, which was weeks ago. I kept doing this, for some reason: comparing everyone I'd just met to everyone else I'd just met, aloud, to their faces. Guys lied about their ages a lot, I said. A 40-year-old said he was 36, and a 48-year-old said he was 44. Should I be lying about my age? I wanted to attract people my age or older than me, I said. If I said I was in my twenties, I could start attracting twentysomethings, whom I hated. Don't you? I asked. He stared forward, blank faced. No thirtysomething man hates twentysomethings, he said. Was I anxious about aging? he asked. The anxiety was what I was supposed to lie about. All thirtysomething women are supposed to say they are excited to finally feel adult and to know themselves. But I didn't lie about that. I said if I was anxious about anything, it was becoming obsolete, in my career and in my sex life. He was surprisingly sympathetic. He wanted to have sex with me, though. I wanted to have sex with someone, so it may as well be him.

NOVEMBER 18, 2017

I WENT WITH C. TO the Women's Entrepreneurship Day fundraising pre-dinner. In the lobby, we told a woman with an iPad who we were, and another girl took us to a private elevator, whose operator knew what floor to take us to. When the doors opened, another attendant took our coats and gave us tickets. A short hallway opened to an apartment painted in bright colors and hung with paintings and artifacts of world travels. Two bichon dogs wearing hot-pink fleece vests and diamante-studded collars clinked around a tiered table full of champagne bottles. A man was filling flutes and placing them on a tray held by another man. Another man was ladling a creamy pink punch into short goblets and handing them to women wearing Chanel suits and costume jewelry.

The publicist who had invited us introduced us to the owner of the apartment, a woman whose face was asymmetrical with botched plastic surgeries. She was wearing a pink fleece vest, too, and furry pink slippers. Many of the attendees looked to be mothers who wore pearls, with daughters who wore Tiffany charm bracelets or Cartier bangles. The publicist and the waitstaff were the only men in the room, until a man walked in with his younger wife. Her Hervé Léger dress squeezed her upper back, giving it a long crease. It took the man only a few minutes to find a reason to talk to a famous model who was sipping a clear cocktail near the window. The trophy wife stood patiently to the side. The owner of the apartment, now holding a dog under each arm, posed in front of a small step-and-repeat that blocked a doorway. Someone handed her a microphone and took one of the dogs from her so she could hold it. She talked for a few minutes about her home, her dogs, and her career as a film producer.

The founder of Women's Entrepreneurship Day, a leading activist, mentioned how close she was to each of the dogs, how much character they had, and how her own dog loved them like sisters. What followed was hard to follow. It was a winding speech about activism—first animal-rights activism, and then something vague about underprivileged women, a half-told anecdote about a stalker, something about writing several books and breaking several Guinness World Records, and then a story that started with, "No one told me that Honduras isn't a vacation spot." If it wasn't for her trip to Honduras—"Which I do not recommend, by the way; it's the most dangerous place in the world, did you guys know this? I didn't"—she would have never met so many women in need of business training. And that was the goal for the fundraiser the following night, to which everyone was required to bring their checkbooks.

NOVEMBER 19, 2017

AT SOME POINT ON SUNDAY, in bed, I googled the owner of the apartment. Her one film credit was a short she'd written, directed, produced, and voiced. It starred her two dogs. Next I googled the speaker. Her books were mostly about her dogs, and her Guinness World Records were for dog with the most expensive wedding and dog photographed with the most celebrities.

NOVEMBER 20, 2017

I SWIPED THROUGH TINDER at work and went on a date with someone I'd matched with hours earlier, J. He looked like an older Ryan Gosling.

"It's weird, because that guy isn't that attractive, right? But because he's so charming, he is. And now I am, only because I look like him."

After one drink, he insisted we talk about the abuse allegations against Al Franken, Louis C.K., and Lars von Trier. Everyone I went out with brought up sexual harassment, which made me uneasy. They all spoke with the same flippant tone about women getting ahead of themselves or making bigger deals about certain things than was productive. It was as if they were making sure I wasn't one of the ones who would get hysterical. At least J. backtracked a little and then let me change the subject. We'd both just seen *The Square* and loved it, and he'd just broken up with someone, too, and 31 seemed so young to him. We went from a bar in Ridgewood to a club in Greenpoint and danced to minimal techno until 2 AM. An obscure song started playing and we both said "I love this song" at the same time. At the end of our date, he put me in a cab and kissed me and said, "We should stay in touch."

NOVEMBER 21, 2017

A GROWING PERCENTAGE of my texts were from men who wanted to "stay in touch." We had inside jokes, we sent each other articles about things we'd discussed on our dates, we even started telling each another about other dates we'd been on, commiserating about what the app was doing to our minds.

There were many men, most of whom I'd met and at least made out with: a lawyer, a garbage man, a magazine editor, a TV camera operator, a CEO, a graphic designer, a social-media analyst, a photojournalist. There was a married woman who had no job. I didn't quite feel rejected by any of them. It was about chemistry, I told myself. Some seemed intimidated by my busy life. Others were hung up on an ex and just wanted to hook up, but found that texting me later was fun, too. I knew that J. wasn't going to want to date me, which only hurt because he was perfect on paper. His detached kiss and all the conversations tapering off into platonic feelings made me sad, and I started to cry, as I often did lately, without warning. Was I not irresistible to anyone? Was being irresistible to men what I wanted the most?

NOVEMBER 22, 2017

I WAS EMAILING A MAN from my past, a new divorcé. "Stop that," said H. I switched to the conversations on Tinder with guys who were old enough to be my father. There were messages I left unanswered, some about sex and others about expensive dates and still others about the full moon that night or the delicious meal they made from scratch, alone. Sometimes they would enter my fantasies, their hunger more interesting than the other, brutish kind of lust. These men were happy to repeatedly ask for my attention, and maybe even happy that our dynamic meant that I often acted callous toward them. I wanted them to continue to want me, but I couldn't imagine becoming exclusive with someone so fascinated by my autonomy. I sent a series of texts to a man in his late forties I'd been on one boring date with. He was away on a business trip in an earlier time zone. "Hello, darling," he wrote back, as if we were in a full-blown relationship. That kind of thing didn't used to bother me so much.

NOVEMBER 23, 2017

H. AND I WENT TO a Thanksgiving party at our friend's West Village apartment. We brought a green-bean casserole and ham. I was surprised to see an acquaintance of my ex, and more surprised to find out that he hadn't heard we'd broken up. "But you guys had some kind of understanding, right? You weren't, like *committed*."

I couldn't help myself. "He wasn't," I said. "I was."

"I never knew, by the way, that you're a writer. Why didn't you tell me?"

"I assumed he would have told you that," I said, stunned again.

"You can never expect anyone to do your promotion," he said. "I learned that the hard way." I knew that he wanted me to ask about his own writing career, but I didn't.

I excused myself to get a glass of wine. A woman I didn't know well sat by me during the dinner. She said she'd gotten back together with her ex, who had broken off their engagement a year earlier. C. was there with her boyfriend, the gallerist. They'd gotten back together, too. After dinner, H., C., and I went to the Thursday night strip club in the basement of the Monster. I had never seen male strippers before. As a woman, I wasn't allowed to get a lap dance, which meant none of the men walking by us would paw my shoulder or kiss my cheeks. They just smiled and winked. "A lot of them are straight," said H. "Like, a lot." Some could pole dance almost as well as female strippers, and others simply stood on the stage and flexed. There wasn't a correlation I could trace between skill and tips, only one between attractiveness and tips. C. got a phone call from her boyfriend and had to leave. I could see tears forming in her eyes when she hugged us to say goodbye. H. disappeared into the lap dance room. I was alone, a handful of ones ready to fold into a waistband if I was impressed enough by a silently dancing man. It was still Thanksgiving, and the emcee hadn't mentioned the holiday once. I was surrounded by older men, but it was like they didn't see me. If I didn't know why, I'd be sad about that, but since I did know why, I was happier than I'd been in months. +

NEW RELEASES
WINTER/SPRING • 2018

ALANIS OBOMSAWIN
Bush Lady

CARLA BOZULICH
Quieter

ERIC CHENAUX
Slowly Paradise

JASON SHARP
Stand Above The Streams

EFRIM MANUEL MENUCK
Pissing Stars

STILL FRESH • 2017

JONI VOID
Selfless

SALTLAND
A Common Truth

JESSICA MOSS
Pools Of Light

ESMERINE
Mechanics Of Dominion
2018 JUNO NOMINEE: ALBUM PACKAGE OF THE YEAR

DO MAKE SAY THINK
Stubborn Persistent Illusions
2018 JUNO NOMINEE: ALBUM PACKAGE OF THE YEAR
INSTRUMENTAL ALBUM OF THE YEAR

GODSPEED YOU! BLACK EMPEROR
Luciferian Towers

CONSTELLATION
CSTRECORDS.COM

IVAN SEAL, *FIRHE IF MAG*. 2011, OIL ON CANVAS. 20 × 16". COURTESY OF CARL FREEDMAN GALLERY, LONDON.
© IVAN SEAL.

YOU CAN'T READ

Rose Réjouis

WHEN IT COMES DOWN TO IT, there's really only one thing we hold against you: you can't read. What does that mean? Just that you cramp our style. You are neither an active verb, a pretty word, nor a useful preposition. You live here in punctuation that is not your own. You imitate. When you're a little less shy, then maybe you're charming, you smile a lot. That's sweet, but it's not enough. You are not from here. You are in our house, and here you are inscrutable—with or without that veil. Whether the veil is your skin or polyester. By the way, where do you people get those scarves? Don't they make you feel like you have tattoos on your face? It's so weird to take attention away from one's face with these motley colors. Sorry, I find it kind of childish, like wearing mommy's clothes.

Now, it's true, sometimes you're really striking, tall and slender. Sometimes you dress stylishly. OK, fine, but . . . what then? It's still going to be exhausting to have lunch with someone who goes on and on about all the obstacles she's had to overcome just to be here in this cute bistro, and we won't be able to sit back and just whine without upsetting her, because the truth is, nestled inside her is that ironclad faith, the naive faith of a little girl squeezing her grandmother's hand. And so then we're forced to feel ashamed—despite the white gleam and gilded riches of modernity—because we did nothing but go clubbing on Saturday and watch TV on Sunday, get into a fight with a friend, or just wallow in the fact that we don't like our job. While for this idiot, the sun sparkles through the window in a special way because she's drinking a café noir with a French friend, sitting on a banquette upholstered with gold studs, and, for a brief moment, life is good. It's a day like any other in Paris—and here she is, just head over heels because she works in an office.

You're head over heels because you don't understand that you don't count. We don't mean you when we talk about the unemployed. You, we don't care about. One more, one less. We're not talking about you but about *him*, out there, who despite his engineering degree has not found a job after five years of looking. We are worried about Dominique. He lives in the apartment his grandmother bought for him and spends half the year traveling to run away from the shame of being unemployed. It is his fate that fills us with rage. When we run into you, well, you do get our mind off things. Yes, why not, let's have coffee, a quick one. What, you don't like your office job that much, after all? And it's not a real position, you just work in the mailroom, and you're afraid to get fired? Well, sure, obviously, I knew your job wasn't a real job. That's what I've been saying. You don't function as a subject in the sentence. You're just a space between words. You are disposable. True, you're an absolute sweetheart, and you do have a beautiful smile, but that's about it. Whether you're here or there makes no difference. We can make do.

You can't possibly understand. He is my *brother*. She is my *cousin*. We have *always* known each other. We have the same *grandmother*. But you, even years later, you remain a stranger. With your big puffy immigrant hair. And your big sensitive immigrant eyes. And your glib immigrant talk. I don't know if you've noticed, but we—the people from here—we measure our words. We don't talk to just anybody. We wait and watch before figuring out whether it's worthwhile. Yes, you, I know, if *you* didn't talk to *everyone*, you might go months without saying a word. You speak to survive. But admit it, you also talk because you come from an oral culture, right? Don't forget you come from somewhere else. All the same, it's really not the same.

What's that you're saying now? Oh, it was your grandmother who didn't know how to read, and you've been in the school system from preschool to college? I see, so you *really* don't get what's going on when people talk to you. Your grandmother, your sister, you, it's all the same. Don't you get it? You believe in assimilation, you only wore a headscarf for a couple of years when you were a teenager—that's fine. But, I mean, we can't just let go and leave what is French in your hands. What about us? What would we do? Who would we be? I mean, what's next? I've noticed that only primitives believe in civilization. Civilization isn't a thing. It's a strategy. You go left, we go right. You set up little workshops, we build huge concrete malls, and the minute you flood our malls, voilà, we rush back to our boutiques and workshops. Gotcha! Good riddance. That's civilization. A strategic occupation of territory. That's all. You make me laugh, you. Really now.

Besides, deciphering something is not the same as reading. You need to know loads of other things. You need to be steeped in the culture to understand—otherwise you get it wrong. You read everything as if it were a user's manual. You don't get that reading is about what you choose to read. You don't read everything just because you know how. For one thing, you're not supposed to read manuals. Or ads. You don't just read whatever . . . You, you come to words as if you were a black ant. The words are in a bigger font than you are. Anyway, no one listens when you speak, you know. That's because you don't speak. You repeat. It's not the same thing. All your words are borrowed. What would you do if we took them back? The ideas simmering in you are not yours . . . Return them to the library . . . I dare you . . . See? You can't read. So if you do ever decide to write a book, no need to look for the needle in a haystack. All you have to do is tell the story of your life. You know, your grandmother, your mother, all that. Don't forget the pain and humiliation. That's what sells books by people like you. Difference. People need to feel that you are not like them, that your hands are worn, that there's an eye or a finger missing, that your body bears scars or burns, that there's a stone in your path and in your throat. In other words, they need to feel you've been properly flayed.

Oh, here's a really good one. My father liked to tell me that he knew lots of Africans with PhDs who would spend all day walking around Paris with empty briefcases to make their families believe they were at work. But no one would hire these men. In their three-piece suits, they took enormous strides through a city they knew better than the backs of their hands. That's one my father used to tell me.

What, you still don't get it? Look, all of French literature *tells* you that you can't read. What exactly do you think Verlaine meant in "Ars Poetica" when he wrote:

> Who can count all Rhyme's mistakes?
> What deaf child or mad Black
> Must have forged this cheap hack?
> Tapped out, it sounds hollow and fake.

Verlaine? Don't know him? I get it, you pretend to be deaf when you hear the word *Black*. So that's your strategy. Nice.

Translated from the French by Grace McQuillan, Rose Réjouis, and Val Vinokur

SHOP.NPLUSONEMAG.COM

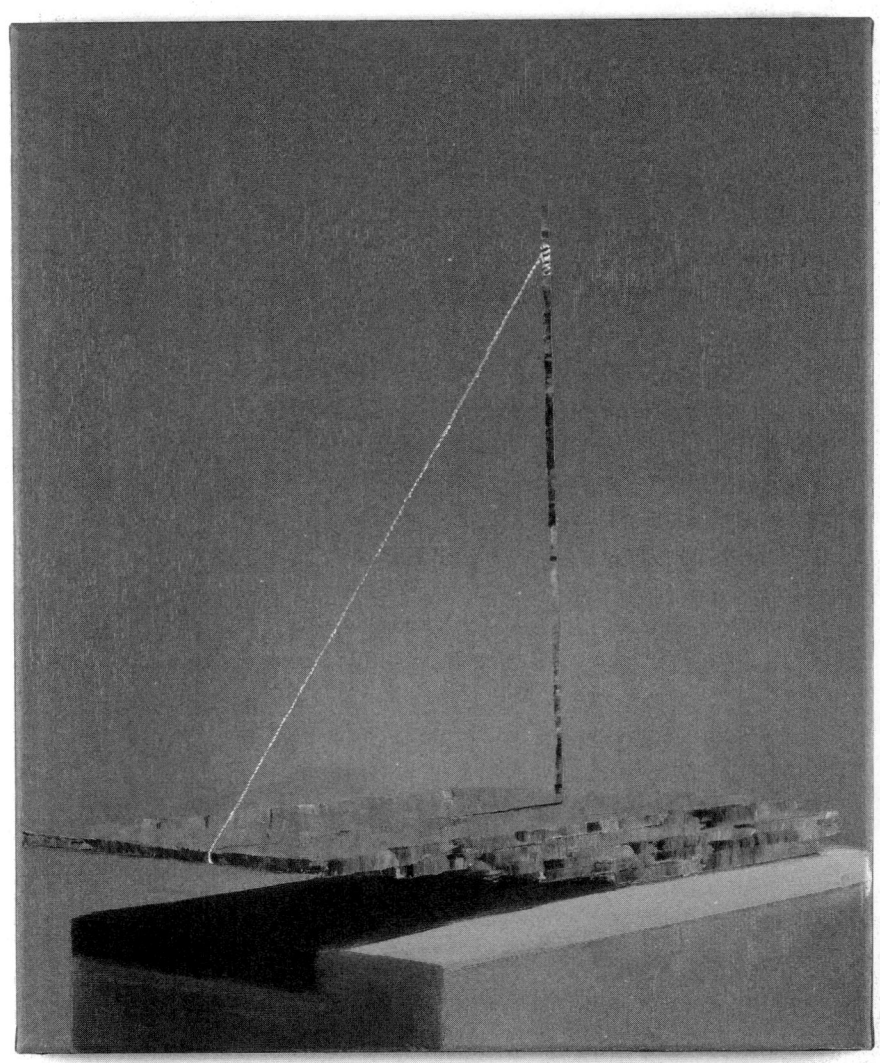

IVAN SEAL, *PROTOTYPE TO GET OUT*. 2011, OIL ON CANVAS. 20.5 × 16.5". COURTESY OF CARL FREEDMAN GALLERY, LONDON. © IVAN SEAL.

LETTER TO FREUD

Rose Réjouis

I'M IMITATING HIM by writing you this letter, but I don't agree with what Yosef Hayim Yerushalmi wrote in his last book about your last book. I don't believe you were thinking about your father and his suggestion not to neglect Torah study when you wrote *Moses and Monotheism*. Your father was on your mind when you were riding a camel in Egypt and reproaching yourself for seeing the pyramids without him. Over and over you tried to say what Egypt meant to you. You even declared that you'd read more archaeology than psychology, and that no one could know the sacrifices you'd made to acquire your collection of Greek, Roman, Egyptian, and Asian artifacts. Oh, the hide-and-seek chiaroscuro in that sentence! I'll tell you that the artist Robert Longo seems to have understood your feelings when he drew some of your statuettes—in charcoal and chalk and on a monumental scale. They shimmer with mystery.

Last summer I devoted myself to reading Spinoza for a month. I read him in English, in Edwin Curley's marvelous translation. I hear his irony, the irony of the *Tractatus Theologico-Politicus*, in your voice, both of you laughing at the audacity of prophets who described a god in their image: a right-handed god for righties, left-handed for lefties. Prophets who imagined victories when they were in a good mood and wars or other misfortunes when they got depressed. "If a triangle could speak, it would say, in like manner, that God is eminently triangular," Spinoza wrote to a friend. Such is the bitter laughter of the lonely philosopher aware of his solitude, laughing to himself. I believe Spinoza's ideas owed something to his past, to the expulsion of the Jews from Portugal during the Inquisition. He expressed himself like a child of refugees, a child whose family was slightly askew with respect to their adopted country, and who could himself expect a skewed fate in this new land—a fate he wisely tried to renounce. His *Ethics* is a manual for the creation of a utopia. I felt like a child again when I tried to imagine, together with him, a society where the citizen would no longer feel the imperious need to persecute his neighbor, because he would recognize his ignorance of the true causes of things and thus act cautiously, reasonably, seeking the God hidden in nature. Well, I'm all for seeking the triangular god who gave his essence to the triangle, but I confess I was a bit disappointed that Spinoza had so little to say about disaster. If what should never happen happens, he says, endure it calmly. Better that than to aggravate and add to a vicious cycle of uncontrollable effects and their tragic consequences.

As for you, you turned toward the future, toward that uncertain future that appeared so clearly to Virginia and Leonard Woolf when they saw the Nazis for themselves in 1935. Later, Leonard joked that they were saved because of Mitzi, their pet marmoset, since "no one who had on his shoulder such a 'dear little thing' could be a Jew." You wrote *Moses and Monotheism* a few years later, saying things enigmatically enough so that no one could accuse you of simplifying anything. You concealed God in a Darwinist and Lamarckian natural history of monotheism. Many people think that you didn't write the book you really wanted to write. Robert Paul actually decided to write it: *Moses and Civilization*, a psychoanalytic anthropology of the origin of civilization. A fascinating correction, but your false note was perfectly deliberate, wasn't it? Didn't you yourself describe it as a "bronze statue with feet of clay"? One false note may conceal another. A collective dissonance, perhaps? The book of Daniel and the *Inferno* both describe a statue made of gold, silver, iron, and bronze and leaning on a clay foot that can't support it. Dante's colossus cries tears of blood as it turns its back to Egypt, to the south and east, and peers west at Rome as if it were a looking glass. You've been trying to warn us against false mirrors. But what can we do? We barely speak the language of our own bodies.

When I lived in Manhattan for two years, on the Upper West Side, I liked to go to the gym at the Jewish Community Center across the street from me, a kind of glass pyramid filled with natural light. After working out, I'd shower with the center's members, Jewish women from the neighborhood, braving the sight, in their eyes, of an unexpected brown body. Naked, staring at the metal pipes as if something else besides hot water could come out of them, I felt it each time: the shock of standing with this community, confronting a still recent history.

IS THAT ENOUGH TALKING about myself? I still have the impression of having rubbed myself out of my own letter. Who is putting this particular stone on your tomb? How can I represent myself? So, okay, after having read Spinoza, I saw this movie by Frances Bodomo, *Afronauts*. Books and films are parables, collective dreams, right? If that's true, then I think this film tells my life story and also, maybe, that of your daughter Anna, who survived you and the four aunts, your sisters, killed at Treblinka and Theresienstadt, and carried on your work, she and her partner, Dorothy. The film, too, is a tale of another kind of hothouse overachievement. It's about Matha, a teenager with albinism who volunteers for the Zambian Space Program in 1969. After a handful of training sessions, she suits up and is launched into space. Several minutes later, the rocket explodes and falls back to earth, without its astronaut. To my eye, the movie becomes a kind of family romance. The older man in charge of the mission is at first bereaved and crazed, but suddenly takes her disappearance as a good sign. He is radiant: his daughter, his favorite child, has reached the moon! The older woman who flickered on the screen at the beginning of the movie, having failed to prevent the mission in the first place, is absent.

Sci-fi, dreams, letters to dead men ... Anything to get to what you called *mea res agitur*—our interminable anxieties. Any cracked mirror will do. I am moved that Yerushalmi succumbed to affect at the end of his book, troubling the smooth surface of an academic essay published by Yale. He found it unbearable to conclude his book without imagining a confrontation with you. Somehow, your solitude is a looking glass for his. And for mine.

Translated from the French by Rose Réjouis, Marco Roth, and Val Vinokur

ROGER BALLEN, *HEADLESS*. 2006, ARCHIVAL PIGMENT PRINT. 19½ × 19½". COURTESY OF THE ARTIST.

DAY OF MEMORY
Bela Shayevich

AUGUST 5, 2014

NOBODY ASKED ME what I was doing at the Memorial Society for the commemoration of Soviet political repressions, scanning NKVD files, coming and going like a big-smiling ghost to a back office packed with files and artifacts like the balls of ore mined by women prisoners gathering dust on the shelves. To get into the office, you took an eyeglasses case off a bookshelf, snapped it open, and took out a five-inch-long key that you snapped back into the case after unlocking the door. I would have gone just for that. None of my relatives were in the gulag; I'm not a journalist or a historian. Summer was dragging in Petersburg, and I'd wanted to go somewhere where there'd be smart people to talk to if I dared to reveal my hideous Russian and ignorance. I didn't dare. No one cared.

My second week at Memorial, in the tiny kitchen where everyone smoked when they didn't want to smoke at their desks, Tanya, the deputy director, suddenly noticed me.

"Oh!" she offered, "do *you* want to come to Solovki?"

"Yes!!!" I said. I'll go anywhere, even if I don't know where it is, especially away from St. Petersburg. Turns out that Solovki is the Solovetsky Islands, home of the first Soviet labor camp, the titular gulag archipelago. According to Wikipedia, there is a 16th-century fortress there that houses the 15th-century monastery on the back of the 500-ruble bill. I didn't have one on me. We left the following Monday.

Jenya was 25, the only one at Memorial my age. She had a pet snail named Hydra she'd found in Novosibirsk and flown back two thousand miles to Petersburg and kept alive for three years, but she kept saying "Geedra" for "Hydra" and I couldn't understand her. We were on the night train to Murmansk, but we would be getting off at Medvezhegorsk and then somehow heading on to the White Sea. There were six of us: me, Jenya, her friends the boys Zhenya and Sasha, and Lena and Natasha, the girls, who were their own friends. The old people coming were all too old for the night train.

At dawn in Medvezhegorsk, Jenya discovered a short, birch-lined road leading us straight from the station to Lake Onega. Wisps of haze steamed off the lake's silver peel; the sun on its skin looked like a nickel glinting in gelatin. The air was so still and blue it felt like a simulation. Jenya wanted to swim naked, but I felt shy around boys I didn't know and maybe they were shy, too, so she said, "Oh, fine," and pulled on a sports bra. I'd packed my swimsuit even though we were going practically to the Arctic Circle; I was just worried that it was wrong to want to go swimming so badly when we were there to see where people were murdered. But Jenya went in first. I followed her into the algid water, squealing.

Between two brows of dark blue rock, the cloud-white water and sky erased the horizon. Jenya bobbed out toward the nothing until she stalled and lay back on the water. I wished I could make her know that I love snails, too, and that I love being naked and cold, but I was already back out on the shore, watching her. Up and down the coast were trees, and behind the trees, more trees, all the way up the hills. Zhenya flopped into the shallows in his boxer briefs and promptly hopped back out onto the log where he and Sasha sat chain-smoking skinny cigarettes, praising the water that clearly had been too cold for him. Lena and Natasha had planted themselves with their backs to the lake reading Solovki prison memoirs. They had each brought their own little stack.

Oldish women started emerging one by one out of the trees, each of them wanting to know, "Are you the ones from yesterday?"

"No," we would chant, "We're the ones from today."

And each would walk away, shaking her head toward the others accumulating packets of cookies and baskets of berries a little bit down the shore, passing around a thermos of hot black tea. They were annoyed because we had taken the spot where they go every morning. Then they took off all their clothes and dawdled into the water, which had begun to sparkle. Splashing handful after handful over their shoulders in a loose ring, talking about children and who's in the hospital, bullying a little white dog on the shore into joining them. Making me feel extra dumb for not going in naked.

Around ten, a text came in from the old people saying that we could proceed to the town center. Not much going on in downtown Medvezhegorsk: a bus stop, a statue of Kirov, and a hulking, pathetic mall/office building with two women in front, in aprons and slippers, hawking an iceless pile of trout. Chartered buses were waiting to take us to Sandarmokh, a mass grave in the forest. It was the first I had heard of it, and by "it" I mean both Sandarmokh and the fact I was going there.

Different people, books, and articles say that different numbers of people—between seven and ten thousand—were shot in Sandarmokh during the purges of the '30s, including exactly 1,111 inmates from the Solovetsky prison camp executed between October 27 and November 4, 1937. For almost sixty years, nobody knew where any of them had been murdered except for the surviving murderers. Sandarmokh lay within a nameless, borderless stretch of pines until 1997, when Veniamin Iofe, the founder of St. Petersburg Memorial, Irina Flige, his then assistant, and Yuri Dmitriev, an independent researcher from Petrozavodsk, discovered it. Dmitriev named it. He would go on to unearth execution protocols until he could also name more than six thousand of the people buried there.

Iofe and Flige had started the search in 1989, when, on their first trip to the Solovetsky Islands, they were approached by the children of a number of missing prisoners and entreated to find them. There were rumors of a massive transit of prisoners that vanished from the islands sometime in the autumn of 1937. It was said that the thousand prisoners were put on a barge and drowned in the White Sea. Iofe and Flige spent years combing the archipelago for their remains, finding no burial on that scale. It wasn't until 1996 that they finally came upon the name of an NKVD operative who'd been deployed to Medvezhegorsk in 1937 to deal with a large transit of "politicals from Solovki." It was a name they'd already heard of, Mikhail Matveyev. He had to have been the one who had killed everyone they were looking for. After a difficult battle with the authorities, they managed to access the case file containing his testimony against two of the other men who murdered the transit from Solovki.

Flige:

> The most astounding thing was his rationality. Everything about why Matveyev tortured prisoners, why he'd invented his barbaric pre-execution procedure, he had a logical reason for.... At a certain point in his complaints and rationalizations, Matveyev states that the site was located nineteen kilometers from where they were keeping the prisoners.... During another interrogation, he mentions... a bad incident on the road leading through a settlement, when an engine stalled out around the village of Pindushi [and a prisoner tried to escape —Trans.]. That was all that we needed from Matveyev's testimony. We now had the most important facts: the site was nineteen kilometers from Medvezhegorsk, down the road that passes through Pindushi.

In the spring of 1997, Iofe and Flige were introduced to Yuri Dmitriev, a self-taught researcher and archaeologist working with the Karelian branch of Memorial. Photos of him from the end of the '90s show a skeletal man with silken gray hair down to his shoulders and a demonic goatee. He is usually smoking and often dressed in head-to-toe camo. By then, he'd been digging up and reburying people executed in the region for almost a decade. They decided to go on a joint expedition to find Matveyev's victims. "On July 1," said Flige, "we began searching at 9 AM. By 1 PM, we had found it."

There'd been some mention in the documents of a quarry. While Iofe, Flige, and a group of soldiers surveyed the quarry, Dmitriev wandered off down an overgrown path accompanied by his dog, Ved'ma ("Witch"), and the soldiers' commander.

Dmitriev:

> From my research, I knew that executions were required to take place at least ten kilometers from the nearest settlement so that the gunshots wouldn't be audible from the road and no one could see the bonfires and headlights, since most executions took place at night. So we're going along, chatting, and the whole time, I'm thinking where I would choose if it were me. We go over one hill, another one—no, it's too early, you'd still be able to hear the gunshots from the highway. We go down a third hill, and as soon as I think to myself that this place would do,

I see an indentation in the ground that's the right shape. A square about two-by-two meters. I look around and see another one, and another one. We go back to the quarry, pick up the soldier boys, and an hour and a half later, I have the first skull in my hands, with the telltale hole in the back of it.

We rode the bus through dead and dying villages scattered through vagrant farmland staked with faded, tumbling-over houses. Many of the fields were overgrown with a monster weed seven or eight feet tall, like a mutant Queen Anne's lace. Jenya was ominous when I asked: these were the *borschiaviki*, she said, dubbed "giant hogweed" and "cow parsnip" by dumb Victorians who'd imported them to England. They're phototoxic: if you touch them, they give you severe chemical burns, swollen welts that leave purple scars. Just a tiny drop of their venom in your eye can make you go blind. "Once they start multiplying," Jenya told me, "they're almost impossible to get rid of." The fields of Pindushi had long been lost to them.

    I sat next to an old woman who'd spent her life among these villages.

"Where did you work?"

"Here and there," she mumbled guardedly.

    She had two little boys with her, twins, sitting behind us and going nuts.

"Who are you going to see?"

"My relatives," she admitted, after a silence. Like it could still get her in trouble.

    We poured into the mass-grave parking lot, into a jumbled procession solemnly striding past a large boulder inscribed with the words PEOPLE, DON'T KILL EACH OTHER. OK. Cameramen hopped ahead of the shawl-swaddled elderly, wobbling and leaning on one another. A gang of black-and-gold-clad Russian Orthodox clergy dragged fragrant smoke through the sunspots, trailed by their flock of kerchiefs. The forest floor was soft with rusted pine needles, cards of bark, and indentations: grave pits yawning shallow between the tree trunks, rippling out in every direction.

    I've read that "ghosts" could be explained by animals experiencing extreme fear releasing pheromones to mark the spot where they felt it. So when you enter a house where somebody was murdered, you could know "it feels bad in there" just from smelling old fear. But there was so much perfume in the air. From Matveyev's testimony, we know that victims were first stripped and searched. In the next room, their wrists and ankles were bound with wire. Then, in the third room, they were knocked over the back of the head with wooden clubs so that they wouldn't scream, so that they could be driven in passed-out heaps of thirty or forty piled under tarps with guards sitting on top of them. Once they got here, they were thrown one by one into pits, where Matveyev stood waiting to personally shoot each one of them in the back of the head. He killed more than two hundred people that way every night.

In his testimony against his fellow murderers (from just two years later, 1939), Matveyev talks about the abuses his so-called procedure had led to:

> Two wooden clubs and two metal bars with sharpened ends were used as weapons. With these objects, without the slightest necessity [!], prisoners were beaten in holding cells and on the trucks on the way to the site. At the location of the execution of their sentences, the accused were unloaded onto the snow in nothing but their underwear and beaten with wooden clubs and the keys from the trucks. . . . MIRONOV, when traveling with the accused, stabbed one prisoner with a metal bar and strangled another one with a towel.

His language is so officious and technical, he's so used to killing, he seems like he could be incapable of seeing "the execution of sentences" itself as a kind of abuse. But maybe I talk like that, too. "Victims" sounds so much like "the accused" and "enemies." What are these "victims" to me but headless white bloodied bodies lit up by headlights in snow? Depersonalized tropes from a blur of movies and books about genocide. "Victims," a thousand different strangers turned into a single, faceless entity. Thinking of "them" in this way feels like a perpetuation of the same forces that killed "them." Maybe that's why all I could smell was sunshine and pines.

PIKKUVIRTA

HANNA

★ 1891 – † 28.12.1938

OSMO

★ 1912 – † 10.2.1938

Tombstone with white script in Latin letters. Finns. Mother and son?

The faces of the dead looked out from everywhere, most of them printed on enameled ovals of tin. There were a few proper granite tombstones, but most of the memorials hung on the pines, which Russians call ship-building pines when they've grown so tall and straight. Between the pines, there were posts topped with small, sloping roofs, like cuckoo clocks, to protect them from snow and rain. Some were traditional Russian Orthodox grave-posts, some had little platforms for lighting candles. There were also a lot of printouts scotch-taped directly to trees, the words and photos washed into black-purple swirls beneath tattered plastic. I played the game where I tried to imagine how black-and-white people would look in full color.

NIKOLAI TROFIMOVICH GORNEV
1900 – 1938

Sepia portrait of a fleshy face, like an overgrown boy. With a crude, rounded collar sticking out of a coarse woolen suit. Looks like a mug shot.

The prettiest were the wooden boxes filled with fake flowers, crosses, and pinecones. Photos, handwritten bios in ballpoint, copies of execution orders. Some were simple aluminum plaques with punched lettering, like braille, listing dates of birth, arrest, and death. Some also included a date of rehabilitation, when the Soviet government formally admitted a person they'd murdered was innocent. Were the rehabilitation dates there to show the government's hypocrisy, or as "proof" that the person really wasn't "a spy for the Japanese," "a spy for the Polish," "a spy for the Italians"? It was hard to understand. I could barely comprehend the names and the faces. There were so many of them, with their eyes all flashing between one another's.

VOLYNETS
FLEGONT IGNATIEVICH
DEPUTY OF THE SEIMAS OF POLAND
8.1.79 – 3.11.37
TOWN OF VILEYKA, BELARUS

Black-and-white photo of a polished man, bald with a narrow halo of black hair. Bushy black-and-silver whiskers. Shot by Matveyev. The old clothes and mustache make him look like a type, like an extra in Night at the Opera.

154   Bela Shayevich

The previous week, I'd spaced out in front of a framed photocopy in a back hallway at Memorial, a dog-eared typewritten order dictating how many "enemies" were required to be arrested in each district of Leningrad for the third quarter of 1937. After I saw their faces hanging from trees, this fact was embodied: these weren't enemies, or even "enemies" by Stalinist standards. They had been taken at random. Most of these people were killed simply to fulfill quotas.

SAGATELOV
ASTSATUR KHACHATUROVICH
10.8.1899 – 4.11.1937

A severe young man with a thick black mustache and a sharp-edged forehead. Also from Solovki. I don't think I could ever have known this person. Then again, sometimes I feel that way about people I know.

UNDERFOOT: SHAGGY GREEN-AND-WHITE moss, lichen, and stones. Unfurling ferns. Blueberries, dark and stiff on their shrubs. If there were a cemetery for the "victims of the opioid epidemic" where tens of thousands were buried, and my friend was buried there with them, I still wouldn't believe that my friend had died in the "opioid epidemic" (though I would be grateful to know that his body was somewhere I could go). The nightmare of that mass burial site would be just one dimension of the nightmare universe of his death. I'd see the life leading up to his death as being what killed him, not something abstract like "heroin." If I knew any one of these people, maybe I'd feel that way about them, too—that it was irrelevant how they were one of thousands, and that their death was a testament to the fact that a government can and will kill you and cover it up. Did anyone here ever know them?

I'd spent so much of my time imagining being murdered, it wasn't until recently that I'd figured out how I could kill. I was walking across a bridge, and suddenly I was easily capable of looking at passing women (just women) and reading each one as "meat." Despising them. Feeling no interest in any of their subjectivities, certain that whatever they thought was a stupid cliché, and that everything they had ever experienced and how they conceived of it was cookie-cut from the dumb core of mass urban liberal culture. That even imagining them as real individuals would be a grotesque misconception. They didn't matter, and it didn't matter if I were to kill any one of them.

NINA PORFIRYEVNA KOSTINA
1905 — SHOT 1.11.1937
GEORGY EVDOKIMOVICH ARTAMONOV
1902 — SHOT 4.11.1937
ALEXANDRA PORFIRYEVNA KATERUHINA
1891 — SHOT 4.11.1937
ZINAIDA PORFIRYEVNA KOSTINA-KHOVRUNOVA
1901 — SHOT 4.11.1937
ANASTASIA IVANOVNA BAKAEVA
1912 — SHOT 4.11.1937

Five simple plaques, inscribed in neat cursive, screwed onto a pole. At least three of them sisters. All Solovki.

Perhaps I was growing out of some of my narcissism. In my past obsessions with genocide, I had related to victims so much because I was so attached to myself, my life, and my pain. My pain as a listener to horror stories. Now that I was older and felt like I mattered less, I was more able to kill. A picture of me from now in digital color looks exactly like millions of other women from now in digital color. If I were to kill, I would be one of millions of murderers. All this is so easy to say.

I watched a family—three generations—settle around one of the pits. One of the women began telling the kids about how their great-grandfather was buried . . . somewhere around here. Most of the people who'd come looked like typical Russians: former Soviets in cheap Chinese clothing. Aging women with blurred figures in clashing florals and surreal bonnets; aging men showing off hairy forearms in ancient gold watches and stomped-out dress shoes. They fussed over memorials, clearing weeds and arranging fake flowers. Some silently wept.

Flige had given Jenya a big digital camera so she could take photos and videos of people installing memorials and interview them for the Sandarmokh website. I caught glimpses of her through the trees. After a while, I stumbled on Zhenya and Sasha smoking in front of the monument to Tatar victims. Zhenya pontificating, Sasha's eyes on the dust. In earshot of people who'd been in mourning for nearly eighty years, or had been born into grief. I was glad that I didn't have the Russian to join in with my smart ideas, trying to understand and bear witness to something that none of us had seen.

The ceremony began. I should have been watching, but I hate being part of a crowd. I drifted deeper into the woods, aiming for where the memorials ended so I could pee. Snippets of speeches reverberated through the tree crowns. At the edge of the site, an old woman sat at a bright yellow pulpit facing an ornate cross, unwrapping the plastic cocoon of her lunch. The noon sun rocked gently down through the branches. I wavered on taking her photo, and decided no.

I had never seen real wild blueberries before. *But who knows where there are other graves secretly scattered, unmarked or marked barely by indentations*—I needed to tell myself this to keep from picking them. When I was 3 or 4, my father had taken me to the Jewish cemetery in Baku, which I remember as being mosaicked in beautiful snail shells; just as I reached for one, I heard him thunder: "NEVER TAKE ANYTHING FROM THE CEMETERY." Then we left, and we left our dead there. I later learned that the locals have taken to coming to Sandarmokh just to gather the berries and mushrooms, and that it's even become a custom for wedding parties to drop by and take photos, the bride and groom smiling and drinking champagne.

I was scared that the ghosts would know that I didn't know who I was crying for. That "they" would think it was dumb that it was for all of them, that it was for none of them. I resisted letting myself feel too much pain, because it is only my pain, and weeping from it would have just been for me. I could still hear the ceremony, recordings of treacly music swelling between the speeches, then cut off abruptly. I thought they would understand that I was just trying not to make up feelings about things I knew nothing about, and would not think I was callous. That they would appreciate my restraint, my knowledge that I knew nothing of them. I already didn't like how suddenly I'd made these "ghosts" so attentively follow my thoughts. Just because they were keeping me from eating blueberries.

And yet: Dmitriev says that although the first Day of Memory at Sandarmokh was windless and still, as soon as people began to get off the buses, the tops of the pines began rustling in greeting. He said it was the souls clamoring to be remembered. He has also said he believes that we go through this life paying for what we did in the last, and what he did in his past life must have been pretty bad for him to have spent the past thirty years with the dead. I wonder if he believes that he was an executioner. A journalist writing a profile of Dmitriev reported being chased by "two devils" with "green faces and glowing eyes," "baring sharp teeth," at Krasny Bor, another mass grave nearby, which Dmitriev also discovered. He'd come in the winter, though, when there was no one else there.

SIDLING BACK INTO THE FRAY, I was in hearing range for the beginning of the speech by the Ukrainian representative. She gave a fake false start in Ukrainian, pretended to abruptly remember that she was in Russia, and switched languages. In recent weeks, Russian troops in unlabeled tanks had penetrated Ukraine's eastern border. There was a war going on, but on TV, the Russian government was blatantly denying it. Independent news outlets published desperate screeds to an echo chamber of oppositionists. I'd read a harrowing interview with a hairdresser from outside of Donetsk, in eastern Ukraine, who'd been arrested, held prisoner, then taken out onto the street, where she was forced to stand up against a pole so she could be spit on and kicked by passersby who supported the Russia-backed insurgents. The Days of Memory at Sandarmokh and on Solovki were usually attended by a large delegation from Ukraine, who were said to be the soul of the proceedings. They were known for their singing. This year, the woman said, they had been turned away at the border.

After the speeches, people broke off into interest groups, clustering around the larger monuments in the path junctures erected on behalf of the murdered "deaf-mutes," "Italians," "Poles," "Estonians," "Turks," "Russian Orthodox clergy," and so on. This is part of Dmitriev's vision for Sandarmokh: he believes that nationality is a force that keeps people from being part of "the general population," a mass that can easily be controlled by the government. Nationality, which unites groups of people with language, culture, traditions, and history, makes people much harder to control, if there are enough nationalities each standing up for their interests. He actively seeks out national groups, shows them his lists of who from their nationality was murdered here, takes them to the site, shows them the monuments that other nationalities have already erected, and successfully gets them to put up their own. Then, he brings them all together at these ceremonies, and each of them honors their dead while also feeling a solidarity with one another over shared grief. And it's true, the authorities really don't like how he brings around foreigners, showing them the blood of their people on Russia's hidden old hands.

I hate the idea of thinking about my nationality, let alone with special pity and pride, but I didn't know where else to go, so I ended up with the Jews. I hung in the back, watching them. They took turns reading from a list of names of the Jews known to be buried there, then one of them poured out a canister of dirt from Jerusalem while another one played the shofar. Please never do this to me if there is any sense that I might feel it, or that I'm watching, unseen, from the trees. I'll roll in my grave. I don't even feel like I'm part of a population. Maybe I'd feel differently if an American politician were to admit that the way Americans disguise mass murder and incarceration in the past and present, refusing to call it by its name, and perpetuate the policies that stem from it isn't so different from what happens in Russia. And if people from all other nations came forward and did the same. If everybody acknowledged themselves as murderers instead of victims or innocents who just didn't know better, maybe then I would feel like there's a real world that I could say I'm part of. Although, as I understand it, only the abstract world is broken up into nations. You'd also have to convince me to merge with a mass. Over my dead body. I went to spy on the others.

The first thing I saw was a Belarusian bureaucrat in tears, giving a television interview while people ran up and pulled on her, vying to tell her their stories in their native language. She listened intently, blinking her sparkling eyes. Standing around a hulking stone cross, the local Ukrainians were passing around a traditional braid of bread on a light blue–and–yellow shawl. I ripped off a piece; having seen this rite so many times on TV, I had to finally try it. Technically, I was born in Kiev. I mean, actually. Tasted like challah. People began milling around, seeing what else they could see before they left.

Chewing, I ambled up to Lena and Natasha, who were being ranted at. I was relieved to see them. Maybe I do have a people that I belong to; my people's culture and tongue is to stand around silently, being ranted at. The ranter pointed to a gaunt man with skin like tanned hide, a Prince Valiant haircut, and a long gray goatee, flanked by two children and a German shepherd. That's Yuri Dmitriev, he told us. I followed him with my eyes, watching his cortege break away from one group only to be detained by the smuggest-faced of the Cossacks. They were there, too. I'd never seen a militia of Cossacks before, only pictures of them in their black-and-gold uniforms, whipping protesters with horsewhips, unhampered by the police. This guy looked like an overfed mushroom with a bulbous mustache, straight out of Gogol. That year, the Cossacks had come to Sandarmokh to install a monument "to the protectors of Russia," which is to say the police. After all, they were victims here, too; for example, Matveyev's testimony got two of his fellow murderers executed.

The mushroom asked Dmitriev to pose for a photo. Dmitriev obliged, with either hand gripping his adopted daughter, Natasha, and his dog's leash. I snuck my own picture of them from the side. It was a rude and obvious gesture to snap up a photo of a man standing next to a man who might try to kill him. I'd already heard that the Cossacks had yelled at Dmitriev during his speech. As it turned out, the cruelty of this moment would play out around the little blond girl at Dmitriev's side, smiling and clasping her hands to her chest, her face split in two by the eerily straight-edged shadow of a pine.

Yuri Dmitriev's eldest daughter, Katya Klodt, to Open Russia, September 2017:

On December 13, 2016, when they took him away, I was at home on medical leave. My dad called me and said that he was at the investigative committee offices. And that it was about some photographs. To be perfectly honest, at first, I didn't think it was a big deal. I thought they would talk it out and then he would come home. But as the day went on, he kept calling me saying they weren't letting him go. By evening, I started getting worried. He kept calling and saying, "Find Natasha, I can't reach her. What's going on with her?" But I couldn't either.

I ran over to his house. She wasn't there. Then she finally called me and told me that she had also been detained and that they'd taken her to a temporary foster care center. My dad kept calling. I'd ask him where he was, but he couldn't say the name of the street and I didn't know where the investigative committee offices were. He couldn't tell me the name of the detective he was talking to or the office number. And then he said, "Daughter, they're giving me eight to fifteen." Like an idiot, I didn't know what he meant.

"Eight to fifteen what? Days?"

"No. Years."

That's when I completely lost it. I freaked out, crying, screaming into the phone. I was screaming so loud everybody could hear me. I couldn't understand what was happening.

On January 10, 2017, an episode of an investigative news show titled "What the Memorial Society Is Hiding" airs on national Russian television:

"... is being accused of taking photographs for the sake of creating pornographic materials."

HOST: That's a quote from the criminal case where the subject of the photos is a young girl, not yet 14. The accused is her adopted father, Yuri Dmitriev, a representative from the Karelian branch of Memorial, a group that calls themselves human rights activists.

In mid-December 2016, the so-called liberal press and blogs lit up in what they considered righteous anger, as though it were the beginning of yet another political trial. [*Video of Dmitriev being dragged down a hallway in handcuffs by a young man with a long nightstick.*] The reason? The arrest of 60-year-old Dmitriev at his apartment, where a computer was confiscated containing these photos [*the blurred-out face of a naked little girl, arms up, with black rectangles over her face, chest, and genitals*]. For obvious reasons, we can't show these photographs without blurring out details, but, even so, any normal person could not possibly feel anything but sick to the stomach when they see these images, except maybe pity for an 11-year-old child [*cut back to Dmitriev being dragged down a hallway in handcuffs by a young man with a long nightstick*].

[*Cut to a decorated police lieutenant in a blue uniform studded with medals and gold buttons.*]

LIEUTENANT: In the course of our investigation, we have found that the accused habitually photographed his daughter in the nude between 2012 and 2015 [*cut to the blurred-out face of a naked little girl, arms up, with black rectangles over her face, chest, and genitals*]. These photographs were used in order to create pornographic materials. At the present time, investigators are moving forward with their investigation, which will include expert analyses that will definitively confirm that these photographic images are indeed pornographic. The accused has been detained and is currently in police custody.

HOST: But we should also tell you about the reaction of those who see this arrest as a provocation from the authorities, despite the factual evidence. As often happens, they created an online petition on the notorious website Change.org, which included the following statements:

Day of Memory

"The absurdity and political character of these accusations are obvious."

"A person like this cannot possibly be the creator and distributor of pornographic materials."

"This is either a case of personal revenge against Yu. A. Dmitriev and Memorial, or an attempt to discredit the Memorial Society."

These statements are rather strange considering the fact that establishing who does or doesn't produce pornography is something that only a court can do. On top of that, Dmitriev is only under arrest at the moment, and it's not like anybody has abolished the presumption of innocence.

However, when you look at the kinds of things Dmitriev himself has said, the behavior of his allies is not too surprising [*cut to video of Dmitriev speaking at Sandarmokh in 2014, while I was in the blueberries*].

DMITRIEV: "The time has really come when coming here to remember the people who were killed by the state represents a certain civic stance. And this stance is not always welcomed by our, should we say, 'political' authorities. So, my dear brothers and sisters, we need to do something about these authorities. But most importantly, don't be afraid. The most they can do to us is kill us."

HOST: What else can we say? And if anyone tried to say it, Dmitriev answered them without his trademark maneuvering and hesitation, but simply and emotionally [*cut to Dmitriev responding to a Cossack yelling at him from the crowd, telling him to stop talking about politics*].

DMITRIEV: "If anyone doesn't like what I'm saying, they may receive satisfaction behind the pines!"

Sergey Krivenko, an International Memorial board member, to Open Russia, July 2017:

Absolutely no proof has been found of his distributing photos of Natasha online or handing them off to another person. They stayed on his home computer. He would photograph his adopted daughter only in aims of documenting her health after having taken her in from an orphanage. When he adopted her, she was malnourished. This also comes out of the kind of person Dmitriev is. He excavates mass graves, travelling all over Karelia. He's obsessed with the idea of documentation, he documents everything: all the bones he finds in the mass graves, all the human remains. And so, from that, he very easily came to the conclusion that the state of the girl's health should be documented in the same way.

Katya Klodt, September 2017:

> I often have nightmares. And the other day, I had one about my father. We were hugging because, for some reason, they had let him out for a few days. He was so thin. I realize that I need to prepare myself for the day when they give him his sentence. But I still have hope, and I believe that all of the people, the thousands, more than ten thousand people, that he dug up, whose graves he found, praying for each of them, letting each of them pass through him, I am sure that their prayers can save him. They are praying for him and they won't let him come to harm. They will help him. This is a very powerful form of support. I am more than positive that my fathers feels it, too.

"There is a dark force," Dmitriev has said, "that goes into whoever touches the pages of these interrogations, these case files, these death sentences." In November 2016, after Memorial published a list of the names of forty thousand NKVD executioners, Dmitriev began receiving threatening anonymous phone calls demanding to know whether he planned to publish a similar list for Karelia. "I'm not interested in those dead, there are other dead people expecting me," he would tell them. Nonetheless, in his book listing the names of people repressed in Karelia, which Dmitriev was still finishing, he included the names of the officials who signed the documents sentencing them. Needless to say, his archive has been seized.

ROLLING BACK INTO Medvezhegorsk, we found ourselves headed down Dzerzhinsky Street, which leads back to the statue of Kirov. The Soviet place-names were unchanged, "Iron Felix" Dzerzhinsky being the founder of the Soviet secret police, and Sergey Kirov, the man whose 1934 murder (rumored to be a Stalin-ordered assassination) had served as the pretext for the purges. It turns out, Jenya told me, as Flige had just told her, that the crumbling mall/office building at Kirov's back isn't simply a mall/office building. In fact, it had been the headquarters of the Belomor Canal camp administration, and housed the hotel for visiting secret-police officers. It used to have two secret basement levels, and a billiards room in the tower, which now bristles with cell phone antennae. It's safe to assume that people were shot in the building, and it's simply a fact that thousands were sentenced to death inside. In effect, thousands more people were killed there than at Sandarmokh. No word on green devils inside the appliance store.

We had a few hours to kill, so we went back to the beach. In our absence, the lake had gone from the morning's cool slate to a choppy green-amber. It was crowded, and Russian pop blared from an impressive beer tent. From what I saw from the water, which was now perfect and warm, the teenagers of Medvezhegorsk have gorgeous bronze skin and they love volleyball. +

COMING SOON FROM
n+1 books

The collected film writing of

A. S. Hamrah

REVIEWS

A. S. HAMRAH
Sanctuaries of Trust and Caring

Darkest Hour

THIS MASTERPIECE OF CINEMA BOMBAST introduces Winston Churchill like he's in a Murnau film. Waking up in bed, he strikes a match to light his first cigar of the day, his face revealed by the flame.

Gary Oldman's performance comes from the Emil Jannings school of German Expressionist acting, heavy on the makeup, with a fat suit to get this thin, stylish actor up to Churchill's disheveled bulk. Oldman's grumbling and mumbling, which explodes in heavy speeches ("the dark and lamentable catalog of human crime," and so on), could come from Fritz Lang's *M*. Kristin Scott Thomas, as Churchill's wife, is made up to resemble Marlene Dietrich, the Dietrich of the 1950s who retained and refined her Weimar-Hollywood look until the end.

It's unclear whether Joe Wright, the film's director, is trying to fight fire with fire in *Darkest Hour* by using a filmic style associated with the rise of Hitler to tell the story of an outmatched England preparing to fight the Nazis. As a product of Brexit Britain, the film must be seen as anti-Europe in the contemporary sense even as it declares itself antifascist. When Oldman's Churchill lumbers into a tube station to speak with the common man, we descend with him into the realm of Capraesque populism, where the will of the people is mined so it can be turned into speeches and wars.

Dunkirk

DUNKIRK ARRIVED ON MOVIE SCREENS FIVE months before *Darkest Hour*. We see Churchill deliver his speech in the second film, after having watched Britons hear it in *Dunkirk*, a reverse echo as we move backward in time.

Christopher Nolan's event-movie drowns out Churchill's speech, replacing it with action, total destruction, a sea on fire. If *Darkest Hour* was bombastic, it still rambled with Churchill in his drunkenness, lurching from crisis to crisis, cutting through a mob of upper-class twits and senile fraidy-cats not unlike the right-wing weirdos who run Britain today. *Dunkirk* wants to be postpolitics, its common men out of the tube and flooding across the Channel in boats.

The action, however, was not memorable to me. It was too seamless. I lost interest in the perfection of the film's technical achievement, which I never doubted for a minute would be anything but complete and astonishing. I longed for just one moment where something wasn't perfect, to remind me that humans had made this study of improvised naval success. Mostly I remember the image of Spitfire pilot Tom Hardy's face in a CPAP mask left over from whichever of Nolan's Batman movies he was in. When soldier Harry Styles survived it all, it was as though "the enemy" had been vanquished so that the real Styles could leave the set, fly to Los Angeles, hop in a car, and drive between palm trees singing the song from *Titanic* on Carpool Karaoke.

Mudbound

DEE REES'S *MUDBOUND* COMPLETES THIS trilogy of 2017 World War II movies, focusing on the damaging effects of war's aftermath when soldiers return home. Since home is the Mississippi of the Jim Crow South, it is not the generic Everytown, USA, that greets the servicemen in *The Best Years of Our Lives* (1946). Life in rural Marietta, Mississippi, we learn, is worse than the war in Europe, which was at least honorable and only slightly gorier.

The webs of family and class relations in rural Marietta are so racist and stifling that they can only break down into lynching, patricide, and cheap burials. *Mudbound* would make a good double feature with 2016's *Hacksaw Ridge* as a liberal version of the same story. It equals and undercuts Mel Gibson's conservative vision in its portrayal of Southern religion, persecution, and masculinity. Significantly, *Mudbound* is the first American war movie directed by a black woman and the only war movie directed in the US by a woman not named Kathryn Bigelow or Angelina Jolie.

Since Netflix produced *Mudbound*, many viewers will watch it on laptops, which is unfortunate because Rachel Morrison's cinematography is so carefully burnished. Or maybe that's not such a bad thing, since *Mudbound* really brings out what life without indoor plumbing was like. When the townspeople inevitably don their Ku Klux Klan hoods the film kicks into high melodrama, but so many terrible things had already happened by then that I, like a farm implement, was worn down. *Mudbound* has the most forlorn semihappy ending I can recall in any war movie. The protagonist (Jason Mitchell), a sharecropper's son who fought as a tank commander in a segregated army unit, survives a lynching, then returns to Germany, where a better home awaits him amid the rubble left behind by Allied air attacks.

The Post

WHEN NATIONAL PUBLIC RADIO WARNS YOU about one of their upcoming pledge drives, they play a spot asking "if you believe democracy requires a free press." Probably everyone listening believes that, but you never know. Steven Spielberg's *The Post* is the perfect movie for those listeners, and for potential viewers who haven't heard that newspapers, like NPR, need money to run.

The real story in this movie is how Daniel Ellsberg (Matthew Rhys) got the Pentagon Papers to *Washington Post* reporter Ben Bagdikian (Bob Odenkirk) so the *Post* could publish them along with the *New York Times* and help bring the Vietnam War to an end. Spielberg for some reason decided that part of the movie lacked drama, and made it a subplot. *The Post* concentrates instead on bosses. We are asked to worry about the conscience of *Post* editor Ben Bradlee (Tom Hanks) and the finances of publisher Katharine Graham (Meryl Streep) as her newspaper launches an IPO while she fiddles with her glasses.

Around all that is good documentary-style footage of linotype machines in operation, terrible documentary-style footage of antiwar protests that the audience laughs at, and telephoto shots of Nixon on the phone with his back to the camera, seen through the windows of the White House. Those looked cheap on purpose, I guess, and reminded me of something from *The Private Files of J. Edgar Hoover* (1977). Democracy dies in darkness, sure, but if Spielberg really wanted to make a movie about the fate of journalism in America, he should have made one about the founding of *USA Today* in 1982.

All the Money in the World

MARK WAHLBERG SPEAKS ARABIC IN THIS movie. Other than that, he does nothing but pussyfoot around in 1970s suits that look like they were tailored for an actor who doesn't even lift. Though Wahlberg is supposed to be a billionaire's fix-it man helping Michelle Williams get her kidnapped son back, Williams struggles by herself as Wahlberg looks on. In addition to being ignored by her son's grandfather, J. Paul Getty (Christopher Plummer), who's too busy skeet shooting or clutching a painting like he's about to utter "Rosebud," and by her ex-husband, JPG Jr. (Andrew Buchan), a drug fiend who hangs out in Morocco with the Rolling Stones, she's also abandoned by a director (Ridley Scott) who works too fast to care.

But, I think, not fast enough. It took Scott only nine days to reshoot the scenes in which Christopher Plummer replaced the tainted Kevin Spacey as the elder Getty, which makes me think Scott could have shot the whole film in a month. Since the film's virtues are its shoddy, knock-off quality and its Seventies phoniness, shooting faster might have brought that out even more. In the future, I urge Scott to work as fast as he can—to make speed the defining characteristic of his late style more than it already is.

Molly's Game

AARON SORKIN TRIES TOO HARD. HE'S THE opposite of Ridley Scott. Buried within *Molly's Game* is what may be the best Hollywood movie on poker, better than *Rounders* (1998), but Sorkin overstuffed it with backstory. Molly Bloom's (Jessica Chastain's) pre-poker career as an Olympic skier, her overachieving family, the lengthy trial after her arrest, her problems with the IRS—none of that was interesting. Nor is Sorkin's exhaustive look at a

blade of grass on a ski slope, something he sees as the film's key image. I came to this movie to play cards, not to learn how to ski. The poker games Bloom runs in Los Angeles and New York, however—*those* are interesting. Attended by a hellish gallery of wealthy dilettantes, gambling addicts, finance guys, and mobsters, the games are psychodramas Bloom presides over in tight, low-cut outfits. A cool observer of obsessive male behavior in this high-stakes, rules-bound microcosm, Chastain looks on with louche disdain while she indulges the players' addictions and confusions and takes large amounts of cash off them. Away from the poker table, Kevin Costner, as Molly's father, sinks the film by park-bench psychologizing Molly's daddy issues, a scene Sorkin should have kept to himself.

I, Tonya

THE ICE SKATING IN *I, TONYA* LEFT ME WANTing more winter sports, not less. The CGI-enhanced explanations of the historic triple axel Tonya Harding executed in 1991 confused me, maybe because I was preoccupied with the way they got Margot Robbie's head on the body of the skater performing it. Whatever digital photo chamber they had to put Robbie in to get that effect, it worked. People used to watch movies and think, *That could be my face up there on the screen.* Now it really could be.

This antitriumph sports movie puts a morally compromised athlete through the ringer, like Scorsese did in *Raging Bull*, going so far as to take advantage of Harding's brief post-skating career as a pro boxer to pound her some more. The film is trashy in a way movies are not usually allowed to be these days, the excuse being that its trashiness is a side effect of the story itself. The main cast is either too boring to pay attention to (the husband) or too beautiful for the part (Robbie really has to Lon Chaney it like Oldman did in *Darkest Hour*). The fat bodyguard is tiresome in his grotesquerie, but Allison Janney goes beyond simple ludicrousness. Her performance, equipped with shoulder parrot and emphysema hose, exhales malice in an anti–*Lady Bird* evocation of working-class motherhood.

The Disaster Artist

ONE CAN NO LONGER ARGUE ABOUT THE SUCcess of Tommy Wiseau's ridiculous movie, *The Room*. Unlike, for instance, all of Edward D. Wood Jr.'s movies, to which it has been compared, *The Room* was a rich man's vanity project. Wiseau made it to get famous, and he has succeeded only slightly below the level of his wildest dreams. So it is fitting that now the Crown Prince of Vanity Projects, James Franco, has made a making-of movie about Wiseau and his antimasterpiece.

Like everything James Franco directs, *The Disaster Artist* is a work of appropriation art. The postcredits sequence, in which scenes from *The Room* are displayed side by side with scenes from this movie, admits as much. By now, Franco has done his Richard Prince act on Kenneth Anger, William Faulkner, the movie *Cruising*, John Steinbeck, River Phoenix, and Cormac McCarthy. Franco does show range in his tastes within the circumscribed genre of the classic masculine outré, but his films are where appropriation art has gone to die.

Call Me by Your Name

EARLY SCENES IN FRITZ LANG'S *METROPOLIS* (1927) show the adult children of the rich at play in a high-rise nature park referred to as "the Eternal Gardens." The gardens sit next to a pre-Riefenstahlian Olympic stadium called "the Club of the Sons," a monumental fitness center. In the gardens, scions and scionesses scamper about in futuristic deco haute couture inspired by prerevolutionary French fashion, while pursuing hookups and vague artistic endeavors. Social reality does not generally intrude on them. If such people were around today and got together to make a film, it would be *Call Me by Your Name*, and the garden where it takes place would be called "the Ageless Ambiguities."

Call Me by Your Name's strength is that it really does seem like the character played by Timothée Chalamet made the film himself. Who else but an actual actor-director would end his film by staring tearfully into a fireplace in winter because he's realized he will always be separate from other human beings, even though he spent last summer having sex in Lombardy with two kind and very attractive people (Armie Hammer and Esther Garrel)? The first Sufjan Stevens song that interrupts the movie so we can concentrate on nature for a few minutes also indicates the hand of Chalamet's Elio at work, as he remembers how beautiful it was and how nothing hurt, before he found out on that last trip that Hammer's Oliver was going to start dancing in public to "Love My Way" again.

Lady Bird

GRETA GERWIG'S *LADY BIRD* IS POPULATED BY actors who, like Gerwig herself, can do no wrong. That enhances the film's goody-goody quality, which falls over the movie like a warm blanket. This goodness and warmth emanate from Lady Bird (Saoirse Ronan) herself, who we know from the beginning is going to be OK even after she throws herself from a moving car during an argument with her mother (Laurie Metcalf). After that great scene, the movie settles into itself and becomes pleasant and forgiving, allowing Lady Bird to get away with a series of dick moves that are necessary to help her achieve her goal of getting out of Sacramento, California, and into a college in New York, Connecticut, or New Hampshire. Her short bursts of insensitivity also help her grow as a person, realize who her real friends are, and love her mom.

She and the film are nice to the nuns and priests who are her teachers but who are people too, with real lives and problems of their own. One of them (Lois Smith) sees right through Lady Bird. "You clearly love Sacramento," Sister Sarah Joan tells her, in a line I had trouble imagining a real person saying. I didn't mind the amount of self-identification the film courted in its audience, even though it was probably higher than in the audience who couldn't wait to see Liam Neeson in *The Commuter*. But having to hear Dave Matthews twice, as clever as that was in context, made me long for, I don't know, Napalm Death.

Logan

A LITTLE GIRL (DAFNE KEEN) SHOPLIFTS Pringles and what looks like a can of Four Loko Frost from a gas-station convenience store in *Logan*, which takes place in the year 2029. Movies have told us our future was dystopian, but it never occurred to me that things would get so bad that Four Loko would still be around a decade from now. Wolverine, by 2029, has deteriorated, too. His claws don't retract as quickly. Working as a limo driver in a black suit and tie, he's slower to recover from his wounds. Hugh

Helen DeWitt
SOME TRICK

"I like dry humor with a stick of dynamite strapped to it. *Some Trick*, by Helen DeWitt, is probably the most recent example. God, it's funny."
—Sloane Crosley,
The New York Times

"DeWitt reasserts herself as one of contemporary fiction's greatest minds in this dazzling collection of stories about misunderstood genius. A gem of a collection."
—**Publishers Weekly (starred review)**

NEW DIRECTIONS
NDBOOKS.COM

Jackman, who also has to play a younger re-cloned Wolverine double, plays the original Logan as a Humphrey Bogart character, world-weary and disinclined to get involved.

James Mangold directs this superhero action movie as part western, part noir. An eerie scene of horses loose on the highway foreshadows the film's dreamlike turn to cynical, gratuitous, and crazed bloodshed. When the little girl jumps on villains' backs and stabs them repeatedly in the head with her Wolverine claws, her frenzy reflects the Logan-like trauma of her past and predicts her violent future. The paradox of Wolverine is that he heals physically but not psychologically. He has always been the best counter to the trauma other action heroes brush off, especially human ones.

In *High Sierra* (1941), Bogart's aging gangster, Roy "Mad Dog" Earle, pays for an operation to fix a young woman's clubfoot before he goes up a mountain for his showdown with death. Here, Wolverine has to care for Laura, the girl, and save a busload of other children, future mutant heroes, before he confronts the same fate as Bogart. The movie is tough and unyielding before overexposure to these kids sets in. The warning in *Logan*'s trailer should have mentioned that it's not mayhem you have to worry about. Saccharin will get you in the end.

Roman J. Israel, Esq.

STUCK IN THE 1970S, IN A JACKET AND trousers tailored by Laurel and Hardy, Roman Israel (Denzel Washington), a lawyer newly out of work, doesn't fit in anywhere. It doesn't matter if the firms he goes to are sharky or woke. Young black lawyers scoff at his afro and dated phraseology (one scoffer is Esperanza Spalding), and middle-aged white lawyers (primarily Colin Farrell) abuse and pity him even after they've realized they can exploit his knowledge and experience. At night, he walks home (in LA!) carrying his heavy briefcase to an apartment building situated among new condo construction, like Jacques Tati's apartment in *Mon Oncle*. There, surrounded by framed photos of Angela Davis and Bayard Rustin, he makes his lonely dinner (peanut butter sandwiches) while listening to Gil Scott-Heron and Pharoah Sanders LPs on his hi-fi.

The Los Angeles of this film is murky—even the ocean water looks muddy—but writer-director Dan Gilroy makes it crystal clear that Roman is a man out of time. Hitting that characterization hard is the film's main strategy. Washington, with his usual excellence, succeeds in making Roman intriguing and admirable rather than pathetic. He plays him as a scholar or monk with a variety of subtle sub-Žižekian tics. When Roman gives up his quest for social justice and sells out, he buys new clothes, goes on a date, and spends a weekend in Santa Monica, a series of normal indulgences he is immediately punished for. The film, at that point, goes from potential comedy to gangster movie, and Roman suffers the same fate as Logan and Bogart. It's an unhappy ending, the wrong unhappy ending for this film. Earlier, the scene of *Goodfellas*-esque paranoia scored to the Chambers Brothers' "Time Has Come Today," a song that is longer than I remembered, signaled that things were not working out in this movie.

The Boss Baby

I'M NOT INTERESTED IN ANIMATED FEATURE films even though I fully understand that Miyazaki is a great artist and I have been told more than once that it is in things like *WALL-E* and *Toy Story 3* that we will locate the zeitgeist. As a child of the terrifying *Watership Down* era, I am surprised anew each time a *Lego Batman Movie* or a *Coco* captures the imagination of anyone I know over 12. Once, a while ago, I was walking to a two-screen movie theater down the street from me to see a French movie called *Strayed*. As I got closer I noticed an unexpectedly long line of adult couples waiting to buy tickets. *Wow*, I thought to myself, *there sure are a lot of André Téchiné fans in this neighborhood*. When I got to the theater I saw that *Finding Nemo* was playing on the other screen.

Last summer I was on an airplane to California that only had two movies showing. I watched the first one, *Paris Can Wait*, which starred Diane Lane as an American held captive in a car by a Frenchman, who drives her around against her will to show her architecture and make her eat snails. Lulled by the Provençal scenery, I decided to watch the second movie, which was *The Boss Baby*. Alec Baldwin played Lane's mostly absent husband in the first film, and now here he was again as the voice of the title cartoon baby. The animation in this movie was kind of 1960s-style, which seemed low-budget and delightful compared with the oppressive anthropomorphism of the animation I have witnessed in trailers for things like *Zootopia*. The principals here were human beings rather than talking yaks and sloths. So I watched it.

The plot began with the surprising revelation that babies are produced in factories and are, at heart, tiny fascistic CEOs concerned only with maximizing profit, which is the love they receive. They work to control every moment of everybody's lives by commandeering their attention so they ignore everything else. Everyone in the family works for the executive baby as his employee. That seemed right to me. And it's exactly the same way animated movies work in our culture today.

Combined with the film's witty conflation of labor as both giving birth and working for a corporation, *The Boss Baby* began with a lot of promise, like most babies. As usual, though, time passed and the baby got annoying. Baldwin's obnoxious CEO voicings, a gloss on his *Glengarry Glen Ross* and *30 Rock* performances, got tiresome as the movie became more frenetic. Chase scenes involved Elvis impersonators, which have not only been done to death but also depend on a real person doing them. The joke is the talent gap between the impersonator's ability to play Elvis and the glory that was Elvis himself, and I wasn't interested in contemplating a cartoon of a cartoon of a cartoon. I made it all the way through *The Boss Baby*, however, newly strong in my conviction that I don't need to see another animated feature for a long, long time. It was like getting a measles vaccination.

Three Billboards Outside Ebbing, Missouri

IF PEOPLE ARE COMPARING YOUR HIT MOVIE to *Crash* (not the Cronenberg one), you have a problem. If half the people who see your movie find it racist, you might want to address that in print somewhere, maybe in a publication with a little more heft than *Entertainment Weekly* or *Deadline Hollywood*. If giving interviews to places like that also serves as awards-season self-promotion, you're starting to make the situation worse. Martin McDonagh is an eminent playwright as well as a screenwriter and film director. He probably could have found a place to write about his movie if he had wanted to.

For now, we only have what's on the screen. McDonagh's subjects are violence, sin, and redemption. The overlooked priest scene in *Three Billboards* is a key to the film. When Mildred (Frances McDormand) is insulting the priest (Nick Searcy) for being a useless part of a corrupt organization, she is expressing the film's theme: *My God, my God, why have you forsaken me?*

What McDonagh believes in is storytelling. Storytelling, like Catholicism, can be plunked down anywhere, and through sheer force it will conquer. So it doesn't matter to McDonagh if he finds himself in Belgium, Joshua Tree National Park, or Missouri: he will tell his story with forceful dialogue and dramatic violence, and he will get his point across—*Repent, sinners!*

At the end of *Three Billboards*, Mildred and Dixon (Sam Rockwell) find themselves in the coy limbo of possible redemption, the same place McDonagh has resided since he's been called to account. If he had not let the sin of pride interfere and had, for instance, cut the pious, godlike speech Sheriff Willoughby (Woody Harrelson) delivers to the racist Dixon in voiceover from beyond the grave, he would not have come off as so manipulative and clueless. A little humility goes a long way, as Saint Darryl F. Zanuck, who is depicted holding a red pencil, once wrote in a memo.

The Shape of Water

ONE THING GUILLERMO DEL TORO'S *THE Shape of Water* has not been accused of is racism. This reimagining of *Creature from the Black Lagoon* (1954) as a cold war love story goes out of its way to be inclusive. In addition to the species-fluid fish-man (Doug Jones), it features a mute lead character (Sally Hawkins) who can't talk because she is the victim of abuse; a gay character who loves movie musicals (Richard Jenkins); a black cleaning lady (Octavia Spencer) who is sick of her husband; a dissident Soviet scientist (Michael Stuhlbarg); and the entire civil rights movement, which is asked to leave a lunch counter. The white men in the film represent The Man in no uncertain terms. Michael Shannon is an abusive torturer who has bad sex with his wife and loves his big Cadillac more than her. The assorted military men and spies around him, both Americans and Russians, concern themselves only with winning and killing.

Despite all the positive representation of marginalized people and the explicit condemnation of men who work for the government, the film takes a gleeful delight in torture and pain. Often morose, it livens up when Shannon is tasering the fish-man or engaged in bloodletting and beatings. It is a kind of horror movie, it's true, but those scenes overpower the film's invocation of desperate forbidden love. When Shannon tortures Stuhlbarg, del Toro revels in the pain the film's villain inflicts on a weak, dying man. In this world of pain, escape into fantasy is the only recourse. The film ends by illustrating the reason W. C. Fields gave for not drinking water: fish fuck in it.

The Big Sick

WHAT DIFFERENTIATES THIS LIGHTWEIGHT rom-com from others is that in this one the girlfriend is in a coma and it's based on a true story. Screenwriter and star Kumail Nanjiani did sit with his real-life future spouse, Emily V. Gordon, who cowrote the screenplay and is here played by Zoe Kazan, while she was unconscious in the hospital. I was surprised there were not more scenes of Nanjiani at Emily's bedside delivering comedy monologues to her unconscious form, which would have been the ultimate in post–*When Harry Met Sally* romance. But it takes the daring of an Albert Brooks for that. It's not something producer Judd Apatow would condone. In the same way, the Smiths song was kept as far away from *The Big Sick* as possible.

Phantom Thread

BACK IN THE 1990S, I PREDICTED—MAYBE IT was after I saw *Happiness*—that sound design would soon get so extreme that there would be a movie in which we heard not just the sound of salt leaving a saltshaker, but also the sound of it *hitting the food*. With *Phantom Thread*, that day has come. From the shaving scene at the beginning with its *scrape* across the cheekbones of Reynolds Woodcock (Daniel Day-Lewis), it was clear this was going to be a film in which sound was prominent. We learn that Reynolds is alert to noises and easily distracted by them. The movie is full of typically memorable Paul Thomas Anderson dialogue that demonstrates how easily disturbed Woodcock is. Toast buttered too loudly at breakfast, for instance, is "like you rode a horse across the room."

Since I have a touch of Roderick Usher in me, I am sympathetic to Woodcock's bristling. As sound design has become more intrusive in movies, my relationship with it has deteriorated. While in real life I do not notice audible eating and drinking, in the movies every moment of intimate conversation over a drink has become a symphony of slurp I can't ignore. People attracted to working in sound design no doubt have sensitive ears. But directors have got to dial this down. Either that or ban breakfast cereal from their movies. In *Logan*, the noise of Dafne Keen eating cornflakes sounded like a recording of John Goodman on a gravel road in work boots. I think she ate one of her teeth. The literalism of this kind of sound design, in which every action depicted on-screen must have an accompanying sound, even if you would never notice that sound in real life, is as distracting as an unasked-for pot of tea shuffled into the room when you are working.

In *Phantom Thread*, Anderson makes the film about that. Woodcock must get over his neurotic sensitivities so he can get on with life and enjoy being fed poison mushrooms by the woman he loves. Sounds become a joke played on this demanding soft-spoken man who is overly conscious of his talent. Romance in *Phantom Thread* swings between gothic horror and comedy. In the end it is hard to figure out what exactly has saved the House of Woodcock from the fate of the House of Usher. Whatever it is, Anderson's sense of macabre humor won't allow Alma (Vicky Krieps) to kill Reynolds. It's weirder to watch him squirm.

The Square

LATELY THE ACTING IN TV COMMERCIALS HAS gotten really good. The other night I saw an ad for some company that helps people get rid of timeshares they don't want anymore and I thought, *Man, that was great, really affecting.* That could have been an episode of *Togetherness* on HBO, if that was still on. Car commercials are particularly satisfying these days. Thirty-second-long one-acts with movie-level production design and cinematography, each one is a humanist masterpiece featuring quality acting that fits right in with streaming drama. In one, a wedding party gets caught in the rain and they can't walk to the outdoor altar so they have to jump in their mini-SUV to get there. You really get a feel for the relationships between these four people in that thirty seconds. Car manufacturers know our little victories are hard-won. Automakers just get us. In other ads, the family drama of auto insurance plays out just as insightfully.

Film criticism has become really humanist, too. The moral arguments against movies including *Good Time* and *The Square* from some of our most prominent movie reviewers really touched me last year. I didn't agree with them at all, but I was moved by the way these critics shooed away potential viewers from such unpleasant fare. I could feel their internal debate as they worried over the existence of such ethically compromised, mean-spirited films. Our top critics, in recent years, have pioneered a new form of panning movies, a soft pan in which they gently wring their hands and conclude that it's just too bad certain things exist in this world. Some of these critics mentioned how a film's formal qualities, its careful framing, the coldness of its photography or its acting revealed a lack of soul. Movies like that do not offer solutions to our present predicament. They just excoriate the bourgeoisie for no reason. After dismissing such films, these critics then turn back to the business of writing weekly roundups of the 1001 Things Streaming on Netflix This Week You Have to See Before You Die.

Ruben Östlund's *The Square* is harsh, sarcastic, unsparing, threatening, unfair, and messed up. While it is formally rather controlled, it is also a cauldron of bad feelings and bad faith. It illustrates, with great patience and wit, something I once read that the artist Kurt Schwitters wrote: "Banality is bourgeois style." The quotation fits this movie, which takes place in a museum of contemporary art. Östlund depicts audience reactions of various kinds, in a shock-series of unforgettable scenes that rankled some critics. These scenes replicate the conditions under which art is viewed in the West, and the way artists are interviewed and feted, and appear in the movie in contrast to the way successful administrators in this administered world curate the poverty and crime they experience outside their galleries.

The square in the film is an outdoor art installation that is described, repeatedly, as "a sanctuary of trust and caring." At the end of the movie, a group of young Swedish cheerleaders performs their routine at a cheerleading competition in a white square against a black background. The squares in the movie double the movie screen. Östlund's was the only movie I saw this year that gave the lie to all the safe spaces most movies design to lure audiences and get them to shout, "Go team!" These spaces within fictional spaces, car interiors in car commercials, get safer and safer. Critics guide readers to the safe ones, steering them away from danger. +

NICHOLAS DAMES
Coming in from the Cold

John le Carré. *A Legacy of Spies*. Viking, 2017.
David Ignatius. *The Quantum Spy*. W. W. Norton & Company, 2017.
Daniel Silva. *House of Spies*. Harper, 2017.

OVER THE PAST YEAR, IT HAS BECOME IMPOSsible to ignore the fact that spy terminology has infiltrated everyday discourse. One does not have to be an intelligence analyst to speak confidently—or at least with knowing, giddy pseudo-confidence—of cut-outs and assets, *dezinformatsiya* and *kompromat*. Politics is less about speeches and party platforms than about declassified files, leaks from grand jury testimonies, and the "dossier." Collectively, we long for interrogation rather than debate; we yearn for the proofs that only a clandestine bureaucracy could offer. What did the President know and when did he know it? What was in the contents of that secret meeting? Only the spies—secreted in tapped wires and behind hidden cameras— know the truth. It all has had a childish glee to it, as well as a childish comfort if the spy world seemed narrower than the one we were used to inhabiting, its confines promised protection and some kind of order, a durable state if not a deep one. So it was that I, assailed and assuaged by agency talk, read spy novels. It was 2017, and I was in need of reassurance. I also needed to know what that reassurance was costing me.

To debrief: there are in the world real spies, in possession of real secrets, hired by real organizations with fantastic—if, according to their recipients, forever inadequate—budgets, who may prevent harm but also, very often, perform it. (John le Carré, writing in 1991, on the cold war intelligence services of the US and the UK: "Both services would have done much less damage to their countries, moral and financial, if they had simply been disbanded.") But the spy is always also a fiction. It isn't simply that the spy relies on "covers," or fictions, for their work. It is that no profession has greater traffic with the business of fiction writing itself. *Studies in Intelligence*, the in-house and partly classified academic journal of the CIA, reviews spy fiction with a connoisseur's discernment for shoddy verisimilitude and thematic flimsiness. Put aside the covert funding of postwar writers by CIA fronts like the Congress for Cultural Freedom. Spy novelists themselves are routinely ex-agents or intelligence personnel—most famously John le Carré, a.k.a. David Cornwell; Ian Fleming; and Graham Greene—while in the US we have the less illustrious examples of ex–CIA officer and Nixonian ratfucker E. Howard Hunt, or blown agent Valerie Plame; and if they are not former agents they are journalists who cover the world of secret intelligence. So tight is the relationship that in burying myself in spy novels I became a cliché of agency life itself, like Robert Redford in *Three Days of the Condor*, working at the American Literary Historical Society, reading thrillers for plot elements and reporting to his superiors on his discoveries.

SPY NOVELS NARROW the world to the dimensions of agencies and their rivals or targets. They are realist in texture, never experimental, resolutely focused. Characters become their functions: agent, handler, mole, director, or operational head. Like Balzac in *La Comédie humaine*, spy novelists reuse characters: though the plots are byzantine, the people are familiar. The locales are far-flung, but in an enclosed, airless way: casinos, hotels, safe houses, clubs, airports, and passport checkpoints. (The spy blends the solitary tourist's isolation with the native's blasé familiarity.) There is, of course, the lingo, which manages to be well-known while parading its exclusivity: walk-ins, babysitters, sleepers; to be burned, rolled up, exfiltrated. Spies in spy novels also read other spy novels—Olen Steinhauer's Milo Weaver reads le Carré; le Carré's Jerry Westerby reads Greene and Conrad as Saigon falls. Thus the weariness of the literate, worldly spy: there is nothing new under the sun.

The limits of its thought-world defined, spy fiction comfortably becomes a literature of expertise—*the* literature, perhaps, of the knowledge worker. Written by former participants and experts, thanks to the conventional alibi that the secrets of their world can only be expressed allegorically or fictionally, the spy novel gives us a world with handles. How-to is as important to the spy novel as it is to Odysseus or Robinson Crusoe, and evoking it is one of the spy novelist's most fundamental tasks. In David Ignatius's *The Quantum Spy*, the novel's putative villain—a mole inside the CIA who passes her Chinese masters scientific information out of the ideological principle that science should not respect borders—is caught, but arranges a plea agreement in which she writes "a manual on tradecraft": "She wrote it in the form of a novel, which captured what she had come to understand about intelligence.... Ford's book was circulated widely within the intelligence community. It gave Ford what she had sought through her career but had only achieved after she became a foreign spy, which was a reputation as a brilliant and intuitive operations officer."

Tradecraft: the spy's professional fetish. The dead drop, the brush pass, the dry clean. Knowing how to evade surveillance, make a convincing legend, encrypt a message. Every action in the spy novel is done badly or well, clumsily or skillfully. The mystique of tradecraft lies somewhere between secrecy and simplicity, the suspicion a reader has that one could, with training, also do these things well. So wrote William Hood, former OSS and CIA officer, who in his 1982 memoir, *Mole*, asserted: "Tradecraft may seem mysterious to outsiders, but it is little more than a compound of commonsense, experience, and certain almost universally accepted security practices.... The fact is that tradecraft is like arithmetic: it has been around for centuries. The basics are easy to learn and good texts can be found in any library." It is also, in its way, fun; when the American Oulipo member Harry Mathews was mistaken for a CIA agent in the early 1970s—as he writes in *My Life in CIA*—he played along: he invented a false travel agency to act as cover, commissioned maps woven into shawls, and left enigmatic chalk marks on Parisian walls.

The neutral respect for a job done well, the professional's code, overrides every other consideration. What is the first thing Robert Ludlum's amnesiac assassin in *The Bourne Identity* learns about his identity? "If he had learned anything about himself during the past forty-eight hours it was that he *was* a professional. Of what he had no idea, but the status was not debatable." James Bond himself, in *On Her Majesty's Secret Service*, observes his abductor, the Corsican ganglord Marc-Ange Draco: "James Bond sipped his drink and watched the other man's face with respect. This was one of the great professionals of the world!"

The ethic of tradecraft is larger than the items that usually constitute it; it saturates the lifeworld of the spy novel. It is dedicated, without irony, to the *art de vivre*. In Fleming, one learns how to play chemin de fer, how to ski, how to seduce. In the work of Howard Hunt, CIA figures cultivate the high-cold-war manner. They smoke pipes and plot grand strategy, are skilled men of action who mingle headmaster with buccaneer in the manner of the OSS. David Morgan, protagonist of Hunt's *The Hargrave Deception*, is the fantasy: New England boarding-school boy turned CIA agent, fluent in various languages, adept at killing, intimate with grand hotels and secret restaurants in various European capitals, always sure of what wine to order. Like a child trapped with an irritatingly well-informed adult, Hunt's reader learns how to fish for dolphin (and that "dolphin was the finest eating-fish in the Caribbean"), how to wrap sidearms in condoms to keep them from corroding in salt air, and how to properly make scrambled eggs, "with a splash of cream and two drops of Worcestershire."

The *art de vivre*, of course, aims to make everything knowable; and a knowable world shades imperceptibly into a world of stereotypes:

> Later they feasted on broiled dolphin and fried *platano*, drinking a chilled chablis-type Paternina that Morgan had come to know in Spain. Afterward he sipped Felipe II brandy while Marisa sang to her guitar, and toward ten o'clock they went to bed where they fell asleep in each other's arms, moonlight filtering through the slatted blinds across their bodies and the bed.

The cartoon earnestness of Hunt's Floridian *espagnolisme*, the fussiness about the proper drink and consort: it offers narcotic comfort. To the spy, no choice is accidental; everything is deliberate. It's as if the spy—or the spy's narrator—wants to weep at the loveliness, and transience, of well-arranged things.

This intensely throttled emotion is a male sentimentality that gives the spy novel its tonality. Few female characters, vanishingly few female authors. So often the spy is fatherless, father haunted, in search of a father figure, or otherwise burdened by the weight of patriarchal lineage: le Carré's Peter Guillam, his father a French Resistance hero murdered by the Gestapo, finds a second father in George Smiley; Steinhauer's Weaver, his father ex-KGB, reemployed in a secret intelligence bureau at the UN, is himself sterile. The service women render as guides to the male spy's self-discovery is classical in its simplicity. How else to explain Jason Bourne, who abducts a young woman who then devotes herself to making sense of his past and making him whole? Or take the textbook case of Graham Greene's *The Quiet American*, where a homosocial struggle over a Vietnamese woman ends in the narrator's strangled quasi apology to his dead rival, an American spy: "Everything had gone right with me since he had died, but how I wished there existed someone to whom I could say that I was sorry."

No genre is more masculine than the spy story, more impervious to revisionary feminist versions. Still, it attempts to inoculate itself against charges of bravado, because it depends on the poignancy of male failure and insufficiency with pitying self-regard. It is filled with male failures and betrayals; with men who let other men down. The paradigm is Kim Philby: the charismatic friend one loved and trusted, color in a gray world, who takes the color with him when he flees into an outed mole's ignominy.

What glamour male heartache still has is suffused with the pathos of obsolescence and the struggle to keep current. Sometimes a cultural code in even the most au courant of these novels would stride confidently out of a couple of generations back: "Flanagan did look like a perpetual undergraduate," Ignatius writes. "He was dressed, as ever, in a tweed jacket, chino pants, and his Bass loafers." Not just a male kind of story, it is a middle-aged one.

As I read these novels in public and stumbled across sentences like these, I began to feel self-conscious. It is the literature of Father's Day gifts and the half-populated shelves of vacation cottages, the leisure reading of think-tank apparatchiks, as smugly incurious in its purview as a well-paid pundit. Yet spy novels are also rights-optioned as thrilling crowd-pleasers and reviewed as serious geopolitical statements. This least cool of genres retains an aura of suavity, insider expertise, cosmopolitanism. (The spy is traditionally of dual nationality or ethnicity: Bond is half Scot and half Swiss.) Could any other popular narrative genre be so given to a critique of Americanism and forgiven for it, celebrated for it? Le Carré's well-known left-leaning politics are closer to the rule than the exception; American spies are naïfs or pallid sidekicks, playing Felix Leiter to various Bonds, in need of British adroitness or, as in Daniel Silva's Gabriel Allon novels, an Israeli gruffness about moral niceties. Like a Henry James heroine traveling on a false passport, the American spy is continually wandering with passionate ignorance into complicated foreign snares.

The spy novel is silly, when it isn't claustrophobic; urgent, but with an urgency severed from any link to the various impending geopolitical alarms—German invasion, Soviet infiltration, Chinese technological advancement, terrorist havoc—that the genre's history continually sounds. There is something in the condition of existence in these novels, the presuppositions of their world, in other words, that seems, finally, to be at once illness and cure.

SINCE THERE HAVE been states, there have been spies. Herodotus tells of Greek spies who infiltrated the court of Xerxes. The modern spy story, however, seems to have its origins in the early 19th century, in the wake of the Napoleonic Wars. In Stendhal's *The Red and the Black*, there is an inconsequential episode of international espionage. The novel's parvenu, Julien Sorel, has been taken on as the secretary to the Marquis de la Mole, who has organized a secret group of reactionaries conniving at the restoration of prerevolutionary norms. But this coterie of plotters needs to make contact with foreign assistance.

Julien craves mentors. He also has a talent for memorization, which makes him the ideal courier. He is tasked with memorizing four pages of notes on a secret meeting; disguised as a fop traveling for leisure; and, at a mysterious chateau inhabited by figures he takes to be priests, given a false passport. His handler, the marquis, worries about infiltration within their group—and on his trip Julien is drugged and has his papers searched by enemies who seem to have been tipped off to his route—but Julien nonetheless arrives safely in foreign territory, where he flashes a prearranged signal to his contact, who might well be, of all people, Prince Metternich. He is led by the prince to a dingy inn to repeat his message, then has to lie low in Strasbourg for twelve days while waiting for a reply, which he duly returns to the marquis and his coconspirators.

If this is a recognizably modern story, it is because of the peculiar linkage of precise tradecraft and broad political impulse. There is the detail—the watch Julien takes out with practiced ordinariness as his princely contact passes on the street, the disguise that fools the alert border guards—and there are the windy generalizations of the reactionary group that Julien, privately a radical, willingly serves. This is the doubled allure: the meticulous techne of navigating a hostile world undetected, linked to the ability to see the secret levers of power, the table of irascible and dangerous men who, be it in a Parisian salon or a Langley boardroom, see the big picture. (As Fleming called them in the opening pages of *Casino Royale*, "those few cold brains that made the whole show work.") It is seductive enough to get the parvenu to risk his life on behalf of exactly the stultifying principle he has otherwise tried to dismantle: maintaining the balance of power. The spy is put in service of *preservation*; and yet that preservation is somehow also thrilling. That paradox gives the secret agent their moral ambivalence, long before Greene or le Carré made it famous. The spy craves the thrill of making sure, with professional élan, that nothing changes.

From Stendhal onward, from Metternich's balance-of-power Europe to realpolitik and into the age of mutual deterrence, the spy story's narrative bones are uncannily similar. It tends to start in a place of becalmed retreat, a literal "safe house" where the spymaster pretends that history has stopped. Le Carré's Smiley is repeatedly dragged from his scholarly pursuit of baroque German literature; Silva's Gabriel Allon labors quietly at restoring old master canvases. Patient, hypercivilized men master arcana in a setting—the research library, the conservation lab, the desk job—where nothing happens, as they try to forget their past, romance, or sense of duty. Then, things lurch into action. Peril is imminent. The agency is compromised by the Soviets from within (le Carré's famous Karla trilogy). An Iraqi terrorist mastermind named Saladin has begun to carry out attacks across Europe (the Allon novels). The Chinese have a source inside the CIA, providing them access to the quantum computing secrets of the US tech industry (*Quantum Spy*). The agency is galvanized. Or—with the invernal coda to a long series—the protagonist emerges from retirement and gathers the band again for a lucrative farewell tour.

What matters, very often, is the *mole*—whether to flush it out or place it. Along with the father or mentor, the mole is the key function of the spy story. Gabriel Allon and the Mossad have to place a mole inside terror networks in Syria and the south of France; Ignatius's CIA operatives have to find the mole in their own ranks. Le Carré popularized the term, and in his first major novel, 1963's *The Spy Who Came in from the Cold*, the plot function is doubled: Smiley places a false defector inside East Germany, one intended to be easily unmasked, as a ruse to protect the real MI6 mole. But it is a function as old as the spy story itself, dating back at least to Joseph Conrad's 1907 *The Secret Agent*, which narrated the attempt of a mole inserted into London revolutionary circles—as an agent provocateur for a foreign power and also an informer for the British police—to initiate a terrorist bombing in order to spur British repression of those circles. The mole offers the spy story its mise en abyme: their every act is at once real and false, an embodied double negative; they threaten at every moment to double or triple themselves.

The mole is a function of the past—generally speaking the betrayal has already happened, has always already had its disastrous effect. One only finds Philby, Burgess, Maclean, or Ames after they have done their work. What the spy does is reconstruct the damage that has been done and stop the bleeding. The open secret of so many spy novels is how little can happen within them, aside from the constant succession

Performance Space New York
East Village Series

Kathy Acker, BRUJAS, Bjarne Melgaard, Yve Laris Cohen, Women's History Museum, Diamanda Galas, Sarah Michelson, Penny Arcade, Tiona Nekkia McClodden, Ishmael Houston-Jones/Dennis Cooper/Chris Cochrane

Through June 30

PerformanceSpaceNewYork.org
150 First Avenue, New York, NY 10009

of interrogations, a type scene that is retrospective. The spy novel gives us the drama of research (files gathered, traces read), a forward momentum that is also a backward pull. But the irreversibility of time hangs over the espionage operation. As Harry Mathews was told by a French intelligence official, "there is no way to unrecruit an agent."

The mole is also a creature of interiors, of getting "inside" and being "blown"; it is the personification of the spy world's endogamy, which involves moving into smaller and smaller spaces. Le Carré, as ever the most alert to his world's schematics, has Smiley arrive at the classic metaphor in *Tinker Tailor Soldier Spy*: "one of those wooden Russian dolls that open up, revealing one person inside the other, and another inside him." Here the spy novel departs from its social-realist cousins, even the police procedural: crime gathers a large web of social interactions; espionage remains sealed off from the world at large. Cause and effect do not ramify outward, in horizontal networks; they move from big, those cold brains in a small room, to little, in a vertical cascade. The answer is inside, but it is also *obvious*, a purloined letter too large for any other genre's frame. Even if the novel's mechanics are complexly baroque, the knotty explanations of the plot finally bend back around, in the genre's post-Euclidian logic, to something truly unsubtle. Why, in Steinhauer's *The Tourist*, is Milo Weaver called back to active duty? Nothing less, and also nothing more complicated, than the need to maintain US hegemony over China. "But the answer that gets the gold star is empire," he is told. "It's about the big picture. That's all it's ever about."

Weaver works for the "Department of Tourism," an elite cadre of black ops specialists run out of an innocuous Manhattan office. Like any high-ranking professional, Weaver's antagonists are other professionals at his level—particularly "the Tiger," the nom de guerre of the field's most well-known figure, whom Weaver corners at the novel's outset. But the Tiger is already dying of poison, and he reveals that he too had been a Tourist, recently hired to kill a Sudanese Islamic radical—and then himself nudged toward death in order to cover the traces. Who gave the order to kill the cleric, and then kill the assassin, is Weaver's opening puzzle. Steinhauer's *syuzhet* proceeds through the usual interrogations, with their static dynamic of question and answer, thrust and parry, and the familiar psychological awkwardness around someone finally telling the truth—as well as some near-miss escapes for Weaver to provide thrills. But the *fabula* is beyond psychology or individual will: the Tiger had been hired by a Russian oligarch, working as a front for the CIA, to kill the Sudanese radical in order to destabilize the Sudanese government and force China to involve itself to protect its oil source there, all to create an Iraq-style quagmire for China—a game not even plotted by the CIA itself, but by a senator. As Weaver muses, "each fragment of order we find is connected to the other fragments in a meta-order that is controlled by a meta-meta-order."

The great realist novel diffuses, the spy novel concentrates. Everything leads back to China; to competition for oil or computing speed; to globalized jihad; to SMERSH or to the Black Stone, the organization contracted by the Germans to help in the invasion of England in John Buchan's *The Thirty-Nine Steps*. From that vast but single cause comes the complexity of the spy story's chess moves. And that cause has a momentum that can be resisted, but not reversed. The successful espionage operation disables a terrorist plot, disrupts an infiltration, fends off disaster for another day. No wonder the spy is so often a closet pedant, like Smiley or Allon in love with the past, conservative in temperament if not always in politics. "Unhappy Europe!" the spymaster of *The Secret Agent* declares on his deathbed. "Thou shalt perish by the moral insanity of thy children!"

The spy *despairs*. The epiphany of Jerry Westerby, the hero of le Carré's underrated 1977 *The Honourable Schoolboy*: "For a moment it was all one vanishing world; here, Phnom Penh, Saigon, London—a world on loan, with the creditors standing at the door, and Jerry himself, in some unfathomable way, a part of the debt that was owed." Even the spy's sexiness is bathetic. Take the *mode retro* FX series *The Americans*: two KGB castaways in the early 1980s, moles in American life, always playing from behind, hoping to keep the cold war game going a little longer even as we know it won't. They spend their secret nights out fucking some echt suburban single person—a lonely executive secretary, an engineer at a bar—not out of desire but out of some sad, misguided attempt to keep the Soviet past alive.

The big picture is there to be seen, but for agency men, it offers no consolation. Le Carré's operatives, raised for greater things, find themselves handling the external affairs of a small island. At their worst these moments have a flimsy grandeur: Allon's mentor Ari Shamron, looking out over Lake Kinneret, muses that "the Jews had managed to pull off one of history's greatest second acts" but that "they were already on borrowed time"; Milo Weaver's boss Tom Grainger muses on "Roman outposts in hostile lands." Such moments seem meant to have a heady and bitter savor, redolent of adult sophistication: all empires are one, and you know this best when the end is in sight.

If the British became identified with spy fiction in the 20th century, it is not because, as some have it, of a native tendency toward deception and secrecy. In the agency, they're wised up and they know nothing lasts.

A POSTULATE, THEN: the spy novel, that peculiar 20th-century genre with roots as far back as early 19th-century reaction, has as its ideological dominant a pessimistic, fatalistic nationalism. Think of a world where the revolution will never come—the world Julien Sorel's clandestine employers try to bring into being; that is the world of spies. Instead of rapid change, the glacial melt of national power. If you doubt the sensitivity of intelligence analysts to the contours of a world like this, read the declassified 1985 CIA report on the demise of French high theory ("France: Defection of the Leftist Intellectuals") and its replacement by the "new philosophy" of André Glucksmann and Bernard-Henri Lévy. The report quotes an anonymous figure at Paris Nanterre, a center of leftist theory, as saying, "This is the permanent nonrevolution." The agency, any agency, doesn't want to tamper with that state of affairs, it wants to preserve it in amber—despite its lingering, melancholy awareness of the world's entropy. This is the importance of le Carré's shabby spy milieu; its slow, dingy decay literalizes the genre's historical position rather than revises it.

Fatalistic about what he serves, the spy is cool—both engaged and detached. The code is already present as early as Kipling's *Kim*, another early spy story, about the recruitment and training of an Irish urchin into a British spy combating Russian influence in Central Asia, although it is presented in split form. Kim oscillates between the breathless excitement of working for the Sahibs—mastering tradecraft, pursuing the Great Game against Russian spies—and the profundity of following his mentor the Lama, a Buddhist monk seeking release from the cycle of rebirth, who offers a world of quasi-stoic detachment. In Kipling, Kim's two worlds are largely a binary, in competition with each other: exuberant, restless adventure against the idea that "all doing is evil," the plotted thriller against static philosophizing. Kim must choose, although he manages for the most part to keep deferring his choice. The later spy novel, on the other hand, merges the two. Doing *is* evil, and the spy reluctantly engages in "doing," or plot—if with a certain embarrassed relish—to keep the world's balance. The traditional spy is both actor *and* contemplative, and when they are drawn into action it is unwillingly.

The ethos of this historical condition, in Western terms, is a muted stoicism, and the spy novel, of all our narrative genres, might be our best guide to it. The Victorians had the novel of religious doubt; we have the spy novel, our story of forlorn service to a vanishing ideal. Instead of the church, we have the agency—that compromised, alluring, ridiculous, frightening, and still durable institution, dedicated to ideals that seem no longer viable. The agency may in fact be the villain in most postwar spy stories: it tries to eliminate Jason Bourne, it traduces its employees like Milo Weaver or David Morgan, it cannot be trusted by George Smiley. But one hates most where one has loved. The Service, be it MI6, CIA, or Mossad, is always being dismantled, always needs reconstructing, never seems healthy, never quite collapses—there's a background sense of some constant partial recovery from a prior disaster. How can you continue to perform your duty to such a flawed thing, a thing whose damage is usually more evident than its healing?

This is not just the agency; it is the liberal order the agency has shielded. That has been

A place full of exciting new releases and beloved classics; hidey-holes for children and books to read in them; gifts for friends and loved ones; picture books; poetry and essays; cookbooks; readings and panels every night of the week; togetherness; and, yes, magic.

Books Are Magic

225 Smith Street

Brooklyn, NY 11231

718-246-BOOK

booksaremagic.net

@booksaremagicbk

John le Carré's insight, and it is Smiley—forever the anti-Bond, the bespectacled small shabby master of counterintelligence—who acts as the last saint of the liberal West, who doubts his cause even as he pursues it. In the Karla trilogy he is both implacable and full of misgivings. He tries to snare his ideologically driven Soviet nemesis while having no strong counterideology to offer. Once, Smiley does trap Karla, in a Delhi interrogation room; but Karla cannot be turned. "Did he not believe, for example, that the political generality was meaningless?" he remembers asking his counterpart. "That only the particular in life had value for him now?" Le Carré's thoughtful spies have a way of sounding like Niebuhr as rewritten by George Eliot, with the added quality of being unsure of their own position. "I behaved like a soft fool," was Smiley's verdict. "The very archetype of a flabby Western liberal. But I would rather be my kind of fool than his, for all that."

Fine enough for the cold war, since Smiley's unpersuaded half-faith ends up prevailing: Karla defects, the hard yields to the soft but persistent. Last year, Smiley returned, in *A Legacy of Spies*, le Carré at 85 extending Smiley's life to cover essentially the entire 20th century. The novel is an exercise in amplifying the spy novel's usual retrospection: the surviving children of the two British nationals (one an agent, one an unwitting coconspirator) killed in *The Spy Who Came in from the Cold* have decided, at some point around the turn of the century, to sue for reparations. Aging former spy Peter Guillam is hauled into the agency's garish new Vauxhall Cross headquarters to be interrogated, every past indiscretion and mistake flayed open by agency counsel for whom the cold war is only a childhood memory. Additional documents are brought forward, deepening the story of the 1963 novel. But only Smiley can offer more than documentary details: a moral defense of the human cost of that long-gone operation. And so in the novel's final pages Guillam finds him, in a Freiburg reading room, alone.

What now is the creed of one of his century's greatest spies—what was all that tradecraft good for?

"For world peace, whatever *that* is? Yes, yes, of course. There will be no war, but in the struggle for peace not a stone will be left standing, as our Russian friends used to say." He fell quiet, only to rally more vigorously: "Or was it all in the great name of *capitalism*? God forbid. Christendom? God forbid again."

A sip of wine, a smile of puzzlement, directed not at me, but at himself.

"So was it all for *England*, then?" he resumed. "There was a time, of course there was. But *whose* England? *Which* England? England all alone, a citizen of nowhere? I'm a European, Peter. If I had a mission—if I was ever aware of one beyond our business with the enemy, it was to Europe. If I was heartless, I was heartless for Europe. If I had an unattainable ideal, it was of leading Europe out of her darkness towards a new age of reason. I have it still."

The Brexit irony draped over the passage—if like some Tiresias of MI6 he had lived to see it, Smiley's heartbreak at the vote would have been mortal—only partially conceals the paradoxes of his confession. Espionage is grubby nationalism for idealistic cosmopolitans, ends-justify-the-means calculation on behalf of sweet reason's balance. It is both utterly disabused and almost innocently idealistic, if one can idealize something so purely notional. No wonder Smiley looks puzzled at himself.

He isn't so unusual. Spies are devoted to the old world—whatever old world one believes in—once it becomes clear the old world is setting. In this, the Marquis de la Mole and Smiley are not so very different. Wistful, self-doubting, almost despairing idealism and the disenchanted exercise of skill: if we're all spies now, it doesn't mean we commit ourselves to any particular politics; it means we commit ourselves to this mood. It's the kind of refuge that suffocates. +

NAMARA SMITH
Both Sides Now

Zadie Smith. *Feel Free: Essays*. Penguin Press, 2018.
Zadie Smith. *Swing Time*. Penguin Press, 2016.

ZADIE SMITH'S FIRST NOVEL, *WHITE TEETH*, begins with its main character, a middle-aged British man named Archie Jones, trying to commit suicide in a parked car. Up to this point, he has concluded, his time on earth has been essentially meaningless: he is a divorced, childless professional paper folder with limited career prospects and few friends. His most eventful moment came in the army during World War II, but he was posted to the front lines too late to do any fighting. Since then, his life has been a series of failures. Even his suicide attempt is less an act of will than an effect of randomness. He flips a coin, his habitual way of making decisions, and when it comes up tails—death—he prepares to go through with it. Archie's plan is thwarted twice over: first, by the halal butcher who finds Archie sitting in his car in front of the butcher's store and warns Archie that his property isn't licensed for suicide; then, later that day, by Clara Bowden, the statuesque 19-year-old Jamaican girl he meets at a New Year's party he has wandered into. Within six weeks, Archie and Clara are married. By the end of the year, Archie has become a father for the first time, at 47.

One way to read Archie's story, and *White Teeth* as a whole, is as an allegory for the revitalization of the UK by the waves of immigrants from its former colonies during the mid-20th century. The first impression the book gives is of tremendous energy. Set in the working-class London neighborhood where Smith grew up, it is animated by an obvious delight in the incongruous juxtapositions of different voices and cultures: the second-generation immigrant children with "first and last names on a direct collision course," the Iraqi brothers named Abdul-Colin and Abdul-Mickey who operate a bar called O'Connell's Poolroom, the Bangladeshi lesbian who sews bondage gear for a sex shop, the Jamaican matriarch who falls in love with a Vespa-riding scenester, the Muslim fundamentalist who loves *Goodfellas*.

The daughter of a white British father and a black Jamaican mother, Smith herself was a living symbol of this transformation, a combination of author and subject that helped make *White Teeth* one of the most successful debut novels of the past two decades. In the early 2000s, you could find copies on the library shelf of every youth hostel from Bali to Marrakech next to dog-eared Lonely Planet guides and the love poems of Rumi, a cultural totem for the Fulbright Scholars, backpacking college students, and NGO workers who embraced it as a symbol of a brave new globalized world of which they saw themselves as privileged intermediaries.

A dissenting view came from the critic James Wood, who famously cited *White Teeth* as an example of a disturbing new literary trend he named "hysterical realism." Behind Smith's energetic style, Wood identified a troubling evasion of the tragedy of the human condition. Rather than a playful

celebration of hybrid forms, he saw a vacuous embrace of novelty for its own sake. In what became the authoritative critical verdict on the novel, he charged Smith with a deficiency of "moral seriousness." Two years later, he repeated this judgment in his review of Smith's second novel, *The Autograph Man*, which he found to have "no moral centre because that place is so neglected by Smith's uncertain wandering."

Reading *White Teeth* now, eighteen years later, it's striking how little the novel resembles the cultural artifact it became. In the memory, it is a breathless celebration of fin-de-siècle cosmopolitanism. But the book itself is, on the whole, a sensitive, intelligent consideration of the privations and humiliations of working-class immigrant life. Like most fiction from the days of dial-up internet, it suffers from a surfeit of undigested information, but many of the details Wood singled out as evidence of reckless, credulity-straining literary speculation—K.E.V.I.N., the Islamist terrorist group with a poorly chosen acronym, for instance—now seem like restrained examples of conventional realism. And the book contains a sharp criticism of the type of person who likes Zadie Smith novels in the form of the smug white middle-class Chalfens, who symbolically align themselves with the principles of diversity—Joyce, the matriarch of the family, is the author of a Michael Pollan–like gardening manual on the virtues of "cross-pollination"—while patronizing and exploiting the representatives of diversity they encounter in their own lives.

Wood's central claim—that the novel lacked moral seriousness—was equally unjustified. The book has an obvious moral center, anchored in its unusually affectionate and sympathetic portrait of the unremarkable middle-aged Englishman, Archie, around whom its plot revolves. Archie's mediocrity and indecisiveness are a recurring joke. ("This was the man," his wife ruefully concludes, "never able to make a decision, never able to state a position.") But in the moral economy Smith constructs, these seemingly negative qualities are badges of quiet heroism. The novel's central theme is the danger of believing too fervently in the rightness of your own point of view. Its characters are almost all absolutists: environmental terrorists, millenarian cultists, Islamic fundamentalists, crusading scientists, teenagers. Archie, by virtue of his recessive qualities, is the only one who can listen to others. In his unassuming way, he is both humane and cosmopolitan. "He liked people to get on with things, Archie," Smith says. "He kind of felt people should just live together, you know, in peace or harmony or something." By the end of the novel, he has become its hero, valiantly taking a bullet to the thigh in the book's final slapstick action scene.

White Teeth is not, in other words, the fevered "World Is Flat"-style tract of its critics' imaginings. The book has its problems—Archie's willingness to sacrifice himself to defend a Nazi scientist would raise eyebrows if it were published today—but these problems do not seem to fit Wood's diagnosis. Its immoderately lively minor characters are not symptoms of a hysterical absence of form; they are an effect of the novel's form, intended to throw the recessive virtues of its protagonist into relief.

The conventional narrative of Smith's artistic development is that, chastened by her youthful excesses, she settled down and began to publish more appropriately soberminded fiction, beginning with *On Beauty*, an understated meditation on the dangers of intellectual precocity, in 2005, and culminating in her most serious and ambitious novel, *NW,* in 2012. But much of the machinery of these later works was already in place by *White Teeth*. Though Smith has experimented over the years with many different voices and stylistic effects, the underlying structure of her first four novels has largely remained constant. Each employs an omniscient narrator able to hold multiple voices in suspension. Each insists on the virtues of listening to others, seeing both sides, pragmatism, humility, and tolerance. Her novels don't really have villains (she's too humane for that), but the objects of their derision—the characters whom we know we're meant to look on with pity and contempt—are invariably the most ambitious, overzealous, and single-minded ones. Lacking the ability to consider the world from more than one perspective, they are often committed, in name, to the values of multiculturalism and "progressive" politics, but hopelessly unable to put them into practice. The heroes are the ones who can distance themselves from their own concerns enough to imaginatively enter into the lives of others.

SMITH'S MOST DETAILED expression of her politics came in a speech she delivered at the New York Public Library after Obama's election in 2008. Later published in the *New York Review of Books* under the title "Speaking in Tongues," the talk begins with a discussion of her speaking voice, and how she learned to speak in a new more polished accent as she grew up and went to college. She didn't see this process as a sacrifice, but as a "synthesis of disparate things," a way of gaining a new, double voice. In the essay, Smith compares her own experience to Obama's: both grew up the children of biracial families; both are, to some measure, double voiced. Like her, he is in a "middling spot," an "interim place," split "between worlds, ideas, cultures." Over the course of the essay, she compares him to Shakespeare, Eliza Doolittle, and Cary Grant—"the Man from Dream City," in Pauline Kael's famous phrase, whose voice, a strange mix of Bristol and New England, seemed to come from nowhere and to be purely self-created.

Like Grant, Obama came from Dream City: "a place of many voices," Smith writes, "where the unified singular self is an illusion. Naturally, Obama was born there. So was I.... In Dream City everything is doubled, everything is various. You have no choice but to cross borders and speak in tongues." What all these figures—Obama, Shakespeare, Cary Grant, Zadie Smith—had in common, according to the speech, was their negative capability: the ability to live with "complicated back stories, messy histories, multiple narratives" without trying to flatten them; to see things from other perspectives; to speak in more than one voice; to value the truth over one's allegiance to any group.

Smith lays out four stages over which this "many-colored voice" develops:

> In this first stage, the voice, by no fault of its own, finds itself trapped between two poles, two competing belief systems. And so this first stage necessitates the second: the voice learns to be flexible between these two fixed points, even to the point of equivocation. Then the third stage: this native flexibility leads to a sense of being able to "see a thing from both sides." And then the final stage, which I think of as the mark of a certain kind of genius: the voice relinquishes ownership of itself, develops a creative sense of disassociation in which the claims that are particular to it seem no stronger than anyone else's.

"Flexibility is a choice, always open to all of us," Smith observes. Yet this kind of openness to other voices takes work: "to live variously cannot simply be a gift, endowed by an accident of birth; it has to be a continual effort, continually renewed." It's an account that assumes that every problem has two opposing sides that need to be balanced, and that the way to balance them is by distancing oneself from both sides and achieving a "creative sense of disassociation." To become, in other words, the third-person narrator of one's own life.

Earlier in the lecture, Smith argues that this talent for seeing both sides is something we tend to value more in our artists than in our presidents. In politics, she suggests, we dismiss pragmatists who "straddle the reviled middle ground" as passive and ineffectual. "We consider pragmatists to be weak. We call men of balance naive fools." This, she thinks, is a mistake: "In this lecture I have been seeking to tentatively suggest that the voice that speaks with such freedom, thus unburdened by dogma and personal bias, thus flooded with empathy, might make a good president." In the equation of negative capability and political pragmatism, you can see the germ of the liberal elevation of Obama's "pragmatism" on, for instance, drone strikes to a sign of his sensitivity and moral character. Also striking in this description is the lack of acknowledgment that any two sides that need to be balanced might not be competing on level terrain.

THE SPEECH ENDS on a hopeful note: Smith at an election-night party, celebrating Obama's victory and nourishing the "audacious hope" that the new President—"a man born and raised between opposing dogmas, between cultures, between voices"—might fulfill the transformational promise of his campaign. This hope was already ebbing when Smith published *NW*, a mournful modernist novel, in 2012. *Swing Time*, which was published four years later, at the end of Obama's second term, darkens to the point of disintegration. Its narrator is a familiar figure in Smith's pantheon: an unnamed woman in her early thirties, the daughter of a white British father and a black Jamaican mother, who grew up in a working-class North London neighborhood and bears a strong resemblance to *White Teeth*'s Irie or *NW*'s Keisha. (A classmate at the narrator's progressive school, "a buck-toothed girl called Irie, always at the top of the class," makes a cameo appearance.) But there is a significant difference: *Swing Time* is the first of Smith's books to abandon the omniscient third person and restrict itself to a single first-person narrator, a shift that has a seismic effect on the novel. As in Smith's previous novels, the narrator is responsible for harmonizing a multiplicity of disparate voices and positions. But by assigning this mediating function to a flesh-and-blood character, *Swing Time* presents it in a new light. Rather than an all-seeing eye, the narrator is now a fallible individual with a necessarily limited perspective. The opposing voices she holds in suspension are no longer abstract—instead, they are attached to specific people, namely her estranged parents. The insistence on seeing both sides, previously a transcendent principle in Smith's work, here looks more like the survival mechanism of a child of divorce trying to reconcile her parents' competing claims on her affection.

The book's title comes from the Ginger Rogers and Fred Astaire musical *Swing Time*, a film the narrator watched "over and over" as a child and to which she attaches considerable symbolic importance. Echoing Smith's speech on Obama, she calls Astaire "a man from nowhere, without parents or siblings, without a nation or people, without obligations of any kind." From his films, she gleans the idea that "it was important to treat oneself as a kind of stranger, to remain unattached and unprejudiced in your own case. I thought you needed to think like that to achieve anything in this world. Yes, I thought that was a very elegant attitude."

But from its first pages, *Swing Time* undercuts this picture of Dream City in a way Smith's previous books have not. The novel is framed as a retrospective examination of its narrator's early life. In the opening scene, set in 2008, the adult narrator is holed up in a rented condo in London after an undisclosed personal catastrophe. On the third day of her seclusion, she ventures outside for the first time and aimlessly buys a ticket to a lecture by a visiting filmmaker. He plays a clip of *Swing Time* to illustrate a point about "pure cinema," and the narrator experiences "a wonderful lightness.... I felt I was losing track of my physical location, rising above my body, viewing my life from a very distant point, hovering over it."

Less fuss.
More food.

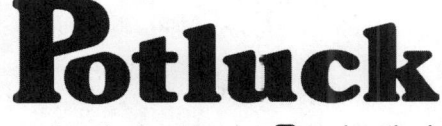

No retail markups.
No single-use gizmos.
Just professional tools for home cooks at a great price.

Potluck

cookpotluck.com   cookpotluck

Later, rewatching the scene on YouTube, she realizes Astaire is in blackface, and that somehow she had "managed to block the childhood image . . . the rolling eyes, the white gloves, the Bojangles grin" from her memory. The question of how she had omitted this aspect of a beloved film of childhood sets the stage for a broader investigation into her past.

In "Speaking in Tongues," Dream City is the place where you could shed your fixed identity and exchange it for that of another. But in *Swing Time*, Smith draws back the curtain to reveal the asymmetry in what feels at first like an equal exchange. Themes of inequitable and violent intimacy recur throughout the book. The narrator's employer, a Madonna-like Australian pop star, becomes enchanted with an unnamed West African country and proceeds to found a girls' school there. She creates a new performance routine based on the traditional dances she observes, becomes romantically involved with a much younger West African man, and, eventually, illegally adopts a baby from the village where the school is being built. The narrator's father loves her mother ("How he loved her! More than she knew or cared to know"), but the novel suggests that this love has a darker side: "She believed my father wanted more children in order to entrap her, and she was basically right about that, although entrapment in this case was only another word for love." In these scenarios, it's not clear who owns what, who gives what to whom, who is acting out what role for whom. What is clear is that this exchange is unequal, a drama whose roles are not always clearly delineated and whose material effects are not evenly distributed.

The novel never entirely develops these insights. There are too many characters, too many overlapping themes and subplots. In another Smith novel this wouldn't be a problem, but here, without the third-person narrator to mediate them, the different voices no longer form a polyphony. By the end of *Swing Time*, Smith's instincts to find the middle ground have reasserted themselves. The final pages hint that the narrator, after a prolonged adolescence, is finally ready to grow up and to enter a responsible adult relationship with a Brazilian development economist, a pragmatist who believes in incremental change, distrusts dramatic gestures, and bases his opinions on carefully gathered facts rather than ideology—a retreat to the shelter of a slightly improved status quo that feels like a way of skirting the problems the book has raised. The strongest impressions that remain after one closes the novel are a few images of the narrator's mother: as a young woman, digging up the grass of their council estate to plant a communal vegetable garden, her hair tied back in a handkerchief; much older, with the man she lived with, a Tobagonian activist, after she left the narrator's father, the two of them smoking a "very poorly constructed spliff" and touching foreheads, murmuring, "Imagine two island kids like us, two barefoot kids from nothing, ending up here"; in hospice near the end of her life, her hands shaking, asking, "Was I a good mother? Was I?"

FEEL FREE, PUBLISHED in 2018 and composed over the same period as *Swing Time*, shows Smith grappling with similar subject matter in a different form. A mixture of speeches and essays, many of them written for the late Bob Silvers at the *New York Review of Books*, addresses "the fictional status of identity itself," the creative freedom of art, and the importance of self-estrangement and openness to experience. Smith's essays are generally more schematic than her fiction, and the ones in this collection touch on a handful of familiar themes. In a profile of the comedians Key and Peele, she celebrates "the antic freedom inherent in sketch." A previously unpublished essay uses the weak pun between Justin Bieber and Martin Buber to emphasize the importance of treating others like people rather than things. Writing on Joni Mitchell, she finds that "her music, her life, has always been about discontinuity. The inconsistency of identity, of personality."

The mood here is bleaker than in her previous essays. "Neither my readers nor I am in the relatively sunlit uplands depicted in *White Teeth* anymore," she writes in "On Optimism and Despair," a lecture given shortly after Trump's election. "I am by nature not a political person and these are the darkest political times I have ever known." In response, she stresses the need to defend liberal values and the importance of incremental progress:

> As the departing president well understood, in this world there is only incremental progress. Only the willfully blind can ignore that the history of human existence is simultaneously the history of pain: of brutality, murder, mass extinction, every form of venality and cyclical horror. No land is free of it; no people are without their bloodstain; no tribe entirely innocent. But there is still this redeeming matter of incremental progress. It might look small to those with apocalyptic perspectives, but to she who not so long ago could not vote, or drink from the same water fountain as her fellow citizens, or marry the person she chose, or live in a certain neighborhood, such incremental change feels enormous.

The highest-profile political intervention in the collection is "Getting In and Out," which addresses the controversy around the white artist Dana Schutz's painting of Emmett Till in the 2017 Whitney Biennial. The famous photographic portrait of Till on which Schutz's work is based, published in *Jet* magazine in 1955 and often credited with sparking the civil rights movement, shows the 14-year-old's body in his casket after he had been beaten and shot in Mississippi for supposedly flirting with a white woman. Schutz's painting reinterprets the portrait in an abstract style. When the painting went on display, the British artist Hannah Black wrote a widely circulated Facebook post calling for the painting to be destroyed. Some months later, Smith published the essay in *Harper's* in response. The crux of Smith's essay is its defense of free speech. Black had asserted that "white free speech and white creative freedom have been founded on the constraint of others, and are not natural rights." In language that oddly echoed Justice Kennedy's argument, in his *Citizens United* decision, that there was no distinction between the free-speech rights of natural and corporate persons, Smith asked what it meant to have "natural rights" to speech: Would she, as a biracial woman, have a right to paint Emmett Till? Would her children? "Whether they like it or not, Americans are one people," the essay concludes, collapsing concrete hierarchies into a vision of unity.

The best essay in the collection, "The Bathroom," is also the least homiletic. In it, Smith considers her childhood through the "retrospective swirl" of becoming a parent herself. Looking back, she understands that her mother and a woman called "Auntie" Ruth, who wasn't actually her aunt, stopped telling the kids what to do after 6 PM because they were "a bit pissed on cheap white wine," and what it meant when her mother would "suddenly go silent and stare at a wall. She just couldn't take *one more second of it*." The focal point of the essay is the family bathroom in their cramped maisonette, which she comes to see in "a new, semi-tragic light" as a "sort of dream space of my parents, mixing memory and desire," where each had attempted to preserve an identity independent of family life. Her mother filled it with "green and tropical-looking and hugely overgrown" plants that made the bathroom look like a corner of Jamaica ("it never occurred to me, as a child, that my mother might be homesick"). Her father, an amateur photographer, used it as a darkroom, "his sleeves rolled up, and the bath full of liquid, and this red light, turning the clean Habitat lines of our modern home into something subterranean and, to me, unnerving. What was this secret room doing in our house?"

In her other essays, Smith uses her family and her childhood as symbols of harmony, tolerance, and cross-cultural connection. Here, a different tone comes through. People are not too far away from each other, but too close: the mood is of a kind of claustrophobic intimacy, of being trapped in someone else's dream, tangled up in a fantasy that seems to come from outside the self. "It's in the nature of the beast that no one gets out of a family unit whole or with everything they want.... However many books and movies and songs declaim the wholesome beauty of family life, the truth is 'the family' is always an event of some violence," Smith writes. "It's only years later, in that retrospective swirl, that you work out who was hurt, in what way, and how badly." +

SUPPORTERS

SUPPORTERS

Jonathan Baskin
The Blumenkranz Family
AJ Brown
Christopher Cox and Georgia Cool
Roberta Denning
Annie Duke
Andrew and Blake Foote
The Garrison Family
Jeremy and Rebecca Glick
Jeff Gramm and Susie Heimbach
Eddie Joyce and Martine Beamon

Gregory Kossinets
Glenn Ligon
Richard Parrino
Chris and Whitney Parris-Lamb
Victoria Roth
Christian Rudder
Mac Simonson
The Tortorici Family
Sarah Whitman-Salkin
Scott Wood-Prince

ADVISORY BOARD

Carla Blumenkranz
Kate Bolick
AJ Brown
Georgia Cool

Christopher Cox
Eddie Joyce
Katy Lederer
Allison Lorentzen

Chris Parris-Lamb
Whitney Parris-Lamb
Henry Rich
Sarah Whitman-Salkin

INSTITUTIONAL SUPPORTERS

Amazon Studios
Audible
The Cheney Agency
Farrar, Straus and Giroux
The Gernert Company
Grove/Atlantic
Hachette Book Group
Harper Perennial

HBO
ICM
Knopf Doubleday Publishing Group
Little, Brown
Massie & McQuilkin
Macmillan
Penguin Random House
W. W. Norton

Special thanks to
Bailey Miller
Lisa Borst
Aaron Braun

Jo Constantz
Joseph Frischmuth
Emma Hager

Lizzy Harding
Eddie Zhang

n+1 is supported, in part, by public funds from the New York State Council on the Arts and New York City Department of Cultural Affairs in partnership with the City Council.

OUR CONTRIBUTORS

Adam Bobbette is a geographer at the University of Cambridge.

Marissa Brostoff is a writer and doctoral student living in New York.

Helen DeWitt is the author of *The Last Samurai* and *Lightning Rods*. "Famous Last Words" and "Improvisation is the Heart of Music" are excerpts from *Some Trick*, her first collection of short fiction, to be published by New Directions in May 2018.

Nicholas Dames is a professor of English and Comparative Literature at Columbia University. His last piece for *n+1* was "Seventies Throwback Fiction" (Issue 21).

A. S. Hamrah is *n+1*'s film critic. His last column, "Cut the Kink," appeared in Issue 30.

Andrea Long Chu is a writer and doctoral candidate in literature at NYU. Her last piece for *n+1* was "On Liking Women" (Issue 30).

Christina Nichol is the author of the novel *Waiting for the Electricity*. She lives in Northern California.

Alex Press is an assistant editor at *Jacobin*.

Rose Réjouis is a professor of literary studies at The New School. "You Can't Read" and "Letter to Freud" originally appeared in the French review, *Esprit*.

Bela Shayevich is a Soviet-American artist, translator, and writer.

Natasha Stagg's first novel, *Surveys*, was published by Semiotext(e) in 2016.

Anthony Veasna So is a writer, cartoonist, and MFA candidate in fiction at Syracuse University.

ACKNOWLEDGEMENTS

"Don't Think Twice, It's All Right." Written by Bob Dylan. Copyright © 1963 by Warner Bros. Inc.; renewed 1991 by Special Rider Music.

"Let's Call the Whole Thing Off" (From *Shall We Dance*). Music and Lyrics by George Gershwin and Ira Gershwin. © 1936 (Renewed) Ira Gershwin Music and George Gershwin Music. All Rights on behalf of Ira Gershwin Music Administered by WB Music Corp. All Rights Reserved. Used by Permission of Alfred Publishing, LLC. Reprinted by permission of Hal Leonard LLC.

LETTERS

On Liking "On Liking Women"

Dear Editors:

Andrea Long Chu's essay "On Liking Women" put into words what I've been feeling for years, as a transfeminine person dissatisfied with most mainstream treatments of transness and trans politics. Popular discourse on trans identities usually essentializes identity as fixed, static, and often biological, or makes all genders equivalent without paying attention to the particular oppression that women and feminine people face. Chu's articulation of being trans as simultaneously a choice and a form of desire—all while demonstrating a deep understanding of the particular context (and limitations) of second-wave feminism—was refreshing, not to mention bitingly funny. I cheered at times, clapped, and exclaimed how moved I was throughout reading it. This is a letter to express my endless gratitude to you, editors, for publishing the piece, and to Andrea for writing it. I look forward to the day when the ideas behind this intervention are commonsense enough that writing them down is no longer necessary.

—*Sarah Pining*

Clickbait Minotaur

Dear Editors,

Reading Dayna Tortorici's "In the Maze," it occurred to me that there was another piece of the puzzle: the crisis in journalism. Many of the pieces that triggered the most vitriolic discussions on social media during the Long 2016 were published in the *Atlantic*, the *Chronicle of Higher Education*, and other publications that were in the midst of shifting from publishing more traditional magazine writing to inflammatory viral reporting as a way of staying alive in an era then dominated by Upworthy and BuzzFeed. The trigger-warning debate became the liberal version of the knockout game, a fake crisis fueled by exploitative online publishers seeking clicks at any cost. (Whether clickbait pushed its male targets further in the direction of misogyny or merely revealed the views already beneath the surface is a different question.) On this grim merry-go-round, the socially conscious humanities majors scapegoated by these pieces graduate to content-farm jobs where they become the producers as well as the consumers of endless new waves of exploitative content.

—*Greg Afinogenov*

Dear Editors,

While I have read many articles about the culture of male resentment, I have encountered very few as insightful as "In the Maze." I consider myself a male feminist, whatever that term connotes these days. Still, I detect hints of the often involuntary negative reaction to cultural trends described in the article in myself. It is, and will likely remain, uncomfortable when you discover that things you consider normal are privileged and not at all self-evident. Moreover, when you learn that behaviors or lifestyles you considered normal, perhaps even desirable, are constructed on the backs of others.

Tortorici writes, "But just as true, and significantly less consoling, is the guarantee that some will find the world less comfortable in the process of making it habitable for others." This is undeniably true and an important insight to keep in mind. However, I think the trauma of losing privilege should be discussed as a source of real emotional pain.

I have been struck, if not surprised, by the visceral anger these trends have inspired in self-described liberal, left-wing, and feminist men. Being one of those specimens myself—a straight, white, highly educated man—I often struggle to reconcile my emotions and reactions to feminist issues, and to weigh feminist issues against other issues I hold dear. Although this fight may never be my fight the way that it is Tortorici's, I believe contemporary feminist debate would benefit from engaging seriously with the reactions and emotions that giving up male supremacy brings.

Now, these are the ruminations of someone who was raised (by) a feminist, who works as a PhD student at the Rachel Carson Center for Environment and Society in Munich (an intersectional stronghold to be sure). In other words, of someone who has read and thought a lot about these issues, and has the tools to thoroughly reflect on his own privilege. If even I have these apprehensions, I find it unsurprising that others with less progressive backgrounds do too.

I fear no durable solution can be found without the support of men, white men. And I don't just mean those like me; I mean the silent majority who, I suspect, still view feminism apprehensively at best. We are all inclined to envision structural progress, but the pendulum could swing the other way, too. We must engage men who have negative reactions, accept the reality of their pain, and acknowledge that, more often than not, they may not be prepared.

—*Jeroen Oomen*